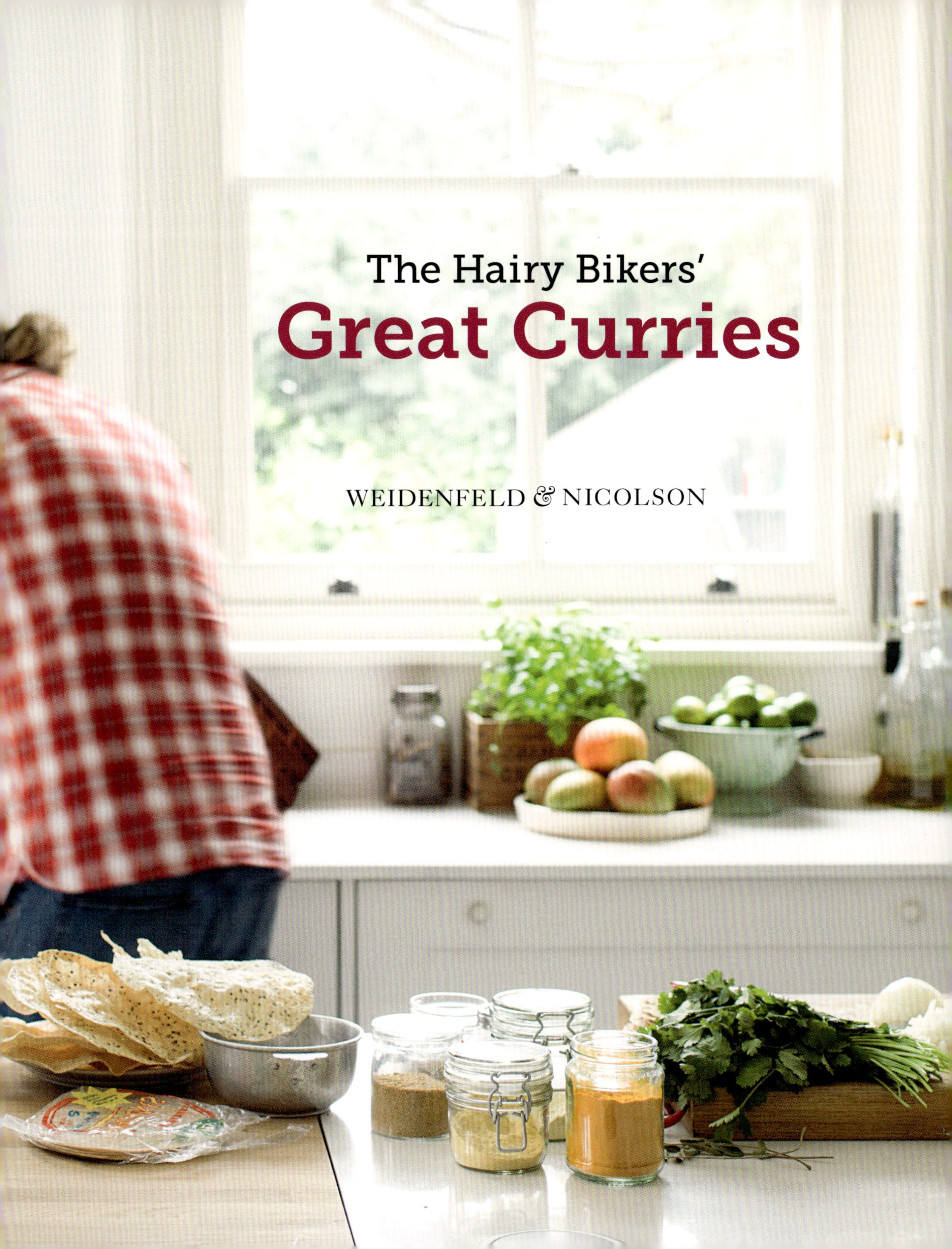

The Hairy Bikers'

Great Curries

WEIDENFELD & NICOLSON

We'd like to dedicate this book with respect and thanks to all the lovely folk from around the world who've brought their fantastic food and recipes to these shores. Their great contribution has made modern Britain a truly exciting place in which to cook and eat – a culinary wonder. Ta very much.

First published in hardback in Great Britain in 2012 by
Weidenfeld & Nicolson, an imprint of the Orion Publishing Group Ltd
Orion House, 5 Upper St Martin's Lane, London WC2H 9EA
an Hachette UK Company

A CIP catalogue record for this book is available from the British Library.

Food consultant: Justine Pattison
Photographer: Cristian Barnett
Food stylists: Lorna Brash and Justine Pattison
Prop stylist: Tamzin Ferdinando
Designers: Kate Barr, Tricia Shiel, Loulou Clark and Andy Campling
Editor: Jinny Johnson
Illustrator: Emma Kelly
Handwritten labels: Abi Hartshorne
Proofreader: Elise See Tai
Indexer: Elizabeth Wiggans
Food director's assistants: Gileng Salter, Lauren Brignell and Kirsty Thomas
Food stylist's assistants: Amber Homan, Sophie Fox, Poppy Campbell and Kathy Kordalis
Photographer's assistant: Roy Baron

Printed and bound in the UK by Butler Tanner & Dennis Ltd

The Orion Publishing Group's policy is to use papers that are natural, renewable and recyclable and made from wood grown in sustainable forests. The logging and manufacturing processes are expected to conform to the environmental regulations of the country of origin.

www.orionbooks.co.uk

CONTENTS

WHO DOESN'T LOVE A CURRY?

Whether it's a take-away korma in your kitchen or a lamb biryani at your local Indian restaurant, a curry is most people's favourite Friday night supper or weekend treat.

But there's so much more to curry than shop-bought or restaurant curries. A proper home-made curry can be an exquisitely fragrant dish, with delicate flavours that surprise and titillate your taste buds. We want to show you how to make the most delicious curries you've ever tasted and share our curry secrets.

This one-stop curry book will demystify curry cooking. It will inspire you to get out your spices and have a go. These recipes will be the best you've ever tasted - fresh, fragrant and fantastic. These are curries for the 21st century.

RECIPES FROM AROUND THE WORLD...

Sadly, home-made curries can turn out bland and muddy – or just mind-bendingly hot. Our recipes are the real deal, using great techniques and secrets we've discovered on our travels in Asia as well as years of cooking curries ourselves. First off, spicy doesn't have to mean hot. A curry can be lip-smackingly good without making you want to reach for the fire extinguisher. In our recipes we explain how to use ingredients to create layers of spicy flavours that will delight you, not burn your tongue off.

We've come up with the best recipes for all your favourites – as well as some you might not have come across – and you'll be amazed how easy they are to make. Try dishes such as our Keralan prawn curry – it takes 10 minutes and tastes fantastic.

We know that those long ingredients lists in some curry recipes can be daunting, but don't worry. We will show you how to build your basic spice collection and learn what goes with what. Soon you'll be using a range of spices as easily as you shake on the salt and pepper, and with great results. All our ingredients are available in the supermarket or online.

In this book we've assembled a wealth of brand-new, tried and tested recipes from around the world – from simple dishes for a quick midweek taste treat to fantastic feasts for a weekend celebration.

You'll also find recipes for the yummy extras, with everything from starters to pickles and chutneys.

We've come up with some fab ideas for refreshing and flavourful sweet dishes, too, that make an ideal final flourish after your curry. And we've included a section on basic techniques to help you prepare ingredients for the best results and explain how to tell your scotch bonnets from your bird's-eyes.

Now, one more thing. As many of you will know, we've lost quite a bit of weight lately and we're proud of ourselves. As you also know, we love our curries and we've found they can be the dieting cook's best friend as a good curry is built on flavour and fortunately there are no calories in flavour. So spice up your taste buds – and your diet – with the recipes in our Light Curries chapter. They're as tasty as the full-throttle versions, but help to keep you trim.

Cooking curry used to be a way of disguising less than perfect ingredients, but nowadays we use the best and enhance flavours, not camouflage them. We've learned from the experts, who make brilliant curries daily, and we want to share our knowledge and passion with you.

Si & Dave

A few little tips from us:

Weigh all the ingredients carefully and use proper teaspoons and tablespoons and a measuring jug. With spices, the difference between half a teaspoon and a teaspoon can really affect the taste and balance of the dish.

All onions, shallots and garlic to be peeled, unless otherwise specified.

We always use free-range eggs and plain natural live yoghurt – full-fat unless otherwise specified.

We specify sunflower oil in most of our recipes, but you can use vegetable oil if you prefer.

Bunches of fresh herbs vary in size. We've mostly used large bunches (50g or so) or small bunches (15–20g).

We've judged the amount of fresh chillies as exactly as we can but their hotness does vary depending on where they come from, so keep tasting. Remember – you can always add more heat but you can't take it out! Long and plump chillies are interchangeable – use whichever you have.

We've made cooking times and temperatures as accurate as we can, but always check that your food is properly cooked.

Starters & Snacks

Crispy, crunchy poppadums make a great start to your meal. You can make your own, but the simplest thing is to buy ready-made uncooked poppadums, fry them up yourself and serve them warm with some home-made dips and chutneys. Fantastic. Some people microwave or grill poppadums, but we think the fried ones taste best. **Makes 12**

MASALA POPPADUMS

600–800ml sunflower oil
12 uncooked poppadums, look out for the flavoured ones
fresh onion and tomato relish, natural yoghurt and fresh coriander, for serving

Pour the oil into a large wide-based saucepan or sauté pan and place it over a medium heat. Put a cooking thermometer in the oil to check the temperature, then heat the oil to 190°C. DO NOT ALLOW THE OIL TO OVERHEAT. NEVER LEAVE HOT OIL UNATTENDED.

As soon as the oil has reached the right temperature, take a poppadum with metal tongs and lower it slowly into the pan (you don't want the hot oil to splash you). Within about 5 seconds the poppadum will have puffed up and grown about a third larger.

Before the poppadum gets the chance to brown, take it out of the hot oil with your metal tongs and place it in an upright position to drain. We put ours in a wide metal toast rack to drain, which works really well, but you could simply lean your poppadums against a clean saucepan with some kitchen paper underneath them to catch the drips.

Continue frying the poppadums until they are all cooked. Watch the temperature of the oil closely as you don't want it to overheat.

When the poppadums are cooked, serve them warm with assorted dips, chutneys, pickles and relish. Or if you prefer, put them on plates and top with fresh onion and tomato relish (see page 276) and some fresh coriander. A drizzle of minted yoghurt sauce (see page 57) goes well too. Break the poppadums apart with your fingers to eat.

Pakoras are a kind of fritter and can be made with lots of different kinds of vegetables as well as fish or meat. The main ingredient is dipped in a spicy batter made from chickpea flour, sometimes called gram or besan flour, and emerges with a wonderful, light-as-air, crispy coating. We love pakoras and this prawn version is one of our favourites. **Makes 20–25**

KING PRAWN PAKORAS

400g peeled raw king or tiger prawns, thawed if frozen
sunflower oil, for deep-frying
lemon wedges, for serving
cucumber raita, for dipping (optional)

Batter

100g gram (chickpea) flour
100g plain natural yoghurt
5 tbsp cold water
1 tsp black mustard seeds
1 long green chilli, deseeded and finely chopped
4 spring onions, trimmed and finely chopped
finely grated zest of ½ well-scrubbed lime
1 tsp fine sea salt

Devein the prawns (see page 355). Rinse them in cold water and pat them dry with kitchen paper – this is important as the drier the prawns are the better they hold the batter.

Pour the oil into a large sturdy saucepan until it is about a third full, and roughly 5cm deep. Heat the oil to 180°C, using a cooking thermometer to check the temperature. Alternatively, heat until a small ball of the batter floats to the surface of the oil as soon as it is added. DO NOT ALLOW THE OIL TO OVERHEAT. NEVER LEAVE HOT OIL UNATTENDED.

While the oil is heating, make the batter. Mix the flour, yoghurt and cold water until smooth and thick, then stir in the mustard seeds, chopped chilli, spring onions, lime zest and salt.

Add the prawns to the batter and toss thoroughly. Using tongs or a couple of forks, lift the prawns out of the batter, 1 at a time. Lower them gently into the hot oil and cook for 2–3 minutes until they are puffed up and golden brown, turning them every now and then. You should be able to fry 6–8 prawns at a time and they should be pink throughout when cooked. Keep an eye on the oil temperature and make sure it doesn't keep rising.

Lift the cooked prawns out with clean tongs or a slotted spoon and drain them on kitchen paper. Keep them warm while you fry the rest. You may need to let the oil return to the correct temperature between batches. Serve with lemon wedges and cucumber raita (see page 285) if you like.

Another pakora treat. Who would have thought a spring onion could taste so delicious? These are cheap to make but have a classy flavour; a really economical snack or starter. **Makes 12**

SPRING ONION PAKORAS

- 1 bunch of spring onions, trimmed
- 100g gram (chickpea) flour
- 1 tsp fine sea salt
- ½ tsp hot chilli powder
- 1 tsp ground turmeric
- 1 tbsp sunflower oil
- 100ml warm water
- sunflower oil, for frying
- chutneys and relishes, for serving

Cut the spring onions into slices about 5mm thick and put them in a large mixing bowl. Add the flour, salt, chilli powder and turmeric and toss everything together lightly. Mix in the sunflower oil with your hand, then slowly pour in the warm water and stir constantly until the batter is smooth and thick.

Pour the oil into a large, wide-based, sturdy saucepan until it is about 3.5cm deep. Heat to 180°C, using a cooking thermometer to check the temperature. Alternatively, heat until a small ball of the batter floats to the surface of the oil as soon as it is added. DO NOT ALLOW THE OIL TO OVERHEAT. NEVER LEAVE HOT OIL UNATTENDED.

Take a dessertspoon of the batter and drop it gently into the hot oil. You may need to use a second spoon to help you do this. Continue adding the batter until you have 4 pakoras frying at the same time. Cook them for 2½–3 minutes until they are well risen and golden brown, turning them occasionally with a slotted spoon or metal tongs.

Lift the pakoras out of the oil with the slotted spoon or tongs and drain them on kitchen paper. Allow the oil to return to the correct temperature and continue cooking the remaining pakoras in exactly the same way. Serve warm with chutneys and relishes for dipping.

This is your luxury pakora, which comes complete with its own handle – a real gourmet item. These are not difficult to make and you can get everything ready ahead of time to dip and fry at the last minute.
Serves 6 as a starter

LAMB CHOP PAKORAS

12–14 small lamb cutlets, French-trimmed
1 tsp cumin seeds
1 tsp coriander seeds
1 tsp black peppercorns
2–3 tbsp sunflower oil, plus extra for deep-frying
chutneys and relishes, for serving

Spice-infused milk
1 cinnamon stick
1 green chilli, thinly sliced
4 whole cloves
8 cardamom pods, crushed
15g chunk of fresh root ginger, peeled and finely grated
½ onion, finely sliced
250ml full-fat milk

Batter
125g gram (chickpea) flour
25g self-raising white flour
½ tsp cayenne pepper
½ tsp fine sea salt

To make the spice-infused milk, put the cinnamon stick, chilli, cloves, cardamom, ginger and onion in a saucepan and pour in the milk. Bring to a gentle simmer and cook for 5 minutes, making sure that the milk doesn't boil over. Remove from the heat and set aside for 20 minutes to allow the spices to infuse.

Make sure the lamb cutlets have been trimmed of any fat and the bones have been scraped clean – you'll use these as little handles when you eat the cutlets. Place a large non-stick frying pan over a medium-high heat and dry fry the cumin and coriander seeds until you can smell them toasting. Tip the seeds into a pestle and mortar, add the peppercorns and pound into a powder. Coat the cutlets on both sides with spices.

Heat 2 tablespoons of oil in the same pan and fry the cutlets in 2–3 batches until browned all over. You'll probably need to cook them for 2 minutes on each side and then a further minute to brown the edges. Cook them in 2 or 3 batches so you don't overcrowd the pan, adding a little extra oil if you need it. Leave the cutlets to rest on a plate.

To make the batter, put both flours, the cayenne and salt in a large bowl and make a well in the centre. Strain the infused milk through a fine sieve into a measuring jug. Slowly pour 200ml of the milk into the flour mixture, stirring it with a metal whisk to make a smooth batter.

Pour the oil into a large, deep saucepan until it is just over one-third full. Heat to 170°C, using a cooking thermometer to keep a check on the temperature. DO NOT ALLOW THE OIL TO OVERHEAT. NEVER LEAVE HOT OIL UNATTENDED. Using tongs, take a cutlet and dip it into the batter. Gently shake off the excess batter and lower the cutlet carefully into the hot oil. Add another 3 cutlets in the same way and fry them for 2–3 minutes, turning them regularly, until the batter is golden brown and crisp.

Using clean tongs or a slotted spoon, transfer the cutlets to a baking tray lined with kitchen paper and keep them warm while you fry the rest. Let the oil return to the correct temperature between batches and take great care that it doesn't start to overheat. Serve the cutlets with a selection of chutneys and relishes.

Everyone loves chicken tikka, which is like a kind of kebab made of marinated meat threaded on to skewers. A popular takeaway dish, this is really easy to make at home. It's great served cold too, so make a double batch and enjoy the rest the next day – perfect for taking on a picnic. **Serves 6**

CHICKEN TIKKA

4 boneless, skinless chicken breasts (or use boneless, skinless thighs if you like)
sliced red onion and tomato, coriander leaves, for serving

Tikka marinade
1 tbsp cumin seeds
1 tbsp coriander seeds
2 whole cloves
½ tsp black peppercorns
½ tsp ground fenugreek
1½ tsp ground turmeric
2 tsp ground paprika
½ tsp hot chilli powder
¼ tsp ground cinnamon
1 tsp flaked sea salt
2 garlic cloves, crushed
20g chunk of fresh root ginger, peeled and finely grated
4 tbsp plain natural yoghurt

Put the cumin and coriander seeds, cloves and black peppercorns in a dry frying pan over a medium heat. Cook and stir for 1–2 minutes, until lightly toasted – you know they're ready when you can smell their spicy aroma. Tip them into a pestle and mortar or an electric spice grinder. Add the fenugreek, turmeric, paprika, chilli powder, cinnamon and salt to the warm spices and grind them all into a fine powder.

Tip the ground spices into a mixing bowl and stir in the garlic, ginger and yoghurt. Mix thoroughly and leave this to stand while you get on with preparing the chicken.

Cut each chicken breast into 7 or 8 bite-sized pieces. Stir them into the spiced yoghurt, cover with cling film and leave in the fridge to marinate for at least 4 hours or ideally overnight.

Take the chicken pieces out of the fridge and thread them on to long metal skewers, leaving 1–2cm between each piece. You should be able to fit about 6 chunks of chicken on each skewer.

Preheat the grill to its hottest setting and place the skewers on a rack over a grill pan lined with foil. Slide the pan on to a shelf as close as possible to the heat and cook the chicken for 5 minutes. Holding the hot skewers with an oven cloth, turn each one and cook on the other side for a further 4–5 minutes or until the chicken is cooked through and lightly charred.

Use a fork to slide the chicken tikka chunks off the skewers and serve with fresh red onion and tomato slices and some chopped coriander. A yoghurt dip is also good with tikka, or serve with some lemon wedges to squeeze over the chicken. If you're saving some of the tikka to eat cold, allow the chicken to cool, then cover it with cling film and keep in the fridge for up to 2 days.

TOP TIP
Use 4 duck breasts instead of the chicken if you like. Remove the skin before cutting into chunks. Cook under the grill for 3 minutes on one side and 2–3 minutes on the other until nicely charred on the outside and hot and juicy in the centre.

Try these variations on the tikka theme. The secret is in the marinade. **Serves 6**

LAMB TIKKA

400g lamb leg meat
lemon wedges, for squeezing

Tikka marinade
1 tbsp cumin seeds
1 tbsp coriander seeds
2 whole cloves
½ tsp black peppercorns
½ tsp ground fenugreek
1½ tsp ground turmeric
2 tsp ground paprika
½ tsp hot chilli powder
¼ tsp ground cinnamon
1 tsp flaked sea salt
2 garlic cloves, crushed
20g chunk of fresh root ginger, peeled and finely grated
4 tbsp plain natural yoghurt

Make the marinade (see page 20). Trim the lamb of any obvious fatty bits and cut the meat into 2.5cm cubes. Put the lamb in the marinade and turn it several times until coated. Cover with cling film and put the meat in the fridge to marinate for at least 6 hours or ideally overnight.

Take the lamb from the fridge and thread the pieces on to long metal skewers, leaving 1–2cm between each chunk. You can add a few chunks of pepper, courgette or onion too if you like. Preheat the grill to its hottest setting and place the skewers on a rack over a grill pan lined with foil. Slide this on to a shelf as close as possible to the heat and cook for 2–3 minutes until the lamb is lightly browned. Turn each skewer, holding it with an oven cloth, and cook on the other side for a further 2–3 minutes or until the lamb is lightly charred but still pink and juicy in the middle. You can also cook this lamb on a barbecue or a lightly oiled griddle with the extractor on full!

Use a fork to slide the tikka chunks off the skewers on to plates. Serve with lemon wedges and some salad and chutneys or dips.

PRAWN TIKKA

400g raw peeled king or tiger prawns, thawed if frozen

Tikka marinade
(see above)

Make the tikka marinade (see page 20). Devein the prawns (see page 355), then put them in the marinade and turn several times until thoroughly coated. Take the prawns and thread them on to long metal skewers, leaving 1–2cm between each prawn. Place the skewers on a small tray lined with cling film, cover them with cling film too and put them in the fridge to marinate for 30–60 minutes.

Preheat the grill to its hottest setting and place the skewers on a rack over a grill pan lined with foil. Slide the pan on to a shelf as close as possible to the heat and cook for 2 minutes. Turn each skewer, holding it with an oven cloth, and cook on the other side for a further 2 minutes or until the prawns are completely pink and lightly charred in places. Use a fork to slide the prawns off the skewers and on to plates. Serve with some chutneys or dips.

Grind spices yourself
for maximum
freshness and flavour
in your curries.

These little deep-fried treasures are a bit like a lovely spicy Indian falafel. They need something juicy alongside them, so serve with some chutneys and dips – we think cucumber raita (see page 284) is just right. **Makes 20**

OUR GOLL BHAJI

- 75g shelled cashew nuts
- 1 tsp fennel seeds
- 100g rice flour
- 100g gram (chickpea) flour
- ½ tsp bicarbonate of soda
- 1 tsp fine sea salt
- ½ tsp ground black pepper
- ½ tsp hot chilli powder
- 20g chunk of fresh root ginger, peeled and finely chopped
- 1 heaped tbsp finely chopped fresh coriander leaves
- 1 medium onion, finely chopped
- 2 tbsp chilled ghee or sunflower oil
- 1 medium egg, beaten
- 4–5 tbsp cold water
- sunflower oil, for deep-frying
- lime wedges, for squeezing

Put the cashew nuts and fennel seeds in a dry frying pan and place over a medium heat. Toast until the nuts are lightly browned, tossing occasionally – keep a close eye on them as they burn easily. Tip the nuts on to a board and let them cool for a few minutes, then chop finely.

Mix both the flours with the bicarbonate of soda, salt and black pepper in a large bowl. Stir in the cashew nuts and fennel seeds, then add the chilli powder, ginger, coriander and onion. Rub the ghee or sunflower oil into the dry ingredients and then stir in the beaten egg. The mixture will look very crumbly at this stage.

Stir in the 4–5 tablespoons of water, a little at a time, and mix with clean hands until you have a firm, slightly sticky dough. Roll the dough into 20 walnut-sized balls and put them on a tray.

Pour the oil into a large, sturdy saucepan until it is about a third full and the oil is roughly 5cm deep. Heat to 170°C, using a cooking thermometer to check the temperature. DO NOT OVERHEAT. NEVER LEAVE HOT OIL UNATTENDED. Alternatively, use an electric deep fat fryer.

Using a slotted spoon, gently lower the balls, 6 or 7 at a time, into the hot oil. Cook them for about 3 minutes until golden brown, turning every now and then. Check the temperature of the oil and make sure it doesn't keep rising.

Lift out 1 of the goll bhajis and cut it open. The bhaji should look fairly dry inside and not at all soggy. If it's not quite cooked, fry for a minute or so more. When the bhajis are ready, lift them out with tongs or a slotted spoon and drain them on kitchen paper. Keep them warm while the next batches are fried. You may need to let the oil return to the correct temperature between batches.

Serve with lime wedges for squeezing over the bhajis and some chutneys and dips if you like.

No argy-bargy about these! Bhajis are really easy to make and great to eat. Home-made versions can be a bit flabby and oily, but not these! We've used beaten egg, which makes our batter extra crisp and golden. For the best results, it's worth investing in a cooking thermometer. They cost less than a tenner and will help you keep your oil at an even temperature. **Makes 12–14**

OUR ONION BHAJIS

- 125g gram (chickpea) flour
- 3 medium onions (about 600g)
- 2 long green chillies
- 1 medium egg
- 1 heaped tsp garam masala (see page 345 or use ready-made)
- ½ tsp hot chilli powder
- 1 tsp fine sea salt
- 5 tbsp cold water
- sunflower oil, for frying
- lemon or lime wedges, for squeezing

Put the flour in a large mixing bowl. Peel the onions, then cut them in half from root to stem and slice fairly finely. Add them to the flour. Cut the chillies in half and remove the seeds (see page 349). Finely chop the chillies and toss them with the onions and flour.

Break the egg into a medium bowl and whisk in the garam masala, chilli powder, salt and water. Stir this into the onion mixture until the onion slices are lightly coated. Add a little more water if the flour remains powdery or isn't coating the onions thoroughly.

Pour the oil into a large saucepan until it rises halfway up the sides. Heat the oil to 170°C using a cooking thermometer. DO NOT OVERHEAT. DO NOT LEAVE HOT OIL UNATTENDED. Take a serving spoon and scoop up a spoonful of the battered onions. Scrape the mixture gently into the pan using a second spoon. The oil will bubble up a little around the onion mound. Add 2 or 3 more spoonfuls, dropping them carefully into the oil in exactly the same way.

Fry the bhajis for 3–3½ minutes, turning them halfway through the cooking time, until they are golden brown and crisp. They will rise to the surface of the oil as they cook. Lift them out of the pan with a slotted spoon or tongs and drain them on kitchen paper. If you are nervous about deep-frying, cook your bhajis in a frying pan in a couple of centimetres of oil instead. Alternatively, cook them in a deep fryer if you have one.

Make the rest of the bhajis in the same way and serve warm with lemon or lime wedges for squeezing and an assortment of chutneys and dips if you like.

Everyone's eaten packet samosas at some time, but the difference between those and a home-made samosa is like chalk and cheese. These are just beautiful – perfect little pies that are great for a snack, a party or any occasion. You can roll and cut the samosa pastry into semi-circles and fold them into cones for filling, but in this recipe we make the samosas out of rectangles of dough and they look and taste fab. To make a template, cut out a 28 x 8cm rectangle from a cereal box or other piece of cardboard and cover it in foil. You can then use this time and time again. If you don't fancy making your own samosa pastry, you can buy ready-made samosa wrappers from Asian grocery stores. **Makes 9**

SAMOSAS

Filling

1 medium potato (about 300g)
1 tbsp sunflower oil
½ medium onion, finely chopped
1 garlic clove, finely chopped
1½ tsp garam masala (see page 345 or use ready-made)
½ tsp ground turmeric
½ tsp black mustard seeds
50g frozen peas, thawed
½ tsp flaked sea salt
freshly ground black pepper

Samosa pastry

250g plain flour, plus extra for rolling
1 tsp fine sea salt
4 tbsp sunflower oil
100ml warm water (50ml just-boiled water and 50ml cold water)
about 1.2 litres sunflower oil, for deep-frying

To make the filling, half fill a medium pan with water and bring it to the boil. Peel the potato and cut it into cubes of about 1cm. Carefully drop the potato cubes into the water and bring it back to the boil. Cook for 4½–5 minutes or until the potato pieces are completely tender. You can test a cube by poking it with the tip of a knife. Drain in a colander and set aside.

Heat the oil in a small non-stick frying pan. Add the onion and garlic and cook over a low heat for 3 minutes until the onion is soft but not coloured, stirring regularly. Sprinkle over the garam masala, turmeric and mustard seeds. Fry for a minute more, stirring constantly.

Tip the potato cubes and peas into the pan and cook for 1 minute, stirring and pressing the potatoes with the back of a wooden spoon to crush them a little. Season with salt and plenty of pepper. Leave to cool.

To make the pastry, mix the flour and the salt in a large bowl. Pour the oil into the bowl and rub it into the flour with clean fingertips until the mixture has the consistency of breadcrumbs. Add the water, stirring with your fingers until the mixture comes together to form a ball. Transfer the dough to a lightly floured surface and knead for a minute, then divide it into 9 equal portions.

Roll a portion of dough out on the floured surface into a rectangle only slightly larger than the template. The dough needs to be extremely thin, so keep rolling until you can make it large enough. Cut around the template and throw away the trimmings.

Place the pastry rectangle with a short side facing you. Fold the right-hand corner across the pastry, so the point is in the very middle, 10cm up the rectangle (just over a third of the way) facing along the length towards the end. There will be a small triangle of pastry overhanging at the bottom of the left hand side. Fold the pastry from the left-hand

continued overleaf…

SAMOSAS CONTINUED…

corner, over the point in the middle, so it meets the right-hand side of the rectangle and creates a cone of pastry that can be filled.

Using a teaspoon, spoon a little of the filling inside the cone shape. Fold the filled pastry back up the pastry length, working from side to side twice more until you have a fully wrapped samosa triangle and a small amount of excess pastry. Dab a little water over the underside of the excess pastry at the end to help it stick and fold over the triangle. Press firmly to seal the samosa. Set aside while you make another 2 samosas in exactly the same way.

Pour the oil into a large saucepan to a depth of about 4cm. Put a cooking thermometer in the oil and place over a medium-high heat. Heat to 160°C. DO NOT ALLOW THE OIL TO OVERHEAT. DO NOT LEAVE HOT OIL UNATTENDED. Using a slotted spoon, lower 3 of the samosas, 1 at a time, into the hot oil where they should immediately begin to sizzle.

Cook the samosas for 6 minutes on each side until the pastry is golden, crisp and lightly puffed. Alternatively, you can cook them in an electric deep fryer. It is important to fry the samosas slowly as the pastry layers need to cook thoroughly and the filling should be hot right through to the middle. Set a timer so you don't forget about them!

While the first samosas are frying, prepare 3 more for cooking. Watch the temperature of the oil in the pan very carefully as you work and make sure it does not overheat. Remove the cooked samosas with a slotted spoon and drain them on kitchen paper.

Continue making and frying the samosas until you've made 9 and used up all the filling. If preparing the samosas in advance, allow them to cool completely, then cover and keep them in the fridge for up to 2 days. Reheat the samosas on a baking tray in a preheated oven at 200°C/Fan 180°C/Gas 6 for about 10 minutes until hot right through. Serve with our minted yoghurt sauce (see page 57).

Top tip from us – cook these kebabs like sausages in a frying pan with a little oil, as they hold together well and are easy to turn. That's what we like to do but if you prefer, shape the mince mixture around skewers and pop them under the grill until cooked through. **Makes 12**

SEEKH KEBABS

- 1 small onion, roughly chopped
- ¼ small green pepper, deseeded and roughly chopped
- 2 plump green chillies (deseeded)
- 15g chunk of fresh root ginger, peeled and roughly chopped
- 3 garlic cloves, roughly chopped
- 1 tsp flaked sea salt
- 2 tsp garam masala (see page 345 or use ready-made)
- ¼ tsp hot chilli powder
- 1 tbsp tomato purée
- 400g lean minced lamb
- 3 tbsp finely chopped fresh coriander leaves
- 1–3 tbsp plain flour (optional)
- 4–5 tbsp sunflower oil
- freshly ground black pepper
- lemon wedges, mixed salad, dips and chutneys, for serving

Put the onion, green pepper, chillies, ginger, garlic, salt, garam masala, chilli powder and tomato purée in a food processor. Season with lots of freshly ground black pepper – and we mean lots. Add more than you imagine you'll need to be sure of a great flavour.

Blitz the ingredients into as smooth a paste as you can make it. You'll need to remove the lid of the food processor and push the mixture down with a spatula a few times. Add the lamb and blitz once more. Tip the mixture into a bowl and stir in the coriander. Cover with cling film and chill for about an hour to allow the mixture to stiffen a little.

Divide the mince mixture into 12 portions and roll them into balls. Then form each ball into a long, fairly thin sausage shape, about 15cm long. If your mince becomes a little sticky, either roll with wet hands or dust your hands with plain flour as you roll.

Heat the oil in a large non-stick frying pan. Gently place a few kebabs into the pan and cook for about 10 minutes over a medium heat until golden brown and cooked through, turning them often. It's best to cook these kebabs in batches of up to 6 at a time, depending on the size of your pan, and keep each batch warm as the next is prepared. You shouldn't need to add any extra oil as some will be released through the fat in the lamb.

Serve the kebabs hot with lemon wedges for squeezing, salad and some dips and chutneys. This mince mixture also makes excellent kofta balls that can also be eaten cold or made in advance and warmed through in a hot pan or on a baking tray in a preheated oven.

This is our take on a shami kebab – first cousin to the seekh. They are usually made with boiled beef and pulses, but we've cut out a few steps to make ours with lean minced lamb and canned chickpeas. They still contain all the traditional spices though and taste delicious served as a snack or starter with a minted yoghurt dip, salad and chutneys. **Makes 12**

SHAMI KEBABS

- 400g can of chickpeas
- ½ medium onion, roughly chopped
- 2 garlic cloves, roughly chopped
- 20g chunk of fresh root ginger, peeled and roughly chopped
- 1 long green chilli, trimmed and roughly chopped
- 1 tbsp garam masala (see page 345 or use ready-made)
- 1 tsp fine sea salt
- 400g lean minced lamb
- small bunch of fresh coriander, leaves finely chopped
- small bunch of fresh mint, leaves finely chopped
- 3 tbsp sunflower oil
- freshly ground black pepper
- minted yoghurt sauce, sliced red onion and chutneys, for serving

Tip the chickpeas into a sieve over the sink and rinse them in cold water. Shake them a few times to drain and transfer them to a food processor. Add the onion, garlic, ginger, chilli, garam masala and salt. Season with a few twists of ground black pepper.

Blitz the mixture to as fine a purée as you can. You may need to remove the lid of the food processor a couple of times and push the mixture down with a rubber spatula until the right consistency is reached.

Add the lamb and herbs and blitz the mixture on the pulse setting until combined. The mince mixture should be thick and paste-like, but don't over blend or it could become too soft. Transfer it to a bowl, cover with cling film and chill for 30–60 minutes. This will help the meat mixture stiffen a little and make it easier to roll.

Take the bowl from the fridge and divide the mixture into 12 portions. Shape these into smooth balls, rolling them between the palms of your hands. Flatten the balls into pattie shapes, about 8cm in diameter, and put them on a tray ready to fry.

Heat the oil in a large non-stick frying pan over a medium heat. Fry the shami kebabs in 2 batches for about 4 minutes on each side until they are lightly browned and cooked through. Keep the first batch warm while you cook the rest. Serve hot with minted yoghurt sauce (see page 57) and some sliced red onion and chutneys if you like.

Eggs and curry – what's not to like? Could this have been the world's first Scotch egg? They're not that hard to make once you get the knack, but as always be very careful with the deep-frying. We love these little goodies for picnics or any time and they're really delicious served warm or cold with some salad, chutney and pickles. **Makes 4**

NARGIS KEBABS

4 medium eggs (fridge cold)
400g lean minced lamb
2 garlic cloves, crushed
15g chunk of fresh root ginger, peeled and finely grated
1 tsp ground coriander
1 tsp ground cumin
1 tsp paprika
¼ tsp cayenne pepper
¼ tsp ground cloves
1 tsp fine sea salt
freshly ground black pepper
salad, chutneys and pickles, for serving

Coating

4 tbsp plain flour
1 medium egg
7 tbsp sesame seeds
sunflower oil, for deep-frying (about 1 litre)

Half fill a medium saucepan with water and bring it to the boil. Gently add the eggs, bring the water back to the boil and cook them for 8 minutes. Cool the eggs under running water, then set them aside in cold water. To prepare the coating for the eggs, put the plain flour in a medium bowl. In a second bowl, beat the egg with a metal whisk until smooth. Sprinkle half of the sesame seeds over a plate.

Put the mince, garlic, ginger, coriander, cumin, paprika, cayenne pepper, cloves and salt in a large bowl. Season well with ground black pepper and mix with clean hands until thoroughly combined. Shell the eggs. Divide the mince mixture into 4 portions and roll them into balls. Place 1 of the balls in the palm of your hand and flatten with the other hand into a round about 1cm thick. It will need to be large enough to wrap around an egg. Dust 1 of the eggs in a little plain flour and place it in the centre of the spiced round of lamb. Wrap the lamb mixture around the egg and smooth any cracks with your fingertips.

Gently roll the egg in a little more flour until the meat is lightly dusted, then dip it into the beaten egg. Lift it out of the egg and gently shake off any excess. Add it to the plate with the sesame seeds and turn a few times until lightly but evenly coated, then set aside. Prepare the other 3 eggs in the same way, replacing the sesame seeds after the first 2 eggs have been coated. This will stop them getting too sticky to use.

Pour the oil into a large saucepan until it is about a third full – you will probably need about 1 litre of oil – and place the pan over a medium-high heat. Put a cooking thermometer in the oil and heat it to 180°C. DO NOT OVERHEAT. DO NOT LEAVE HOT OIL UNATTENDED. Very gently lower 2 of the coated eggs into the hot oil using a slotted spoon. The temperature will drop a little once they are added, but it will slowly rise up again. The eggs don't have to be completely submerged.

Cook the eggs for 6 minutes or until they are golden brown and the mince is cooked. Turn the eggs regularly so they cook evenly. Using a slotted spoon, lift the eggs out of the oil and drain them on kitchen paper. Bring the oil back up to the correct temperature and cook the rest of the eggs in the same way.

Dosas are one of our very favourite things. Can you believe that in India we shared a 10-foot one for lunch? This is our version and we've reduced the preparation time drastically – literally by a day – but we reckon that no one will know the difference. These ones are stuffed with delicious masala potatoes that go perfectly with the crisp pancakes. **Makes 6**

QUICK AND EASY MASALA DOSAS

Masala potatoes

- 900g potatoes, preferably Maris Pipers, peeled and cut into 2.5cm chunks
- 3 tbsp sunflower oil
- 2 tsp cumin seeds
- 2 tsp yellow mustard seeds
- 1 medium onion, finely sliced
- 1 plump green chilli, trimmed and finely sliced (deseed first if you like)
- ½ tsp ground turmeric
- 1 heaped tsp ground coriander
- ¼ tsp garam masala
- pinch of asafoetida
- 1½ tsp flaked sea salt
- 2 tsp fresh lemon juice

Dosas

- 125g gram (chickpea) flour
- 50g rice flour
- 50g plain white flour
- ¼ tsp ground fenugreek
- ½ tsp fine sea salt
- 1 tsp bicarbonate of soda
- 50g plain natural yoghurt
- 675ml water (375ml just-boiled and 300ml cold)
- 2 tbsp sunflower oil, for frying

Half fill a large pan with water and bring it to the boil. Add the potatoes, return to a fast simmer, then cook for 8–10 minutes or until they are tender. Drain the potatoes and leave them to stand while you prepare the spice mix. Preheat the oven to 150°C/Fan 130°C/Gas 2.

While the potatoes are draining, heat the oil in a large non-stick frying pan and fry the cumin and mustard seeds for a few seconds until they begin to pop. Add the onion and chilli and cook for 2 minutes over a medium heat, stirring constantly. Add the potatoes and sprinkle over the turmeric, coriander, garam masala, asafoetida and salt. Stir-fry for 2–3 minutes more, turning the potatoes in the spices until they are lightly coated and beginning to soften around the edges, then sprinkle them with the lemon juice and toss together. Scatter the potatoes on to a baking tray, cover with foil and put them in the oven to keep warm.

To make the dosas, put all the flours in a big bowl. Stir in the fenugreek, salt and bicarbonate of soda. Mix the yoghurt with the water and slowly stir it into the dry ingredients, then whisk the batter until smooth. Pour the batter into a jug and leave it to stand for 10 minutes.

Once the dosa batter has rested, place a large non-stick frying pan over a medium heat and brush with a little of the oil until well greased. Don't have the hob temperature too high as the dosa will burn before it has a chance to dry and become crisp. Stir the dosa batter then, working quickly, hold the handle of the pan and tilt it. Pour a little of the batter into the frying pan and swirl it around until the base is thinly but completely covered. Cook for 2–3 minutes or until the bottom of the dosa is golden brown. It should be dry and crisp – especially at the edges. There is no need to turn the dosa but you should loosen it with a heatproof palette knife before filling.

Spoon about a sixth of the warm potatoes on to 1 side of the dosa and roll it up firmly. Remove it from the pan with a couple of spatulas and serve immediately with a minted yoghurt sauce (see page 57) for drizzling. Make the rest of the dosas in the same way. (They can be kept warm on a baking tray in a low oven, but they won't be quite as crisp.)

Satay comes from Southeast Asian countries, such as Indonesia and Thailand, but is now much loved in this country. It's made from strips of chicken, meat or fish, usually marinated, then threaded on to skewers before cooking. Use metal or wooden skewers, but always soak the wooden ones in water first so they don't burn. Delicious served with gado gado salad (see page 45). **Makes 12 skewers**

THE VERY BEST SATAY

2 x 225g beef sirloin steaks, about 2cm thick
or 2 boneless, skinless chicken breasts (each about 225g)
or 400g raw peeled large king or tiger prawns, thawed, if frozen
2 tsp sunflower oil, for greasing

Satay sauce

100g crunchy peanut butter
180ml sachet of coconut milk
3 tbsp Thai sweet chilli dipping sauce
1 tbsp dark soy sauce
1 tsp fresh lime juice

If you're using wooden skewers, place them in a shallow rectangular dish, or something similar, and cover with cold water. Leave them to soak for at least 30 minutes so they don't burn when you cook the satay.

Next make the marinade. Put the lemon grass, ginger, garlic, chillies, cumin, coriander, sugar, fish sauce, soy sauce, turmeric and oil in a food processor and blitz to a paste. You may need to remove the lid a couple of times and push the mixture down with a spatula until the right consistency is reached. You want the ingredients in the paste to be as finely chopped as possible.

Scrape this mixture into a bowl and season with a few twists of ground black pepper. Trim the beef of any thick fat and cut it slightly diagonally but lengthways into long, thin strips. Your steak will have been cut to around 2cm, so your strips will be about 2cm wide and 9cm long, according to the size of the sirloin.

Cut the chicken breasts in the same way, at a slight diagonal angle but in fairly long strips. You don't want the beef or chicken strips to be too long for the sticks, so 8–9cm in length should be fine. Add the strips to the marinade and stir well. Devein the prawns (see page 355) and add them to the marinade without further preparation.

Thread the beef or chicken strips, or the prawns on to skewers, making sure they aren't threaded too tightly as the heat needs to penetrate. The meat should be fairly flat so it cooks evenly once threaded. As soon as each skewer is threaded, put it on a plate. Cover and leave in the fridge for several hours or overnight.

To make the satay sauce, put the peanut butter, coconut milk, chilli dipping sauce, soy sauce and lime juice in a small non-stick saucepan and heat gently until the peanut butter melts and the mixture comes together to form a thick sauce.

Stir the sauce constantly as it heats, then simmer for 30 seconds, continuing to stir. Remove from the heat and pour the mixture into a heatproof serving bowl. The sauce will thicken as it cools.

Heat a griddle pan until very hot, then brush with a little oil. Cook the beef satay sticks for 1–2 minutes on each side or until nicely browned but still pink and juicy inside.

The chicken satay will need 2–3 minutes on each side or until cooked throughout with no pink remaining. The prawns will need 3–4 minutes on each side until hot and completely pink. While the satay are cooking, press down lightly with a spatula to ensure the meat, chicken or prawns have full contact with the grill. The satay will create a bit of smoke, so make sure you are cooking them in a well ventilated area.

If you prefer, you can grill the satay. Place the sticks on a rack above a baking tray or grill pan lined with foil. Cook under a preheated hot grill for the same times as above, turning once until lightly charred and cooked throughout. If you're using wooden skewers, try to ensure that the part without the meat is sticking out of the grill to help prevent the sticks burning. Fantastic cooked on a barbecue too.

Serve the hot satay with the warm sauce for dipping. Lime wedges are also good for squeezing over the satay.

2 lemon grass stalks, trimmed with white part roughly chopped
20g chunk of fresh root ginger, peeled and roughly chopped
4 garlic cloves, peeled
2 red bird's-eye chillies, stalks trimmed off
2 tsp ground cumin
2 tsp ground coriander
1 tbsp light soft brown sugar
2 tsp Thai fish sauce (nam pla)
2 tsp dark soy sauce
½ tsp ground turmeric
3 tbsp sunflower or groundnut oil
freshly ground black pepper
lime wedges, for squeezing

We make no claims that this is totally authentic, but we've taken bits of a traditional gado gado salad and made it our own. It makes a great starter before Indonesian-style dishes and a lovely salad just as it is. The peanut dressing is meant to be used fairly generously, but if you end up with lots left over, cover it with cling film and keep it in the fridge for up to three days. It's great with satay or other grilled meats. **Serves 4 as a starter or accompaniment or 2 as a main course**

OUR GADO GADO SALAD

- 3 large eggs, fridge cold
- 300g firm tofu, drained
- sunflower oil, for frying
- ½ small head of Chinese leaf, well rinsed
- 1 small round lettuce, leaves separated, rinsed and drained
- ⅓ of a cucumber
- 2 shallots, finely sliced
- 2 medium carrots
- 100g bean sprouts, rinsed and drained
- small handful of little mint leaves (optional)

Peanut dressing

- 75g smooth peanut butter
- 175ml coconut milk
- 1 tbsp Thai sweet chilli dipping sauce
- 1 tbsp dark soy sauce
- 2½ tsp white wine vinegar

To make the peanut dressing, put the peanut butter, coconut milk, dipping sauce, soy sauce and vinegar in a small saucepan. Heat gently and keep stirring constantly until the sauce is smooth. Pour into a heatproof serving jug and leave to cool.

Half fill a medium pan with water and bring to the boil. Gently lower the eggs into the water and return to the boil. Cook for 9 minutes exactly. Drain the eggs in a colander and rinse under running water until the shells feel cold. Put the eggs in a bowl of very cold water and leave them while you prepare the rest of the salad.

Press the tofu on to folded kitchen paper, turning every now and then and replacing the paper until you have soaked up as much of the excess liquid as possible. Put the tofu on a board and cut it into 2cm cubes.

Pour the oil into a medium wide-based saucepan until it is about 1.5cm deep. It's best to use a saucepan rather than a frying pan as the oil can spit once the tofu is added. A sauté pan would also do the job. Place the oil over a medium heat and as soon as it is hot, add the tofu pieces. DO NOT ALLOW THE OIL TO OVERHEAT. DO NOT LEAVE HOT OIL UNATTENDED.

Fry the tofu for about 4 minutes, turning once or twice until golden brown. Watch out for splashes and turn with a long-handled slotted spoon or tongs. Remove when crisp and drain on folded kitchen paper.

Cut the Chinese leaf head into 1–1.5cm slices, discarding the root end, and put the slices in a shallow serving bowl Add the round lettuce leaves, tearing any larger leaves in half. Cut the cucumber into 5cm long sticks and finely slice the shallots. Add these to the salad. Peel the carrots, then continue peeling them into long thin strips with the vegetable peeler. Add the strips to the salad. Scatter the bean sprouts and mint leaves, if using, on top and toss the salad together lightly.

Peel the eggs and cut them into quarters. Arrange the eggs and tofu over the salad. Drizzle with some dressing and serve the rest separately.

We usually use small squid for this but see what's available in your fish shop. Your fishmonger will be happy to clean the squid for you. Medium squid will weigh 175–200g so you'll need two of them. You can buy ready-prepared squid rings, but using whole squid means that you can cut them into ribbons that fry into lovely scoop shapes, ideal for dipping. Make sure to pat the squid dry with kitchen paper before mixing it with the spices. **Serves 4 as a light starter to share or with drinks**

SALT AND PEPPER SQUID
with chilli and garlic dipping sauce

- 5 x 75g squid, cleaned and patted dry
- 2 heaped tsp Szechuan peppercorns (Sichuan pepper)
- 2 heaped tsp black peppercorns
- ½ tsp dried chilli flakes
- 1 tbsp flaked sea salt
- 5 tbsp self-raising flour
- 5 tbsp cornflour
- sunflower oil, for frying (about 500ml)

Dipping sauce

- 100g caster sugar
- 50ml cold water
- 2 tbsp white wine vinegar
- 1 long red chilli, finely chopped (deseed first if you like)
- 2 garlic cloves, finely chopped
- 15g chunk of fresh root ginger, peeled and finely chopped
- 1 tbsp chopped fresh coriander leaves

To make the dipping sauce, put the sugar, water and 1 tablespoon of the vinegar in a small saucepan. Heat gently until the sugar dissolves, stirring constantly, then bring to the boil and cook for 1 minute. Add the chilli, garlic and ginger and cook for 1 minute more, stirring occasionally. Remove the pan from the heat, stir in the remaining vinegar and leave to cool. The sauce will thicken as it cools.

Cut the squid cones up one side and open them out. Score the inside of the cone in a criss-cross pattern with the tip of a knife, working diagonally across the flesh. Cut the flesh into 1.5cm ribbons. Cut the tentacles into halves or quarters, depending on size. Pat the squid pieces lightly with kitchen paper and set aside.

Put the Szechuan and black peppercorns, chilli flakes and salt in a small pan and heat gently until you can smell the peppery aromas – this helps to release the flavour. Tip everything into a pestle and mortar and pound hard until everything is about the texture of freshly ground black pepper. Transfer the pepper mixture to a medium bowl and stir in the self-raising flour and cornflour. Drop the squid into the bowl and toss together until the squid is well coated with the spiced flour. Pour the sauce into a small bowl set on a plate or serving platter and stir in the coriander just before serving.

Pour 2cm of sunflower oil into a large saucepan and place over a medium-high heat. Put a cooking thermometer in the pan and heat the oil to 180°C. DO NOT ALLOW THE OIL TO OVERHEAT. DO NOT LEAVE HOT OIL UNATTENDED. When the oil reaches the right temperature, use tongs to drop a few pieces of the squid into the pan – add them 1 at a time so they don't clump together. Fry the squid for 1–1½ minutes until golden brown and crisp. Lift the squid out with a slotted spoon and drain it on kitchen paper while you fry the next batch.

As soon as a batch is cooked, wait for the oil to get back to the right temperature and cook the next. Re-toss the uncooked squid in the seasoned flour between batches so it has a good coating. Eat as soon as possible. Don't let the squid cool or it will go soggy.

This prawn curry is lovely with any Indian breads and is especially good served with puris. To make them, follow our recipe on page 255 and make 6 large puris, each about 16cm in diameter, instead of 12 smaller ones. It's a good idea to get all the ingredients assembled and prepared before you cook the puris. That way they will stay hot while you finish off the curry. Use ordinary cooked peeled prawns for this recipe, but make sure you thaw them well and don't overcook them or they will go hard. If you don't fancy prawns, use small cubes of chicken breast instead. **Serves 6**

PRAWNS ON PURI

3 fresh ripe tomatoes
4 tbsp sunflower oil
1 medium onion, finely sliced
1 long green chilli, deseeded and finely chopped
20g chunk of fresh root ginger, peeled and finely grated
3 garlic cloves, crushed
1½ tsp garam masala (see page 345 or use ready-made)
¼ tsp cayenne pepper
3 tbsp fresh lemon juice
1 tbsp caster sugar
½ tsp flaked sea salt
400g cooked peeled prawns, thawed if frozen
3 heaped tbsp finely chopped coriander, plus extra sprigs for garnishing
freshly ground black pepper
lemon wedges, for squeezing

Skin and roughly chop the tomatoes. Place a large non-stick frying pan or wok over a medium-high heat. When it's hot, add the oil, then stir-fry the onion and chilli for 3 minutes, stirring constantly. Reduce the heat slightly and add the ginger and garlic and stir-fry for 2 minutes more. Sprinkle with the garam masala and cayenne pepper and cook together, stirring constantly for 30 seconds.

Tip the tomatoes into the pan and add the lemon juice, sugar and salt. Cook for 5 minutes, stirring constantly until the tomatoes soften and create a spicy sauce.

Add the prawns to the pan, along with any thawing liquid, season with a little freshly ground black pepper and cook for 1½–2 minutes until hot, stirring constantly. Remove from the heat and stir in the coriander.

Divide the puris between warmed plates. Don't worry if they have sunk a little while you were cooking the prawns. Spoon the prawn mixture into the centre of each puri and garnish with sprigs of coriander. Serve with lemon wedges for squeezing over the prawns – delicious.

Light Curries

We first cooked this on a houseboat in Kerala when we were travelling round the country. We ate it with some plain rice and chutney and we were very content. This is an easy recipe and fish doesn't need marinating for long – an hour is usually enough. **Serves 4**

SOUTH INDIAN MASALA FISH CURRY

4 x 125g skinless firm white fish fillets, ideally hake or swordfish
2 tbsp plain natural yoghurt
1 tbsp garam masala (see page 345 or use ready-made), plus ½ tsp
1 tsp black mustard seeds
1 tsp cumin seeds
½ tsp hot chilli powder
½ tsp flaked sea salt, plus extra to season
2 tbsp sunflower oil
1 medium onion, finely sliced
2 large fresh ripe tomatoes, skinned
150ml cold water
2 lime wedges, for squeezing
plain natural yoghurt, for serving

197 calories per portion

Pat the fish with kitchen paper to remove any excess moisture. Mix the yoghurt, 1 tablespoon of garam masala, mustard seeds, cumin seeds, chilli powder and ½ teaspoon of salt in a shallow bowl until well combined. Add the fish and turn to coat the fish in the marinade, then cover with cling film and chill for 1 hour in the fridge.

Heat a tablespoon of the oil in a large non-stick frying pan. Take the fish fillets from the marinade and place them in the pan over a medium-high heat. Fry for 2 minutes on each side, depending on the thickness, until just cooked. While the fish is cooking, cut the skinned tomatoes in half, then scoop out the seeds and chuck them away. Cut the tomato flesh into 1cm dice.

Remove the fish from the pan and add the sliced onion. Fry for 4–5 minutes over a medium heat until golden, stirring constantly. Pour the remaining 1 tablespoon of oil into the same pan, then add the diced tomatoes and water. Season with the remaining ½ teaspoon of garam masala and a pinch of salt. Cook for 3–4 minutes, stirring constantly, until the tomatoes soften and the sauce is fairly thick.

Return the fish to the pan and reheat it in the hot sauce for 1–2 minutes. Serve with a good squeeze of lime and a generous spoonful of yoghurt. This goes well with plainly cooked basmati rice, a mixed salad and some chutney.

We're all told to eat more oily fish and sardines are some of our favourites. This is great way of enjoying them – sort of Portugal meets the Punjab! You could also cook these sardines on a barbecue and perhaps butterfly them first, if you like. **Serves 2 as a main course or 3 as starter**

GRILLED MASALA SARDINES

To make the marinade, put the cumin, coriander and mustard seeds with the black peppercorns in a small frying pan and toast them for 1–2 minutes until you can smell the fab aromas. Tip the warm spices into a pestle and mortar and pound them to a powder. Then tip the pounded spices into a bowl and add the garam masala, chilli powder, salt and lime zest. Stir the mixture together.

Slash the sardines 3–4 times down each side and toss them in the marinade until lightly coated all over. Sprinkle with the lime juice and toss again.

Preheat the grill to its hottest setting. Line a grill pan with foil and put a rack on top. Place the sardines on the rack and grill them for 3 minutes on each side until the skin is crisp. Turn the fish carefully so they don't fall apart.

Divide the sardines between your plates and drizzle over any juices that have collected in the grill pan. Serve with lime or lemon wedges for squeezing.

6 fresh sardines, cleaned and heads removed

Marinade

1 tsp cumin seeds
1 tsp coriander seeds
1 tsp yellow mustard seeds
½ tsp black peppercorns
1 tsp garam masala (see page 345 or use ready-made)
½ tsp hot chilli powder
1 tsp flaked sea salt
finely grated zest of 1 well-scrubbed lime
1 tsp fresh lime juice
lime or lemon wedges, for squeezing

---

330 calories per portion (if serving 2) or 220 calories per portion (if serving 3)

Curry can be quite rich and high in calories, but we couldn't give it up while on our weight-loss regime. So, we came up with this great recipe that's going to remain one of our favourites, whether dieting or not. It's a completely guilt-free indulgence and light in fat but full-on in flavour. Delicious served with veg and the minted yoghurt sauce. **Serves 4–5**

MASALA ROASTED CHICKEN
with minted yoghurt sauce

1.65kg chicken
1 lime, quartered
freshly ground black pepper
fresh watercress or baby leaf salad, for serving

Marinade
6 cardamom pods
2 tbsp cumin seeds
2 tbsp coriander seeds
4 whole cloves
1 tsp black peppercorns
1 tsp ground fenugreek
2 tsp ground turmeric
1 tbsp paprika
1–2 tsp hot chilli powder (the more you use, the spicier the dish)
½ tsp ground cinnamon
1 tsp flaked sea salt
4 garlic cloves, crushed
40g chunk of fresh root ginger, peeled and finely grated
100g low-fat natural yoghurt

To make the marinade, split the cardamom pods and remove the seeds. Put the cardamom seeds in a dry non-stick frying pan and throw away the husks. Add the cumin and coriander seeds, the cloves and black peppercorns and place the pan over a medium heat. Cook for 1–2 minutes, stirring regularly until the spices are lightly toasted – you know they're ready when you can smell their spicy aroma.

Tip the toasted spices into a pestle and mortar, or an electric spice grinder, and pound to a fine powder. Transfer these ground spices to a mixing bowl and stir in the fenugreek, turmeric, paprika, chilli powder, cinnamon and salt. Add the garlic, ginger and yoghurt, then mix well and leave to stand while you prepare the chicken.

Place the chicken on its breast on a sturdy chopping board and cut carefully along either side of the backbone with good scissors or poultry shears. Chuck out the bone and cut off the foot joints and wing tips.

Strip all the skin off the bird apart from the ends of the wings (which are easier to remove after cooking). You'll find this simpler to do if you snip the membrane between the skin and the chicken flesh as you go. Cut off and discard any obvious fat – it will be a creamy white colour. Open out the chicken and place it on the board so the breast side is facing upwards.

Press down heavily with the palms of your hands to break the breastbone and flatten the chicken as evenly as possible. This will help it cook more quickly. Slash the meat with a knife through the thickest parts of the legs and breasts. Place the chicken in a shallow non-metallic dish – a lasagne dish is ideal – and tuck in the legs and wings.

Spoon over the marinade and massage it into the chicken on both sides, ensuring that every bit of the bird is well coated – get your hands in there and really go for it. Cover the dish with some cling film and put the chicken in the fridge to marinate for at least 4 hours or, even better, overnight.

Preheat the oven to 210°C/Fan 190°C/Gas 6½. Take the chicken out of the dish and place it on a rack inside a large baking tray, breast-side up. Squeeze over some juice from the lime and season with ground black pepper.

Roast for 45–50 minutes until the chicken is lightly browned and cooked throughout, tossing the lime quarters on to the rack for the last 20 minutes to cook alongside. The limes will be good for squeezing over the meat later. Check that the chicken is properly cooked – the juices should run clear when you pierce the thickest part of a thigh with a skewer. Cover the chicken loosely with foil and leave to rest for 10 minutes before carving.

While the chicken is resting, make the sauce. Spoon the yoghurt into a serving bowl and stir in the mint sauce and sugar until thoroughly combined. Transfer the chicken to a plate or wooden board and carve into slices, discarding any skin if you're watching your weight. Serve with the sauce and a garnish or some watercress or salad and enjoy!

Minted yoghurt sauce

200g low-fat natural yoghurt
2–3 tsp ready-made mint sauce
½–1 tsp sugar, according to taste

---

320 calories per portion (if serving 4) or 256 calories per portion (if serving 5)

This is another of the recipes we enjoyed while trimming our tums. We love chicken korma and our light version is lower in fat than the trad recipe but still very good to eat. Add extra chilli if you like your curry kicking hot and call it a balti. **Serves 4**

LIGHT CHICKEN KORMA

- 4 fairly small boneless, skinless chicken breasts (about 600g)
- 25g low-fat natural yoghurt
- 1 tbsp sunflower oil
- 2 medium-large onions, chopped (400g prepared weight)
- 20g chunk of fresh root ginger, peeled and finely grated
- 4 garlic cloves, sliced
- ½ tsp ground cardamom
- 1 tbsp ground cumin
- 1 tbsp ground coriander
- ½ heaped tsp ground turmeric
- ¼ tsp hot chilli powder
- 1 bay leaf
- 4 whole cloves
- 300ml cold water
- 1 tbsp plain flour
- small pinch of saffron
- 2 tsp caster sugar
- ½ tsp fine sea salt, plus extra to season
- 3 tbsp double cream
- freshly ground black pepper
- fresh coriander, to garnish (optional)

---

294 calories per portion

Cut each chicken breast into 8 or 9 bite-sized pieces, season with black pepper and put them in a non-metallic bowl. Stir in the yoghurt, cover the bowl with cling film and chill for at least 30 minutes, but ideally for 2–6 hours.

Heat the oil in a large non-stick saucepan and add the onions, garlic and ginger. Cover and cook over a low heat for 15 minutes until everything is very soft and lightly coloured. Stir the onions occasionally so they don't start to stick.

Once the onions are softened, stir in the cardamom, cumin, coriander, turmeric, chilli powder and bay leaf. Pinch off the ends of the cloves and add them to the pan; throw away the stalks. Cook the spices with the onions for 5 minutes, stirring constantly.

Stir in the flour, saffron, sugar and ½ teaspoon of salt, then slowly pour the water into the pan, stirring constantly. Bring to a gentle simmer, then cover and cook for 10 minutes, stirring occasionally. Remove the pan from the heat, take out the bay leaf and blitz the onion mixture with a stick blender until it is as smooth as possible. You can do this in a food processor if you prefer. The sauce can now be used right away or cooled, covered and chilled until 10 minutes before serving.

Drain the chicken in a colander over the sink, shaking it a few times – you want the meat to have just a light coating of yoghurt. Place a non-stick frying pan on the heat, add the sauce and bring it to a simmer. Add the chicken and cream and cook for about 10 minutes or until the chicken is tender and cooked through, stirring regularly. Exactly how long the chicken takes will depend on the size of your pieces, so check a couple after 8 minutes – there should be no pink remaining.

Adjust the seasoning to taste, spoon into a warmed serving dish and serve garnished with fresh coriander if you like.

Lemon grass – peel it, bang it, chop it. It's the aroma of Asia.

Another of our special curries that are light in calories but high in flavour. We like to use heaped tablespoons of curry paste for a good hot taste, but reduce this if you like a milder curry. We also like this recipe made with chicken thighs or even firm white fish, such as monkfish. Whatever you use, be sure to cut it into thin slices so it cooks quickly and thoroughly. **Serves 4**

VERY EASY THAI CHICKEN AND COCONUT CURRY

- 1 large red pepper
- 1 large yellow pepper
- 3 boneless, skinless chicken breasts
- 1 tbsp sunflower oil
- 400ml can of half-fat coconut milk
- 250ml cold water, plus 2 tbsp
- 2 heaped tbsp Thai green or red curry paste
- 6 kaffir lime leaves, dried or fresh
- 4 tsp Thai fish sauce (nam pla)
- 1 tsp caster sugar
- 150g mangetout, trimmed
- 2 tbsp cornflour
- small bunch of fresh coriander, roughly torn (optional)
- small bunch of fresh basil, leaves roughly torn (optional)

Deseed the peppers and cut them into thin strips. Cut the chicken breasts into thin slices. Heat the oil in a large non-stick saucepan, deep frying pan or wok, then stir-fry the chicken and peppers for 1 minute. Pour over the coconut milk and add the 250ml water, curry paste, lime leaves, fish sauce and caster sugar. Bring everything to a gentle simmer and cook for 5 minutes.

Add the mangetout and bring the curry back to a simmer. Mix the cornflour with the remaining 2 tablespoons of cold water and stir this into the pan. Cook for a further 2–3 minutes until the vegetables are tender and the spiced coconut milk has thickened, stirring regularly. Make sure the chicken is cooked through and no trace of pinkness remains.

Serve this curry in deep bowls, scattered with fresh coriander or basil, if using. Don't be tempted to eat the lime leaves though!

TOP TIP

Serve this curry with jasmine rice or basmati rice. If you're watching your weight, cook just 50g of rice per person, so 200g in total. Press the freshly boiled rice into a 200ml metal pudding basin that you've oiled lightly and lined with cling film, then turn it out into the bowls before adding the hot curry. You only need 1 basin or mould, as you can reuse it for all the servings.

286 calories per portion

We're big fans of Vietnamese cooking and this dish uses all the characteristic flavours to make a light, flavoursome supper. It's good cooked on a barbecue as well. **Serves 4**

VIETNAMESE-STYLE CHICKEN

4 boneless, skinless chicken breasts
2 spring onions, white and green parts diagonally sliced

Marinade

4 garlic cloves
2 shallots, roughly chopped
1 lemon grass stalk, outer leaves removed and white tender part finely sliced
2 bird's-eye chillies, trimmed and thickly sliced
1 tbsp Thai fish sauce (nam pla)
1 tsp dark soy sauce
2 tbsp soft light brown sugar
1 tsp sunflower oil

---

197 calories per portion

To make the marinade, put all the ingredients in a small food processor and blend until everything is as finely chopped as possible. You may need to remove the lid and push the mixture down a few times until the right consistency is reached. Scrape the mixture into a large bowl.

Put the chicken breasts on a board and slash each one diagonally 4 times, cutting about halfway through. Place the chicken in the marinade and turn until it's all thickly coated with the mixture. Cover and chill for at least 30 minutes and up to 8 hours.

Line a grill pan with foil and place a rack on top. Take the chicken breasts from the marinade and place them on the grill rack. Preheat the grill to its hottest setting. Place the chicken under the grill and cook for 6–8 minutes on each side until lightly browned, charred in places and cooked throughout. Sprinkle with spring onions – make sure you have lots of green slices – and serve with a salad.

This recipe is inspired by a curry made by a friend who grew up in Singapore. Look out for fresh galangal for this dish as it makes all the difference. Also, it is important to use the tiny dried bird's-eye chillies and good-quality braising steak. Just the thing when you want a banging-hot curry.
Serves 6

INDONESIAN BEEF CURRY

- 1 fairly large bulb of garlic
- 30g chunk of fresh galangal, peeled and roughly chopped
- 50g chunk of fresh root ginger, peeled and roughly chopped
- 12 shallots (about 350g)
- 20 dried extra-hot chillies (bird's-eye)
- 1 tbsp caster sugar, preferably golden
- 1.2kg beef chuck steak or other braising steak, trimmed and cut into 2.5cm cubes
- 125ml dark soy sauce
- 1 tbsp sunflower oil
- 1 cinnamon stick
- 600ml beef stock (made with 1 beef stock cube)

335 calories per portion

Break the garlic into separate cloves and set aside 4 of the cloves. Peel the rest of the garlic and put it in a food processor, then add the galangal and ginger. Put 8 of the shallots in the processor and keep 4 for frying later on. Add the chillies and sugar, then blend until the mixture is as finely chopped as possible. You may need to remove the lid and push the mixture down a few times with a rubber spatula.

Put the pieces of beef in a large bowl. Add the shallot mixture and pour over the soy sauce. Mix together well with a wooden spoon until the meat is nicely coated with the soy sauce and the shallot marinade. Cover with cling film and leave to stand for 30 minutes.

Thinly slice the reserved shallots and finely slice the 4 garlic cloves. Place a large flameproof casserole dish over a high heat. Add the oil, then the sliced shallots, garlic and cinnamon and fry for 1–2 minutes or until just before the shallots begin to brown, stirring constantly.

Add all the meat and its marinade and fry for 5 minutes, turning until the meat is lightly sealed and the liquid looks rich and dark. Pour over the stock and bring to a simmer, stirring frequently. Reduce the heat slightly, cover loosely with a lid and simmer the curry gently for 1 hour. Remove the lid and stir every 10 minutes or so, topping up the water when necessary. The liquid should always cover the meat for the first stage of cooking.

After the hour is up, remove the lid from the casserole dish and continue cooking the beef for a further 45–60 minutes or until it is meltingly tender. Stir often, as the liquid reduces to a thick, meaty sauce. This curry is meant to be fairly dry and dark, but it mustn't be allowed to burn, so you will need to watch it carefully as it cooks. Don't be afraid to add extra water if necessary, as you can always increase the heat and bubble the excess liquid away later. The longer the curry cooks, the deeper and richer it will become.

Chicken Curries

Rich and creamy, chicken korma is the curry for people who think they don't like curries. It shouldn't be hot, but the layering of spices makes it wonderfully fragrant and never bland. Although some kormas need long slow cooking, our version is quick to make and just as tasty. **Serves 4**

CREAMY CHICKEN KORMA

4 tbsp ghee or 3 tbsp butter and 1 tbsp sunflower oil
2 medium onions, chopped
20g chunk of fresh root ginger, peeled and finely grated
4 garlic cloves, sliced
½ tsp ground cardamom
1 tbsp ground cumin
1 tbsp ground coriander
½ tsp ground turmeric
¼ tsp hot chilli powder
1 bay leaf
4 cloves
small pinch of saffron (optional)
3 tbsp ground almonds
1 tbsp caster sugar
1½ tsp flaked sea salt, plus extra to season
300ml cold water
2 tbsp sunflower oil
4 boneless, skinless chicken breasts
100ml double cream
freshly ground black pepper

Melt the ghee, or butter and oil, in a large non-stick saucepan and add the onions, ginger and garlic. Cover the pan and cook over a low heat for 10 minutes, then stir in the cardamom, cumin, coriander, turmeric, chilli powder and bay leaf. Pinch the ends off the cloves and add them to the pan; throw away the stalks. Cook for 5 minutes more without covering the pan until the onions are very soft, stirring occasionally.

Stir the saffron, if using, almonds, sugar, salt and water into the pan and bring to a gentle simmer. Cook for 5 minutes, stirring regularly, then remove the pan from the heat and set aside. Remove the bay leaf.

Cut each chicken breast into 7 or 8 bite-sized pieces and season with salt and freshly ground black pepper. Heat the sunflower oil in a large non-stick frying pan. Fry the chicken over a medium heat for 3–4 minutes until lightly coloured on all sides, turning regularly. While the chicken is cooking, blitz the onion mixture with a stick blender or in a food processor until it is as smooth as possible.

Tip the spiced onion purée into the pan with the chicken. Bring it to a simmer and cook for 5–6 minutes or until the chicken is tender and just cooked through, stirring occasionally. Stir in the double cream, then return to a gentle simmer, stirring constantly. Serve with rice.

We think our tandoori chicken is pretty close to the real thing, even though it's not cooked in a traditional tandoor. Try to get some kashmiri chilli powder for the marinade, but if you can't, use two teaspoons of paprika and one teaspoon of hot chilli powder instead. A little red food colouring can make the tandoori the bright scarlet colour that people expect. Using poussins will ensure the chicken marinates beautifully and cooks quickly without becoming dry, but you can use skinless chicken pieces if you prefer. Adjust the cooking time accordingly. You can also bake this in the oven at its hottest setting – watch out for your eyebrows! **Serves 2–3 as a main course or 4 as a starter**

TANDOORI CHICKEN

- 2 young chickens (poussins), about 450g each
- lemon wedges, for squeezing

Marinade

- 10 cardamom pods
- 2 tsp cumin seeds
- 2 tsp coriander seeds
- 1 tsp ground turmeric
- ½ teaspoon ground cinnamon
- ¼ tsp ground cloves
- a good grating of nutmeg
- 1 tbsp kashmiri chilli powder
- ¼ tsp cayenne pepper
- 1 tsp fine sea salt
- 25g chunk of fresh root ginger, peeled and finely grated
- 4 garlic cloves, peeled and crushed
- 150g full-fat yoghurt
- 2 tbsp fresh lemon juice
- red food colouring paste (optional)

To make the marinade, put the cardamom pods in a pestle and mortar and pound lightly until the husks split. Split each pod open and scrape the seeds back into the mortar. Add the cumin and coriander seeds and pound them to a powder. This may take a while – but you can always grind them in a spice grinder instead. Tip the ground spices into a large mixing bowl and add the turmeric, cinnamon, cloves, nutmeg, chilli powder, cayenne pepper and salt. Stir well. Add the ginger, garlic, yoghurt and lemon juice to the bowl and mix well together. Dab in a little food colouring paste if you like, using the end of a teaspoon.

Strip all the skin from the poussins. Separate the skin from the meat with your fingers and use the tip of a small knife to help lift any stubborn areas (you may find the skin around the wing tips easier to remove once the chicken has been quartered). Using poultry shears or really good kitchen scissors, cut the chickens into 4 quarters through the bones. Start by taking the legs off where they join the body. If you twist each leg backwards to break the joint before you cut, it will make life a bit easier. The drumstick needs to remain attached to the thigh.

Next, cut up through the backbone and then through the centre of the breast bone to separate each breast and wing. Flatten the chicken out a little by pressing it with the palms of your hands but watch out for small sharp bones. Slash the thicker parts of each chicken piece – that will be the breasts and thighs – a few times with a knife. Put the chicken in the marinade and turn to coat it all. Cover with cling film and leave to marinate in the fridge for at least 3 hours or overnight.

Preheat the grill to its hottest setting. Line a baking tray or grill pan with foil and place a rack on top. Take the chicken pieces from the marinade, shake off any excess and place them on the rack. Cook under the hot grill, fairly close to the element so the chicken chars, for 6–8 minutes on each side. Check the chicken is cooked by piercing the thickest part of each thigh with a skewer – any juices should run clear and there should be no pink remaining. Serve the chicken hot with a salad garnish and perhaps some minted yoghurt sauce (see page 57). Put some lemon wedges alongside for squeezing over the chicken.

This is a fantastic dish of chicken stir-fried with lots of green chillies and garlic – jalfrezi means 'hot-fry'. We use the long thin green chillies for this – they're not as hot as some but they add lots of flavour. Our jalfrezi has a lovely fresh taste but it's still spicy so you might like to serve it with a raita to temper the chilli heat. You can also make this with boneless, skinless chicken thighs if you prefer. **Serves 4**

CHICKEN JALFREZI

- 6 long green chillies
- 4 boneless, skinless chicken breasts
- 8 tbsp sunflower oil or ghee
- 2 garlic cloves, finely chopped
- 5 fresh ripe tomatoes, 3 of them chopped and 2 quartered
- 1 tbsp ground cumin
- 1 tbsp garam masala (see page 345 or use ready-made)
- 1 tsp ground turmeric
- 1 tbsp caster sugar
- 1 tsp flaked sea salt
- 200ml cold water
- 2 tbsp plain natural yoghurt
- 1 medium onion, cut into 12 wedges
- 1 green pepper, deseeded and cut into 3cm chunks

Place the chillies on a board and finely chop 4 of them. Deseed them first if you don't like your food very spicy (see page 349). Split the other 2 chillies from stalk to tip on one side without opening or removing the seeds. Cut each chicken breast into 6 or 7 bite-sized chunks.

Heat 6 tablespoons of the oil or ghee in a large, fairly deep, non-stick frying pan (or a wok) over a high heat. Add the garlic, chopped chillies, chopped tomatoes, cumin, garam masala, turmeric, sugar and salt, then stir-fry for 3–4 minutes, until the vegetables soften. Don't let the garlic and spices burn or they will make the sauce taste bitter.

Next, add the chicken pieces and whole chillies and cook for 3 minutes, turning the chicken regularly. Pour over the water, stir in the yoghurt and reduce the heat slightly. Cook for 8–10 minutes, stirring occasionally, until the chicken is tender and cooked through and the sauce has thickened. The yoghurt may separate to begin with, but it will disappear into the sauce.

While the chicken is cooking, heat the remaining 2 tablespoons of oil in a clean frying pan and stir-fry the onion and pepper for 2 minutes. Add the quartered tomatoes and fry for another 3–4 minutes, stirring, until the vegetables are just tender and lightly browned.

When the chicken is cooked, stir in the fried vegetables and toss together lightly. Serve immediately.

A North Indian dish with a spicy butter-based sauce, chicken makhani is beautifully aromatic and luxurious. Grilling gives the chicken a lovely charred flavour and keeps it juicy. This dish is often called butter chicken – makhan is the Hindi word for butter. Fab we call it. **Serves 6**

CHICKEN MAKHANI

6 boneless, skinless chicken breasts
sunflower oil, for greasing skewers

Marinade

1½ tbsp cumin seeds
1½ tbsp coriander seeds
½ tsp cardamom seeds (from pods)
4 cloves
½ tsp black peppercorns
2 tsp ground fenugreek
1 tsp ground turmeric
2 tsp ground paprika
1 tsp hot chilli powder
1 tsp flaked sea salt
2 garlic cloves, crushed
25g chunk of fresh root ginger, peeled and finely grated
4 tbsp plain natural yoghurt

Butter sauce

175g ghee, or 150g butter and 3 tbsp sunflower oil
2 medium onions, roughly chopped
6 garlic cloves, crushed
35g chunk of fresh root ginger, peeled and finely grated
1 tsp ground turmeric
4 fresh ripe tomatoes, chopped
3 tbsp tomato purée
1 tbsp caster sugar
1 tsp flaked sea salt
100ml double cream
handful of fresh coriander, chopped

First prepare the marinade. Put the cumin, coriander, cardamom, cloves and peppercorns in a dry frying pan over a medium heat. Cook for 1–2 minutes, stirring regularly until lightly toasted. Tip everything into a pestle and mortar or spice grinder, then add the fenugreek, turmeric, paprika, chilli powder and salt and grind everything into a fine powder. Spoon 3 tablespoons of the spice mixture into a bowl and stir in the garlic, ginger and yoghurt. Cut each chicken breast into 7 or 8 bite-sized pieces. Stir these into the spiced yoghurt, cover with cling film and put them in the fridge to marinate for at least 4 hours or ideally overnight.

To make the butter sauce, heat 125g of the ghee (or 100g of butter and 3 tablespoons of oil) in a large non-stick saucepan and add the onions, garlic and ginger. Cover the pan with a lid and cook over a low heat for 10 minutes, stirring occasionally. Remove the lid, increase the heat slightly and stir in the rest of the powdered spices you prepared for the marinade and the turmeric. Fry for 3 minutes, stirring regularly.

Stir in the tomatoes, tomato purée, sugar and salt and fry for 5 minutes, stirring constantly until the tomatoes have softened. Add 200m of cold water, bring to a gentle simmer and cook for 10 minutes more, adding the cream for the last 2 minutes of the cooking time. Remove from the heat, and blitz with a stick blender or in a food processor until smooth. Pour the sauce into a heatproof bowl, cover with cling film, cool and chill until you are ready to cook the chicken.

Preheat the grill to its hottest setting. Thread the chicken pieces on to 7 or 8 lightly greased, long metal skewers, keeping 1–2cm between each piece. Place the skewers on a rack over a grill pan lined with foil. Slide the pan on to a shelf as close as possible to the heat and cook the chicken for 5 minutes. Holding the hot skewers with an oven cloth, turn them and cook them on the other side for 4–5 minutes or until the chicken is cooked through and lightly charred.

Meanwhile, melt the remaining 50g of ghee or butter in a non-stick frying pan and stir in the butter sauce. Bring to a gentle simmer and cook for 5 minutes, stirring regularly. Take the chicken and, sliding a fork down each skewer, plop the chicken pieces into the hot sauce. Stir well and bubble for a few seconds more. Sprinkle with freshly chopped coriander and serve hot with rice.

We know there are lots of ingredients here, but please give this a go. This recipe is simple to prepare and tastes fantastic. It's by far the best home-made chicken tikka masala we've ever cooked and it's as close to a restaurant dish that you're ever likely to find. Truly a national treasure of a dish. **Serves 4**

CHICKEN TIKKA MASALA

2 tbsp cumin seeds
2 tbsp coriander seeds
2 whole cloves
1 tsp black peppercorns
small piece of cinnamon stick
½ tsp ground fenugreek
1½ tsp ground turmeric
2 tsp ground paprika
½–1 tsp hot chilli powder
1 tsp flaked sea salt
2 garlic cloves, crushed
20g chunk of fresh root ginger, peeled and grated
4 tbsp plain natural yoghurt
4 boneless, skinless chicken breasts, each cut into 7 or 8 pieces
sunflower oil, for greasing skewers

Masala sauce
4 tbsp ghee, or 2 tbsp softened butter and 2 tbsp sunflower oil
3 medium onions, chopped
4 garlic cloves, crushed
25g chunk of fresh root ginger, peeled and finely grated
½ tsp ground turmeric
3 tbsp tomato purée
2 tsp caster sugar
1 tsp flaked sea salt
400ml cold water
2 tbsp double cream

Put the cumin and coriander seeds, cloves, peppercorns and cinnamon stick in a dry frying pan over a medium heat. Cook for 1–2 minutes, stirring regularly until lightly toasted – you know they're ready when you can smell the wonderful spicy aroma. Tip everything into a pestle and mortar or electric spice grinder. Add the fenugreek, turmeric, paprika, chilli powder and salt and grind everything to a fine powder.

Spoon 3 tablespoons of this spice mixture into a mixing bowl and stir in the garlic, ginger and yoghurt. Mix thoroughly and set aside. Stir the chicken pieces into the spiced yoghurt, cover with cling film and put them in the fridge to marinate for at least 4 hours or ideally overnight.

To make the masala sauce, heat the ghee (or butter and oil) in a large non-stick saucepan and add the onions, garlic and ginger. Cover and cook over a low heat for 10 minutes, stirring occasionally. Remove the lid, increase the heat slightly and stir in the rest of the powdered spices, plus the ½ teaspoon of turmeric. Fry for 3 minutes, stirring regularly.

Stir in the tomato purée, sugar and salt and fry for 2–3 minutes, stirring constantly. Add the water, bring to a gentle simmer and cook for 5 minutes more, adding the cream for the last 30 seconds of the cooking time. Remove from the heat and blitz with a stick blender or in a food processor until you have a sauce that's as smooth as possible. Pour this into a heatproof bowl, cover with cling film, cool and chill until you're ready to cook the chicken.

Thread the chicken pieces on to lightly greased, long metal skewers. You should be able to fit about 6 chunks of chicken on to each skewer, leaving 1–2cm between each piece. Preheat the grill to its hottest setting and place the skewers on a rack over a grill pan lined with foil. Slide the pan on to a shelf, putting it as close as possible to the heat, and cook the chicken for 5 minutes. Turn each skewer, holding it with an oven cloth, and cook on the other side for another 4–5 minutes or until the chicken is cooked through and lightly charred.

While the chicken is grilling, tip the masala sauce into a large non-stick frying pan. Bring to a gentle simmer and cook for 2–3 minutes, stirring regularly. Take the chicken skewers from under the grill and slide a fork down the length of each skewer to plop the pieces into the hot sauce. Stir well and bubble for a few seconds more. Serve hot with rice.

Balti has become the Brummies' own and is the quickest of all curries. Balti means bucket and is the name of the pot traditionally used for cooking this dish. The pot looks a bit like a two-handled wok, but an ordinary frying pan with a lid works just fine. This is our version of this wonderful one-pot meal – really simple but tastes rich and delicious. Add an extra spoonful of curry paste if you like your curry hot, or fry a chopped red chilli with the garlic and ginger instead. **Serves 4**

VERY GOOD BALTI CHICKEN

- 15g butter
- 2 tbsp sunflower oil
- 2 large onions, roughly chopped
- 3 garlic cloves, sliced
- 25g chunk of fresh root ginger, peeled and roughly chopped
- 2–3 tbsp medium curry paste or balti curry paste
- 1 tbsp tomato purée
- 4 boneless, skinless chicken breasts
- 175ml just-boiled water
- ½ tsp flaked sea salt
- 1 tsp caster sugar
- 4 fresh ripe tomatoes, quartered
- 200–225g bag of baby spinach leaves

To prepare the sauce base, melt the butter with 1 tablespoon of the oil in a large non-stick frying pan. You need a pan with a lid, so if you don't have one handy, use a large non-stick saucepan instead. Add the onions, garlic and ginger to the pan, then cover with a lid and cook over a low heat for 15 minutes until very soft. Stir occasionally.

Remove the lid from the pan and turn up the heat. Cook the onion mixture for 2–3 minutes more, stirring constantly, until well coloured. Add the curry paste to the pan, turn down the heat slightly and cook with the onions for 3 minutes more, stirring frequently. Remove the pan from the heat and stir in the tomato purée.

Blitz the spiced onions with a stick blender or tip them into a food processor and blend until as smooth as possible. Tip the onion mixture into a bowl and set aside. If you like, you can keep the mixture, covered, in the fridge for up to 3 days.

Cut each chicken breast into 7 or 8 bite-sized chunks. Place the pan used to cook the onion mixture back over a medium heat and add the remaining oil and the chicken pieces. Fry the chicken for 3 minutes, turning often, until lightly coloured all over.

Next, add all the spiced onion mixture, water, salt, sugar and tomatoes, bring to a simmer and cook for 4 minutes. Add the spinach in a few handfuls, allowing each to soften a little before adding the next. Cook for a further minute, stirring regularly, or until the chicken is cooked through, the tomatoes are softened and the spinach has wilted. Serve with warmed naan bread or freshly cooked rice.

We love one-pot dishes and this is a great one – meat, rice and veg all in one pan and served up in next to no time. A perfect mid-week supper that all the family will enjoy. **Serves 4**

QUICK CHICKEN PILAU

Scatter the almonds into a large, deep non-stick frying pan, wide saucepan or sauté pan and place it over a medium heat. Cook the almonds for 1–2 minutes until they are golden, tossing occasionally, then tip them into a heatproof bowl. Stir the saffron, if using, into the hot chicken stock and leave to stand. Snip any visible fat off the chicken thighs with a good pair of kitchen scissors, then cut them in half.

Return the non-stick pan to the heat and add the sunflower oil and sliced onion. Gently fry the onion for about 5 minutes or until softened and turning golden brown, stirring regularly. Add the chicken pieces and fry for 3–4 minutes or until lightly coloured all over. Add the garlic, pepper and beans and cook for 1 minute more, stirring constantly.

Spoon the curry paste into the pan and cook with the chicken and vegetables for about 3 minutes, stirring constantly. Tip the rice on top, pour over all the saffron-infused stock and bring to a simmer. Stir in the sultanas and toasted almonds and cover the pan with a lid. Leave to cook over a low heat, allowing the stock to simmer gently, for 12 minutes by which time the chicken should be cooked, the rice tender and almost all the liquid absorbed.

Remove the pan from the heat and leave to stand, covered, for a further 3–5 minutes. Take the lid off and give the rice a good fluff up with a fork, then serve steaming hot.

3 heaped tbsp flaked almonds
good pinch of saffron (optional)
900ml hot chicken stock (made with 1 chicken stock cube)
6 boneless, skinless chicken thighs, cut in half
2 tbsp sunflower oil
1 medium onion, halved and sliced
2 garlic cloves, crushed
1 red pepper, deseeded and cut into rough 2cm chunks
100g green beans, trimmed and cut into 3cm lengths
4 tbsp medium curry paste
300g basmati rice, rinsed and drained
25g sultanas

There are times when only a chicken madras will do – that's what we say. This is a stalwart in our curry repertoire and it's a fiery curry loved by millions and we're no exception. If you like your food a little milder, reduce the chillies to just two and remove all the seeds – you should still get the great flavour but less of the heat. You might think this recipe contains a lot of oil but it will help make the sauce taste great. Use boneless, skinless chicken thighs instead of the breasts if you like. **Serves 4**

QUICK CHICKEN MADRAS

- 4 long red chillies
- 4 boneless, skinless chicken breasts
- 4 tbsp sunflower oil
- ½ medium onion, finely chopped
- 2 garlic cloves, crushed
- 227g can of chopped tomatoes
- 2 tsp ground cumin
- 2 tsp kashmiri chilli powder (or ½ tsp hot chilli powder and 2 tsp paprika)
- 1 tbsp garam masala (see page 345 or use ready-made)
- 1 tsp ground turmeric
- 1 tbsp caster sugar
- 1 tsp flaked sea salt
- 200ml cold water
- 2 tbsp double cream (optional)

Place the chillies on a board and finely chop 2 of them. (Deseed them first if you don't like very spicy food – see page 349.) Split the other chillies from stalk to tip on one side without opening or removing the seeds. Cut each chicken breast into 7 or 8 bite-sized chunks.

Heat the oil in a large, fairly deep, non-stick frying pan (or wok) over a high heat. Add the onion, garlic, chopped chillies, chopped tomatoes, cumin, chilli powder, garam masala, turmeric, sugar and salt. Stir-fry for 5 minutes, stirring until the vegetables soften and the oil begins to split from the sauce. Do not allow the garlic or spices to burn as they will add a bitter flavour to the sauce.

Next, add the chicken pieces and whole chillies to the pan and cook for 2 minutes, turning the chicken regularly. Pour over the water, stir in the cream, if using, and reduce the heat slightly. Cook for 8–10 minutes, stirring occasionally until the chicken is tender and cooked through and the sauce has thickened. Don't let the chicken overcook or it will toughen. Serve immediately with freshly cooked rice.

Shallots have a milder flavour than onions and are just right for this dish. The long banana shallots or the round ones are fine and if you have any left over, fry them up to make a garnish for your curry. You can buy shrimp paste in Asian grocers and online. It adds a lovely savoury flavour and does make all the difference to the results. **Serves 4**

MALAYSIAN CHICKEN

- 4 chicken legs (with thighs and drumsticks)
- 1 cinnamon stick
- 5 cloves
- 3 star anise
- 6 cardamom pods, lightly crushed
- 400ml can of coconut milk
- 350ml cold water
- 600g waxy potatoes, such as Charlottes, peeled and cut into 4cm chunks
- 1 tsp fine sea salt, plus extra for seasoning
- freshly ground black pepper

Curry paste

- 300g shallots, peeled
- 20g chunk of fresh root ginger, peeled and roughly chopped
- 6 garlic cloves
- 2 tbsp Malaysian curry powder or medium curry powder
- 1 tsp ground turmeric
- 10 dried extra-hot chillies (bird's-eye)
- 10g shrimp paste
- 3 tbsp sunflower oil

Garnish (optional)

- 2 tbsp sunflower oil
- 100g shallots, finely sliced into rings

To make the curry paste, put the shallots, ginger, garlic, curry powder, turmeric, chillies, shrimp paste and sunflower oil in a food processor and blitz them to a paste. You'll need to remove the lid and push the mixture down a couple of times with a rubber spatula until you get the right consistency.

Take a chicken leg and bend the drumstick away from the thigh until you hear a small crack. Put the chicken leg on a board and use a sharp knife to separate the drumstick and thigh, cutting carefully between the joints. Do the same thing with the rest of the chicken legs and season them all with a little salt and some black pepper.

Put the cinnamon stick, cloves, star anise and cardamom in a large flameproof casserole dish or a very large non-stick saucepan – you need something large enough to hold the chicken and liquid later when simmering. Place the pan over a medium heat and toast the spices for 1–2 minutes, stirring until you can smell their aroma. Immediately add the curry paste to the pan and cook it with the whole spices for 2–3 minutes, stirring constantly and scraping the bottom of the pan with a wooden spoon so nothing sticks. Place the chicken pieces in the same pan and fry them in the spices for 5 minutes, turning regularly until very lightly coloured. Keep watching that the spices don't stick.

Pour the coconut milk and water into the pan, then sprinkle with the salt and stir well. Cover the pan loosely with a lid, bring to a gentle simmer and cook for 15 minutes. Remove the lid and add the potatoes to the pan, making sure they are all submerged.

Return to a gentle simmer without covering and cook for another 30–40 minutes until the chicken is tender and the sauce has reduced by about a third. Stir every 15 minutes. Once it's cooked, let the curry stand for 5 minutes, then skim off any fat that has risen to the surface.

To prepare the garnish, if using, heat the oil in a large non-stick frying pan. Fry the shallots for 5–8 minutes, stirring them frequently with a wooden spoon until they are lightly browned and crisp. Drain on kitchen paper, then sprinkle over the chicken before serving.

We know you can buy ready-made green curry paste, but our home-made version is a million miles away from shop-bought and unequalled in freshness and flavour. Fish sauce or nam pla is an important ingredient in Thai curries and it's essential for that authentic taste. It's easy to find in supermarkets now so be sure to add it to your larder. This recipe makes a fairly mild curry, but if you like your curries spicier, add one or two extra chillies. **Serves 3–4**

THAI GREEN CHICKEN CURRY

6 boneless, skinless chicken thighs
1 tbsp sunflower oil
1 x 400ml can of coconut milk
handful of fresh basil leaves
handful of fresh coriander, chopped

Green curry paste

2 tsp coriander seeds
3 long red or green chillies, halved and deseeded
2 garlic cloves
2 lemon grass stalks, outer leaves removed and white part roughly chopped
5 spring onions, trimmed and sliced into short lengths
25g chunk of fresh root ginger, peeled and chopped
6 kaffir lime leaves (dried or fresh)
large bunch of fresh coriander, trimmed
1 tbsp Thai fish sauce (nam pla)
1 tbsp demerara sugar
flaked sea salt
freshly ground black pepper

First make the curry paste. Put the coriander seeds in a small pan and place over a high heat. Cook for 1–2 minutes until they begin to release their delicious spicy aroma, giving the pan a good shake now and again. Tip the seeds into a pestle and mortar and pound until they are crushed to a powder.

Transfer the crushed coriander to a food processor and add the chillies, garlic, lemon grass, spring onions, ginger, lime leaves, coriander, fish sauce and sugar. Blitz until all the ingredients are very finely chopped and form a thick paste. You may need to push the mixture down a couple of times with a spatula. Season with a good pinch of salt and plenty of ground black pepper and whizz for a few seconds more.

Cut each chicken thigh into 6 pieces. Heat the oil in a large non-stick frying pan or wok and stir-fry the chicken for 1–2 minutes over a medium-high heat until it is no longer pink. Add the curry paste and cook with the chicken for 2–3 minutes more. Pour over the coconut milk, bring to a simmer and cook for 4 minutes. Check that the chicken is cooked through, but don't let it overcook.

Stir in the basil and coriander leaves and ladle the curry into bowls. Serve with some freshly cooked jasmine rice.

Crushed, chopped or whole,
garlic is the bedrock
of a good curry.

Bruce Lee meets Colonel Sanders – this is one of those dishes that just works. We've experimented with lots of variations and this is our favourite – it has a lovely slightly aniseedy taste. Panko breadcrumbs are a must so keep some in your store cupboard. **Serves 4**

JAPANESE CHICKEN KATSU CURRY

4 x 175g boneless, skinless chicken breasts
50g plain flour
1 large egg
100g Japanese panko breadcrumbs or dry white breadcrumbs
200ml sunflower oil
hot mounds of steamed rice, for serving

Sauce

3 tbsp sunflower oil
2 medium onions, roughly chopped
25g chunk of fresh root ginger, peeled and finely chopped
4 garlic cloves, sliced
1 tbsp medium curry powder
½ tsp ground star anise
½ tsp ground turmeric
20g plain flour
500ml chicken stock (made with 1 chicken stock cube)
2 tsp tomato purée
freshly ground black pepper

First make the sauce. Heat the oil in a large non-stick saucepan and add the chopped onions. Cover with a lid and gently fry the onions for 8–10 minutes until well softened, stirring occasionally. Remove the lid, increase the heat a little and cook for 3 minutes more, stirring often, until the onions are pale golden brown. Reduce the heat, add the ginger and garlic and simmer gently for 5 minutes, stirring occasionally.

Stir the curry powder, star anise, turmeric and a few twists of ground black pepper into the onions. Cook for 2 minutes, stirring frequently. Sprinkle over the plain flour and stir well. Gradually add the chicken stock, stirring constantly until it is all incorporated. Add the tomato purée and bring to a simmer, then cook for 5 minutes, stirring occasionally. Remove from the heat and blitz with a stick blender until smooth. If you don't have a stick blender, let the sauce cool for a few minutes and blend in a food processor until smooth. Cover with cling film and set aside while you prepare the chicken.

One at a time, place the chicken breasts on a board and cover with cling film. Bash the thickest part of the chicken with a rolling pin until the pieces have an even depth – just under 2cm. Sift the flour on to a large plate. Beat the egg in a medium bowl with a metal whisk until smooth. Sprinkle half the breadcrumbs over a small tray. Take a chicken breast and dust it in the flour. Shake off any excess and dip it straight into the beaten egg, then coat it in the breadcrumbs until evenly covered. Put the chicken breast on a tray while you coat the rest, adding the reserved breadcrumbs after coating 2 breasts. Chill for 30–60 minutes if you have time, as this will help the breadcrumb coating to 'set'.

Pour the oil into a deep non-stick frying pan and set over a medium heat. DO NOT ALLOW THE OIL TO OVERHEAT AND NEVER LEAVE HOT OIL UNATTENDED. Using tongs, gently lower 2 of the chicken breasts into the hot oil. Cook for 5–6 minutes on each side until the chicken is crisp, golden brown and cooked through – there should be no pinkness remaining in the centre. Keep these chicken breasts warm while you cook the others. Five minutes before the chicken is ready, remove the cling film from the curry sauce and pour it into a pan over a low heat. Slowly bring to a gentle simmer, stirring constantly. Simmer for a couple of minutes. Slice the crisp chicken breasts thickly and serve on warmed plates with steamed rice and some hot sauce, or place the sauce in small dishes to serve alongside. Serve immediately.

Don't diss curry powder. It's a really useful ingredient for some dishes and here it is used to good effect in this great everyday curry from the Philippines. Enjoy. **Serves 4**

FILIPINO SPICY CURRY

- 8 chicken thighs, with skin and bones
- 2 tbsp sunflower or groundnut oil
- 1 medium onion, roughly chopped
- 4 garlic cloves, finely sliced
- 2 tbsp medium curry powder
- 400ml can of coconut milk
- 150ml cold water
- 1½ tbsp Thai fish sauce (nam pla)
- 500g potatoes, preferably Maris Pipers
- 1 large red pepper, deseeded and cut into 3cm chunks
- 1 large green pepper, deseeded and cut into 3cm chunks
- flaked sea salt
- freshly ground black pepper

Take the skin off the chicken thighs and season them with salt and pepper. Chuck away the skins. Heat the oil in a large, wide non-stick saucepan or sauté pan and fry the chicken until it is lightly browned on both sides, then transfer to a plate. You'll need to brown the chicken in 2 batches so you don't overcrowd the pan.

Add the onion to the pan and stir-fry for 3 minutes until it's beginning to soften. Stir in the garlic and curry powder and cook for 1 minute more. Pour the coconut milk and water into the pan, then stir in the fish sauce.

Put the chicken pieces back in the pan along with any resting juices, cover loosely with a lid and bring to a gentle simmer. Cook over a medium heat for 20 minutes. Remove the lid a couple of times and turn the chicken as it cooks.

Half fill a medium pan with water and bring to the boil. Peel the potatoes and cut them into chunks of about 2.5cm. Drop the potatoes carefully into the boiling water and bring the water back to a fast simmer. Cook the potatoes for 8–10 minutes or until just tender – test a couple with the tip of a knife. Drain them in a colander in the sink and leave to stand.

After the 20 minutes is up, remove the lid from the chicken curry and stir in the potatoes and peppers. Cook uncovered at a fast simmer for a further 10 minutes or until the chicken and peppers are tender and the potatoes are hot, stirring regularly. The final curry should be thicker than a Thai green curry but still nice and saucy.

This sumptuously rich, creamy curry from the Rajasthan area in northern India is fit for a maharajah's birthday. Saffron, or kesar, comes from the dried stigmas of crocus flowers and is the most expensive of all spices. You need 70,000 flowers to get just 450 grams of saffron, but luckily a little goes a long way! Take care not to add too much as you don't want it to overpower the other spices in this delicately fragrant dish. If you buy your saffron in sachets, you'll need about half a 0.4 gram sachet for this recipe. Use four boneless, skinless chicken breasts instead of the thighs if you prefer. **Serves 3–4**

RAJASTHANI KESAR MURG

Saffron chicken curry

6 boneless, skinless chicken thighs
150g plain natural yoghurt
150ml double cream
good pinch of saffron
2 tbsp ghee or sunflower oil
1 medium onion, halved and finely sliced
4 garlic cloves, finely sliced
20g chunk of fresh root ginger, peeled and finely grated
50g cashew nuts or ground almonds
4 cloves
1 bay leaf
6 green cardamon pods, crushed
1 heaped tsp ground coriander
½ tsp cayenne pepper
½ tsp ground turmeric
1 tsp flaked sea salt
1 tsp caster sugar
300ml cold water
freshly ground black pepper

Cut each chicken thigh into 2 pieces, removing any obvious fatty bits. Season with a little black pepper, then put the chicken in a bowl and add the yoghurt. Turn the chicken pieces in the yoghurt to coat them, then cover and leave to marinate in the fridge for 30–60 minutes.

Pour the cream into a small saucepan and add the saffron. Bring to a gentle simmer, then remove from the heat and leave to stand. This standing time will give the saffron time to infuse into the warm cream. Heat the ghee or sunflower oil in a large non-stick saucepan or sauté pan and gently fry the onion, garlic and ginger for 8–10 minutes until well softened and the onions are lightly browned. While the onions are cooking, put the cashew nuts in a food processor and blitz them into fine crumbs.

Once the onions are done, take a clove and, holding it over the frying pan, crumble off the top part with your fingertips and sprinkle the powder into the onion mixture. Repeat with the remaining cloves, then add the clove stalks, bay leaf, cardamom pods, coriander, cayenne pepper, turmeric, salt and sugar. Cook together for 2–3 minutes, stirring constantly. The onions should be a rich brown colour by now.

Add the chicken and yoghurt to the pan and fry over a medium heat for 5 minutes, turning every now and then until the chicken is very lightly coloured all over. The yoghurt will separate to begin with, but as the chicken cooks, it will thicken. Stir in the ground nuts and cook for a few seconds, stirring constantly.

Pour in the saffron-infused cream and the water and stir well. Bring to a low simmer and cook for 10 minutes or until the chicken is tender and cooked through and the sauce has thickened, stirring and turning the chicken in the sauce occasionally. Take care not to bite on the cloves and cardamom when you come to eat the curry.

Fish & Shellfish Curries

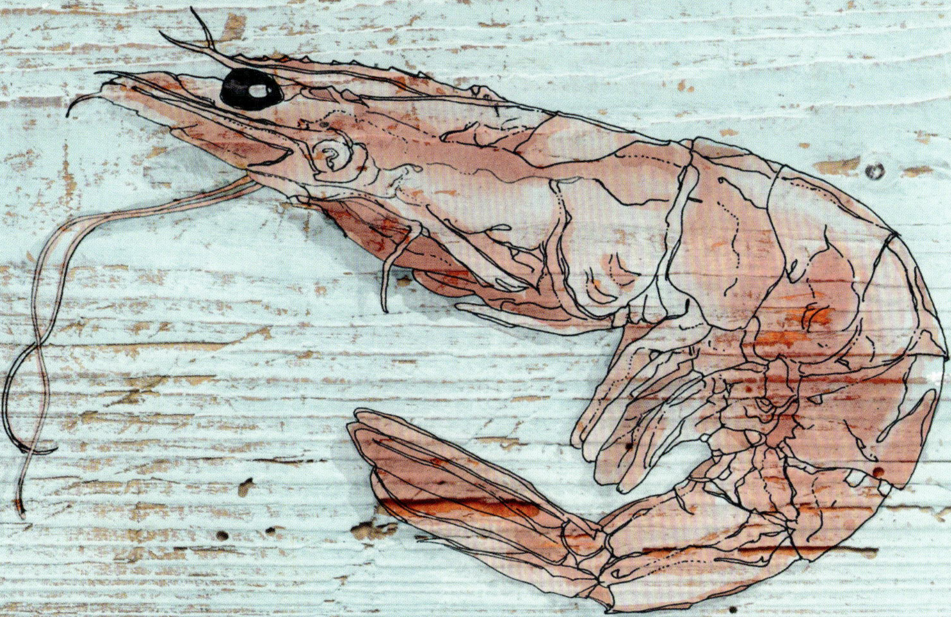

Mussels are a great favourite of ours and they work well with a light curry sauce. This makes a nice change from the usual Mediterranean-style mussels and you could treat yourself to some warm naan bread (see page 247) for mopping up the juices. Be sure to give your mussels a good scrub and chuck out any that don't behave themselves. **Serves 2–3**

SIMPLE MUSSELS
in a fragrant curry sauce

- 1kg fresh live mussels
- 2 tbsp sunflower oil
- 1 medium onion, finely chopped
- 4 garlic cloves, finely sliced
- 15g chunk of galangal or 20g chunk of fresh root ginger, peeled and very finely chopped
- 1 tbsp red or green Thai curry paste
- 4 fresh kaffir lime leaves or 6 dry lime leaves
- 400ml can of coconut milk
- 1 tbsp Thai fish sauce (nam pla)
- large bunch of fresh coriander, leaves roughly chopped
- freshly ground black pepper

Scrub the mussels really well and scrape off any barnacles that might be hitching a ride. Remove the beards. Chuck away any mussels that are damaged in any way or that don't close when you tap them on the side of the sink. Put the mussels in a bowl or colander and set aside.

Heat the oil in a large non-stick frying pan that has a lid over a low heat – you could also use a sauté pan. Very gently fry the onion, garlic and galangal or ginger for 8–10 minutes, without covering, until well softened but not coloured, stirring regularly. Stir in the curry paste and lime leaves and cook for 1 minute more, stirring constantly.

Pour over the coconut milk and stir in the fish sauce and coriander, then season with black pepper. Bring to a simmer and cook for 5 minutes. Add the mussels, cover the pan with a lid and cook until all the mussels have steamed open. Remove the lid after 2 minutes of cooking and turn the mussels with a spoon to ensure they cook evenly. Cover again and cook for a further 1–2 minutes, giving the pan a good shake now and again. The total steaming time shouldn't be longer than about 4 minutes.

Remove the pan from the heat and, using a slotted spoon, serve the mussels into wide, warmed bowls. Throw away any mussels that haven't opened. Pour the cooking liquor over the top and give everyone spoons so they can slurp up the delicious sauce.

This is a dry, spicy curry, flavoured with the sourness of tamarind and the heat of chillies in a thick sauce that clings to the prawns. Traditionally made with freshly grated coconut. **Serves 4**

SOUTH INDIAN PRAWN CURRY

- 400g peeled raw large tiger or king prawns, thawed if frozen
- 2 tbsp sunflower oil
- 1 medium onion, finely chopped
- 2 garlic cloves, finely chopped
- 25g chunk of fresh root ginger, peeled and finely chopped
- 2 long green chillies, deseeded and finely chopped
- 2 tsp garam masala (see page 345 or use ready-made)
- 1 tsp hot chilli powder
- 1 tsp ground turmeric
- 4 fresh ripe tomatoes, roughly chopped
- 1 tsp tamarind paste
- 2 tsp runny honey
- 50ml cold water
- 4 tbsp desiccated coconut
- small bunch of fresh coriander, leaves roughly chopped
- rice or chapatis, for serving

Devein the prawns (see page 355). Heat the oil in a large non-stick frying pan and gently fry the onion for 5 minutes until softened. Add the garlic, ginger and chillies and cook for 2 minutes more, stirring.

Sprinkle over the garam masala, chilli powder and turmeric and cook for 30 seconds, stirring vigorously. Watch that the spices don't burn. Tip the tomatoes into the pan and stir in the tamarind paste, honey and water. Simmer for 10 minutes, stirring regularly, until the tomatoes are softened and the sauce has thickened.

Stir in the coconut and prawns and cook for 2–3 minutes or until the prawns turn pink. Stir constantly while the prawns are cooking and don't allow them to overcook or they won't be as succulent. Sprinkle the curry with freshly chopped coriander and serve with rice or chapatis.

Plump prawns make perfect curries, but make sure you clean them properly first.

We based this recipe on the amazing dishes that we've eaten and enjoyed in Kerala, in South India and it's a real keeper. It's so quick to make that we used to make this on our stage tour round Britain. We cooked it on 80 nights – and left lots of folk hanging over the balcony licking their lips. **Serves 3–4**

KERALAN KING PRAWN CURRY

500g jumbo tiger prawns, thawed, if frozen
1 onion, peeled and roughly chopped
1 long red chilli, deseeded
2 garlic cloves
25g chunk of fresh root ginger, peeled and roughly chopped
2 tbsp sunflower oil
12 fresh curry leaves
1 tsp black mustard seeds
½ tsp ground fenugreek
pinch of asafoetida
1 tbsp cold water
½ tsp ground turmeric
200ml coconut milk
juice of 1 lime
flaked sea salt
freshly ground black pepper
4 tbsp chopped fresh coriander leaves and 1 lime cut into wedges, for serving

First peel the prawns, removing their heads but leaving the tails on to look decorative. Slit the prawns down the back and remove the black stuff – it's not good to eat.

Put the onion, chilli, garlic and ginger in a food processor and blitz them to a paste. You might need to remove the lid of the food processor and push the mixture down with a rubber spatula a few times.

Heat the sunflower oil in a frying pan over a medium heat. Add the curry leaves, mustard seeds, fenugreek and asafoetida, then fry for 20–30 seconds, or until you smell the delicious aroma. Add the onion, chilli, garlic and ginger paste and fry for another 1–2 minutes.

Then add the water, turmeric and prawns and cook for 1–2 minutes or until the prawns are pink and the water has evaporated. Stir well to cover the prawns in the spice mixture.

Pour in the coconut milk and season to taste with salt and freshly ground black pepper. Bring the mixture to a simmer and cook for 1–2 minutes until the coconut milk is warmed through and the prawns are done. Squeeze over the lime juice.

Garnish with the chopped coriander and lime wedges and serve with our delicious Keralan parathas (see page 250).

Crabs can carry flavour and spices like no other crustacean – this is a crab-picker's paradise. We use cooked crabs here but you might prefer to cook your own if you're a seasoned crab chef. **Serves 4–6**

SRI LANKAN CRAB CURRY

2 x 1 kg large brown crabs, freshly cooked and cooled
3 tbsp sunflower oil or groundnut oil
2 medium onions, halved and finely sliced
6 garlic cloves, thinly sliced
35g chunk of fresh root ginger, peeled and finely grated
3 fresh bird's-eye chillies, trimmed and finely sliced
2 tsp cumin seeds, lightly crushed
1 tsp coriander seeds, lightly crushed
1 tsp black mustard seeds
1 tsp ground turmeric
½ tsp hot chilli powder
½ tsp ground fenugreek
14 dry curry leaves or 7 fresh curry leaves
½ cinnamon stick
400ml can of coconut milk
500ml cold water
1 tsp flaked sea salt
freshly squeezed juice of 1 lime (about 2½ tbsp)
2 tbsp roughly chopped fresh coriander, to garnish
25g toasted flaked coconut (optional)

To prepare the crab, take a large chopping board and put it on a couple of sheets of folded damp kitchen paper to help secure it firmly to the surface while you work. Place a crab on its back and remove the tail flap from between its back legs. Holding the large claws at the point at which they meet the crab's body, twist and pull them off. Using a meat mallet or the end of a rolling pin, crack them so the crabby flavour can permeate the sauce when the curry cooks. Break the large claws into 3 sections and put them in a large bowl.

Bang the crab firmly on the board to loosen the main shell. Prise the central body section away from the shell and remove and discard the gills (dead man's fingers) away from the sides. Discard the intestines – grey globby bits attached to the shell or clinging to the body – leaving the body clean with only the white flesh showing. Don't throw away the deep orange-coloured crab meat as this has lots of flavour. Scrape it into the bowl with the claws. Remove the first 3 segments from each leg and put them in the bowl with the rest of the prepared crab.

Cut the body section in half lengthways then in half again so you end up with 4 pieces. Prise away the mouthparts and sand sack from the main shell and discard them. Place the shell on the chopping board, hollow side down and with a firm, clean tap, crack it in half. That's 1 crab done but you'll need to do the same thing with the other.

Once all the crab is prepared, heat the oil in a very large flameproof casserole dish or your biggest saucepan over a medium heat, then fry the onions for 5 minutes or until softened, stirring regularly. Increase the heat and cook for a couple of minutes more until golden, stirring constantly. Reduce the heat and stir in the garlic, ginger and chillies. Cook for 2 minutes, while stirring. Add the cumin and coriander seeds, mustard seeds, turmeric, chilli powder, fenugreek, curry leaves and cinnamon and cook together for a further 2 minutes, stirring.

Pour the coconut milk into the casserole or pan and stir in the water, salt and lime juice. Bring to a gentle simmer and cook for 10 minutes, stirring occasionally. Add all the crab, and any of its juices, and return to a simmer. Cover and cook for a further 10 minutes, stirring 3 times and crushing the crab against the sides of the pan to release as much flavour as possible. Take off the heat and scoop any meat out of the larger pieces of shell but leave the claws and legs intact. Garnish with the coriander and some coconut if you like and serve with rice or bread.

A favourite dish from the Kerala region of India, fish molee is fish cooked in coconut milk. It's really flavoursome and fragrant but shouldn't be too hot. You can also use salmon steaks for this recipe, or chunky pieces of white fish fillet if you don't fancy picking around the bones. You'll need 650–750 grams of boneless, skinless fish fillet instead of the steaks. **Serves 4**

KERALAN FISH MOLEE

4 x 285g white fish steaks, ideally hake, about 2.5cm thick
1 tbsp fresh lemon juice
1 tsp ground turmeric
2 tsp plain flour
1 tsp flaked sea salt
2–3 tbsp sunflower oil
freshly ground black pepper

Sauce

2 long green chillies
2 tbsp sunflower oil
1 red medium onion, finely sliced
20g chunk of fresh root ginger, peeled and finely chopped
2–3 fresh ripe tomatoes (about 250g), skinned
10 fresh curry leaves or 15 dried curry leaves
5cm piece of cinnamon
½ tsp ground turmeric
½ tsp garam masala (see page 345 or use ready-made)
400ml can of coconut milk
150ml cold water
1 tsp flaked sea salt, plus extra to season

First you need to marinate the fish. Sprinkle the fish steaks with the lemon juice. Spread the turmeric and flour on a plate and season with a few twists of ground black pepper. Rub the salt between your fingertips and sprinkle it on top. Dust both sides of the fish steaks with the spice mixture, making sure you use it all up. Put the fish on a plate when coated, cover and chill for 30 minutes.

To make the sauce, trim and finely chop 1 of the green chillies. Split the other with a knife from the tip to the stalk but do not cut it in half – the idea is to get flavour into the sauce without too much heat. Place a large non-stick saucepan over a medium heat. Add the sunflower oil and, when it's hot, add the onion, ginger and chopped and split chilli. Cook for 8 minutes until the onion is softened and lightly browned, stirring regularly.

Roughly chop the tomatoes and add them to the pan. Stir in the curry leaves, cinnamon, turmeric and garam masala. Cook together for 2–3 minutes, stirring constantly until the tomatoes soften. Pour the coconut milk into the pan, add the water and salt and bring to a simmer. Reduce the heat, cover with a tight-fitting lid, then leave to simmer for 20 minutes. Take the lid off every now and then and give the sauce a good stir. Season the curry sauce with a little extra salt and pepper if necessary and remove from the heat.

Just before the sauce is ready, heat 2 tablespoons of oil in a large non-stick frying pan. Fry the fish for 2 minutes on each side until nicely browned but not cooked through. Turn the fish carefully with a spatula or fish slice so it doesn't break up and add another tablespoon of oil if the pan starts to look too dry.

Pour the sauce over the fish and nestle the steaks into the curry sauce. Bring to a simmer and cook for 5 minutes more or until the fish is cooked through. Shake the pan gently every now and then, without lifting it off the hob, to swirl the sauce around the fish as it cooks. Serve with rice and watch out for the bones.

This recipe is traditionally made with mustard oil, but we've found that a combination of mustard seeds and English mustard powder brings just the right level of heat and flavour. This is a light-tasting curry but don't be tempted to cut down the amount of oil in the recipe as you need it to help thicken the sauce. Any fish fillets can be used or you can make it with fish steaks instead – as they often do in India. You'll need to increase the cooking time accordingly. **Serves 2**

BENGALI FISH CURRY

- 2 sea bass or sea bream fillets (each about 175g), scaled but skin left on
- 1 tsp flaked sea salt, plus extra to season
- ¼ tsp cayenne pepper
- 300ml cold water
- 2½ tsp dry English mustard powder
- 4 tbsp sunflower oil
- 1 heaped tsp yellow mustard seeds
- ½ heaped tsp black mustard seeds
- ½ heaped tsp cumin seeds
- 1 medium onion, halved and finely sliced
- 2 long green chillies, trimmed and cut in half lengthways
- 1 bay leaf
- ½ tsp ground turmeric
- ½ tsp garam masala (see page 345 or use ready-made)
- freshly ground black pepper

Cut the fish fillets in half widthways. Put them in a bowl and toss them with the teaspoon of salt, cayenne pepper, ½ teaspoon of the mustard powder and lots of freshly ground back pepper. Mix the water with the remaining 2 teaspoons of mustard powder, adding it gradually and stirring constantly until you have a thin yellow liquid.

Heat the oil in a large non-stick frying pan and fry the fish over a high heat, skin-side down, for 1 minute until the skin begins to crisp – we love crispy skin, but you can remove it if you prefer. Carefully turn the fillets over and cook them on the other side for a further minute. Take the fish out of the pan and put the fillets on a plate. Don't let the fish get crowded in the pan or it will be difficult to turn. If your pan isn't large enough, cook the fish in 2 batches instead.

As soon as the fish is cooked, put the pan back on the heat and add the mustard seeds and cumin seeds. Cook for a few seconds, stirring constantly. Add the sliced onion, chillies and bay leaf, then cook for about 5 minutes or until the onion is softened and pale golden brown, stirring constantly. Sprinkle over the turmeric and garam masala and cook for 2 minutes more, stirring constantly.

Stir in the reserved mustard liquid and bring to a simmer. Cook for 3 minutes until the sauce has thickened and reduced by about a third and the spices have mellowed – the sauce should lightly coat the back of a spoon. Put the fish back in the pan and warm through in the bubbling sauce for 2 minutes until hot and cooked through. Serve with rice.

TOP TIP

You can also add 1 or 2 large chopped tomatoes to this curry. Put them in with the turmeric and garam masala.

This curry is a cinch to make and is bursting with flavour. It's our take on curries we've eaten and enjoyed in Southeast Asia and it should be ready to serve in less than 30 minutes. Add extra vegetables or even a few kaffir lime leaves if you have any handy. **Serves 4**

SOUTHEAST ASIAN PRAWN CURRY

- 40g roasted, unsalted cashew nuts, roughly chopped
- 350g raw peeled king prawns, thawed if frozen
- 2 tbsp sunflower or groundnut oil
- 4 shallots or 1 small onion, finely sliced into rings
- 1 garlic clove, finely sliced
- 50g good-quality massaman curry paste or Thai red curry paste
- 1 cinnamon stick
- 1 star anise
- 400ml can of half-fat coconut milk
- 200ml cold water
- 1½ tbsp Thai fish sauce (nam pla)
- 1 tbsp soft light brown sugar or palm sugar
- 1 red pepper, deseeded and cut into 3cm chunks
- 150g sugar snap peas, trimmed and stringed

Heat a large non-stick sauté pan or wok. Add the chopped cashew nuts and dry fry them for about 3 minutes over a medium heat until lightly browned, stirring regularly. Tip the nuts into a heatproof bowl and set them aside. Devein the prawns (see page 355) and set aside.

Place the pan back on the heat and add the oil followed by the shallots or onion. Stir-fry over a medium-high heat for 2–3 minutes until lightly browned. Add the curry paste, cinnamon stick and star anise to the pan and cook for 1 minute, while stirring. Pour in the coconut milk, then add the water, fish sauce and sugar. Bring everything to a simmer and cook for 5 minutes, stirring occasionally. Add the red pepper, sugar snap peas and cashew nuts, then simmer for 5 minutes more, stirring regularly.

Add the prawns and bring back to a simmer, then continue cooking for a further 2–3 minutes until the prawns are cooked and completely pink, stirring occasionally. Do not allow them to overcook or they will get tough. Don't forget to take out the cinnamon stick and star anise. Serve the curry with freshly boiled rice.

These Thai fishcakes make expensive sea bass fillet go a long way – and what's more, they will be the best you've ever had. You can make your own red curry paste if you like, but you can get away with a good-quality bought one. The secret to forming the quite sloppy mixture is to have wet hands – believe us, it works. **Makes 18–20**

THAI SEA BASS FISHCAKES
with a honey and cucumber dip

- 1 lemon grass stalk
- 500g sea bass fillet, skinned and pin boned
- 1 tbsp Thai fish sauce (nam pla)
- 2 tsp Thai red curry paste
- 1 kaffir lime leaf, very finely shredded
- 30g chunk of galangal, peeled and finely chopped
- 1 tbsp finely chopped fresh coriander
- 1 medium egg
- 1 tsp grated palm sugar or soft brown sugar
- 50g snake beans, trimmed and thinly sliced (or use fine green beans)
- freshly squeezed juice of ½ lime
- plain flour, for dusting
- 3 tbsp sunflower oil, for shallow frying
- banana leaf and lambs lettuce, for serving (optional)

Dip

- 2 tbsp rice wine vinegar
- 2 tbsp runny honey
- 2 tbsp cold water
- freshly squeezed juice juice of ½ lime
- 1 tbsp Thai fish sauce (nam pla)
- 100g cucumber peeled, deseeded and diced
- 1 small carrot, peeled and finely diced
- 1 shallot, finely diced
- 2 bird's-eye chillies, deseeded and thinly sliced

Trim the lemon grass, remove the outer leaves, then slice the tender inner part. Place the sea bass, fish sauce, red curry paste, kaffir lime leaf, galangal, lemon grass, chopped coriander, egg, sugar, beans and lime juice in a food processor and blitz to a paste. You'll need to remove the lid of the processor and push the mixture down with a spatula a few times. Carefully remove the blade of the processor and tip the mixture into a bowl.

Sprinkle a little flour on to a plate. Wet your hands, then take a walnut-sized piece of the mixture, roll it into a ball and flatten it into a thin disc. Lay the fishcake on the floured plate and make the rest in the same way until you've used all the mixture. Cover the fishcakes and chill them in the fridge until you're ready to cook.

Meanwhile, make the dip. Put the vinegar, honey, water, lime juice and fish sauce in a bowl and beat with a hand whisk. Taste and adjust the amount of honey and lime juice, depending on how sweet or sour you want the dip to be. Add the diced cucumber, carrot, shallot and sliced chillies – this dip is really more like a salsa.

Heat the oil in a large non-stick frying pan. Cook the fishcakes, a few at a time, for a couple of minutes, then turn them and cook for another 2 minutes. They should be golden on both sides and cooked through.

For an extra flourish, serve the fishcakes on a banana leaf, with the dip in a little dish. Garnish the fishcakes with some lamb's lettuce if you like. We like to drizzle the fishcakes with a little of the dip and pile some of the chunky bits on top.

In this recipe the fish is cooked with a lovely fragrant garam masala crust. The sauce is a perfect match as it doesn't swamp the fish's delicate flavour. We think about 1/4 of a teaspoon of cayenne pepper is about right but add another 1/4 of a teaspoon if you like your curries extra spicy. Serve with spoonfuls of cool refreshing yoghurt. For a more economical dish you could use haddock or lemon sole. **Serves 4**

SPICED FISH CURRY

- 2 tsp garam masala (see page 345 or use ready-made)
- 2 tsp plain flour
- ½ tsp flaked sea salt
- 2 tbsp ghee or sunflower oil
- 4 x 150–200g sea bream or sea bass fillets, scaled and pin boned
- 4–6 tbsp plain natural yoghurt, for serving
- roughly chopped parsley or coriander, to garnish
- lime wedges, for squeezing

Sauce

- 1 medium onion, quartered
- 4 garlic cloves
- 15g chunk of fresh root ginger, peeled and roughly chopped
- 4 tbsp ghee or sunflower oil
- 1 tsp yellow mustard seeds
- 1 tsp cumin seeds
- 1 tsp fennel seeds
- ½ tsp coriander seeds
- 8 cardamom pods, lightly crushed
- 2 long green chillies, trimmed and halved lengthways
- 200g canned chopped tomatoes
- ¼ –½ tsp cayenne pepper
- 2 tbsp tomato purée
- 300ml cold water

To make the sauce, put the onion, peeled garlic and ginger in a food processor and blitz to make a purée. You may need to remove the lid and push the mixture down a few times with a spatula until you have the right consistency. Heat the ghee or oil in a large non-stick saucepan or sauté pan and add the mustard, cumin, fennel and coriander seeds and the cardamom pods. Cook for about 10 seconds, stirring constantly over a medium heat.

Add the puréed onion mixture, chillies, tomatoes, cayenne pepper and tomato purée. Stir in the water and bring to a simmer, then cover the pan and reduce the heat. Leave to simmer gently over a low heat for 30 minutes. Remove the lid and stir the sauce occasionally. It should look thick and glossy at the end of the cooking time but you'll need to watch carefully so it doesn't stick. The sauce can be cooled and chilled at this point then reheated when you are ready to fry the fish.

When the sauce is nearly ready, cook the fish. Sprinkle the garam masala and flour on to a plate. Rub the salt between your fingertips and sprinkle it on top. Dust both sides of the fish fillets with the spice mix, making sure you use it all up, and put the dusted fillets on a plate.

Place a large non-stick frying pan over a medium-high heat. Add the ghee or oil and, when hot, fry the fish for 2 minutes on each side until golden and crisp on the outside and succulent within. You will only have room for a couple of fillets in the pan at one time, so cook them in 2 batches and transfer them to warm plates as soon as the fillets are done. The cooking time is quite short, so they should remain hot. Turn the fish carefully with a fish slice or wide spatula so it doesn't break up.

When all the fish is fried, spoon the spiced tomato sauce mixture on top (or it could go underneath and the fish on top if you prefer). Finish with spoonfuls of yoghurt and roughly chopped parsley or coriander. Serve hot with lime wedges for squeezing.

A really quick and simple supper dish. Use good-quality coconut milk without stabilisers – you want the thick coconut cream that floats to the top of the can for this recipe. And don't shake the can before you open it or the coconut cream won't be separated. It's well worth searching out some fresh kaffir lime leaves for this dish as they make all the difference. You can freeze the ones you don't use. If using dry leaves, add an extra couple to the sauce to help bring out the citrusy flavour. **Serves 2**

PENANG FISH CURRY

- 400ml can of coconut milk (without stabilisers)
- 2 tbsp Thai yellow curry paste or massaman paste
- 4 kaffir lime leaves, preferably fresh
- 1 tbsp Thai fish sauce (nam pla)
- 2 tsp palm sugar or soft light brown sugar
- 400g fresh thick white fish fillet (such as cod or haddock), skinned
- 1 very finely shredded fresh kaffir lime leaf to garnish (optional)

Place a large non-stick frying pan or wok over a medium-high heat. Open the can of coconut milk and scoop out the thick coconut cream that will have floated to the surface and add it to the pan. Use a slotted spoon if the separation isn't clear. Sizzle the coconut cream, stirring constantly until it begins to separate, then add the curry paste and cook for 1 minute, stirring constantly.

Stir the lime leaves, fish sauce and sugar into the pan and cook together for 2 minutes more. The coconut cream should be thick but not so thick that it begins to burn on the bottom of the pan. Once the 2 minutes is up, add the rest of the coconut milk and bring to a simmer. Cook for 2–3 minutes or until the sauce has reduced by about half, stirring regularly.

While the sauce is simmering, cut the fish into chunks of about 3cm. Add them to the pan, reduce the heat slightly and cook in the bubbling sauce for 4–5 minutes. Keep shaking the pan, spooning over the sauce and turning the fish every now and then until it is cooked throughout. Don't be too rough with the fish, though, or it may break up. You will see it beginning to flake when it is ready. The sauce should be thick with a slight oily slick floating on the top.

Remove the pan from the heat and divide the curry between 2 plates. Scatter the finely shredded kaffir lime leaf on top, if using, and serve with rice.

Lots of ingredients, but this is actually a doddle to make. We find it's best to get everything ready before you start, as the cooking time is really short and you don't want to be faffing around looking for your garlic at the last minute. Make with king prawns instead of white fish fillets if you like – it'll be just as delicious. Goa, a state in western India, was a Portuguese colony and has a unique cuisine of which this curry is a good example. The vinegar in the recipe is a classic Portuguese touch. **Serves 4**

GOAN FISH CURRY

- 2 tsp coriander seeds
- 2 tsp cumin seeds
- 6 cloves
- ½ tsp black peppercorns
- 1½ tsp kashmiri chilli powder
- ½ tsp hot chilli powder
- ½ tsp ground turmeric
- 6 tbsp sunflower oil
- 1 tsp black mustard seeds
- 10 fresh curry leaves
- 1 medium onion, sliced
- 4 garlic cloves, crushed
- 25g chunk of fresh root ginger, peeled and finely grated
- 2 fresh ripe tomatoes, chopped
- 2 long green chillies, slit lengthways
- 1½–2 tbsp white wine or cider vinegar
- 250ml water
- 200ml coconut milk
- 1 tsp flaked sea salt
- 1 tsp caster sugar
- 500g thick firm white fish fillet, such as monkfish, skinned

Place a dry frying pan over a medium heat and add the coriander and cumin seeds, cloves and peppercorns. Heat for about a minute or until you can smell the spices, tossing them every now and then.

Remove the pan from the heat and tip the spices into a pestle and mortar. Add the chilli powders and turmeric, then pound everything into as fine a powder as you can. Alternatively, you can blitz the spices in a spice grinder. Leave to stand.

Heat 2 tablespoons of the oil in a large non-stick frying pan over a high heat and add the mustard seeds and curry leaves. Fry for a few seconds until the mustard seeds begin to pop, then add the rest of the oil and the sliced onion. Fry for 5 minutes, stirring regularly, then add the garlic and ginger and cook for 2 minutes more, stirring.

Sprinkle the ground spices into the pan and fry with the onion, garlic and ginger for 2 minutes, stirring constantly. Don't let the spices burn or they will make the sauce bitter. If the pan seems a little dry, add some extra oil. Scrape the chopped tomatoes and slit whole chillies into the same pan and add 1 tablespoon of vinegar and 4 tablespoons of the water. Bring to a simmer and cook for 3–4 minutes until the tomatoes are well softened, stirring regularly.

Pour the coconut milk into the pan, then add the remaining water, salt and sugar. Bring to a gentle simmer and cook for 2 minutes, stirring occasionally. While the sauce is simmering, cut the fish into chunks of about 3cm – enough for 1 mouthful. If using monkfish, remove the fine membrane covering the fish before cutting into chunks.

Stir the fish into the curry sauce and simmer for 3–5 minutes or until just cooked. The exact timing will depend on how large your pieces are and how dense the fish is. Give the pan a little shake every now and then as it cooks but try not to stir as you'll break up the fish. If using fresh monkfish, which is very firm, turn it halfway through cooking.

Adjust the seasoning to taste, adding 2–3 teaspoons more vinegar to bring out the flavour. Serve with rice to soak up the delicious sauce.

Lamb, Beef & Pork Curries

Lamb and lentils are perfect together and our version of the popular dhansak is deliciously hot, with a hint of sourness provided by the lime juice. You can reduce the amount of chillies if you like a milder curry. Dhansak is traditionally served with rice. **Serves 6**

ALL-IN-ONE LAMB DHANSAK

- 800g boneless lamb leg meat
- 2 tbsp sunflower oil
- 2 medium onions, finely sliced
- 4 garlic cloves, crushed
- 2 plump green chillies, finely chopped (deseed if you like a milder curry)
- 25g chunk of fresh root ginger, peeled and finely grated
- 4 tbsp medium curry paste
- 150g red lentils, rinsed and drained
- 1 tsp flaked sea salt, plus extra for seasoning
- 2 bay leaves
- 800ml water
- 1 small butternut squash (about 500g)
- freshly squeezed juice of 1 lime (about 2½ tbsp)
- freshly ground black pepper
- plain natural yoghurt and chopped coriander, for serving

Trim the lamb, discarding any really hard lumps of fat and sinew. You need a bit of fat to add flavour and succulence to the meat. Cut the lamb into chunks of about 3cm. Season with a little salt and pepper.

Heat a tablespoon of the sunflower oil in a large flameproof casserole dish and fry the lamb over a high heat for 4–5 minutes or until lightly browned on all sides. Do this in a couple of batches so you don't overcrowd the pan. Transfer the browned lamb to a plate.

Pour the remaining oil into the casserole dish and cook the sliced onions very gently over a medium-low heat for 15 minutes until they are softened and lightly browned, stirring occasionally. Preheat the oven to 180°C/Fan 160°C/Gas 4.

Add the garlic, chillies and ginger to the casserole dish with the onions and cook for 2 minutes more, stirring. Spoon in the curry paste and stir well over a medium heat for 2 minutes. Add the lentils, salt, bay leaves and water, then put the lamb back in the pan and stir until the ingredients are thoroughly combined.

Bring to a gentle simmer, then take the casserole dish off the heat. Cover the surface of the curry with a piece of baking parchment, pop a lid on top and put it in the oven to cook for 1 hour. Just before the hour is up, peel the butternut squash and remove the seeds. Cut the squash into rough 3cm chunks.

Take the casserole dish out of the oven and stir the squash and lime juice into the curry. Cover with baking parchment and the lid and continue to cook for a further 45 minutes or until the lamb and squash are very tender and the sauce is thick. Serve with spoonfuls of yoghurt and chopped coriander and some rice or naan bread (see page 247).

Pasanda has a creamy sauce enriched with ground almonds and is a favourite treat. In fact, the word pasanda means 'liked' or 'favourite' in Urdu. It's traditionally made with lamb that is flattened and marinated before cooking in a mildly spicy sauce. **Serves 6**

LAMB PASANDA

1kg boneless lamb leg meat
2 tbsp ghee or sunflower oil
2 medium onions, sliced
7 cardamom pods, crushed
1½ tsp fenugreek seeds
1 tbsp garam masala (see page 345 or use ready-made)
2 tbsp ground almonds
1 tsp caster sugar
1 tsp flaked sea salt
1 cinnamon stick
500ml cold water
2 bay leaves or 2 tsp dried fenugreek leaves
5–6 tbsp double cream

Marinade

200g plain natural yoghurt
2 tsp ground coriander
2 tsp ground cumin
1 tsp ground turmeric
¼ tsp hot chilli powder
3 garlic cloves, peeled
25g chunk of fresh root ginger, peeled and roughly chopped

Put the marinade ingredients in a food processor or blender and blitz until it is as smooth as possible. Scrape the mixture into a bowl. Trim the lamb, removing any visible fat or sinew and cut into rough 3cm chunks. Place a few at a time between 2 sheets of cling film and bash with a rolling pin or the flat side of a meat mallet until they are about 5mm thick.

Stir the meat into the marinade and turn the pieces to coat all of them. Cover the bowl with cling film and leave the lamb to marinate in the fridge for at least 1 hour before cooking. You can prepare the meat in the morning, then leave it in the fridge all day before cooking in the evening if you like.

To make the sauce, heat the ghee or oil in a large flameproof casserole dish or non-stick saucepan. Add the onions and fry for about 10 minutes or until softened and lightly browned, stirring regularly. Start off over a low heat, then once the onions are soft, increase the heat so they can brown. Make sure you stir regularly, especially towards the end of the cooking time so the onions brown without burning. Remove the onions from the heat and blitz them with a stick blender until they are as smooth as possible. Alternatively, let the onions cool for a few minutes and tip them into a food processor for blending.

Return the pan to the heat and add the cardamom pods, fenugreek seeds and garam masala. Cook for 2 minutes more, stirring constantly. Tip the lamb mixture and all its marinade into the pan and cook over a medium heat for 2–3 minutes, stirring constantly. Add the ground almonds, sugar, salt, cinnamon and water. Drop the bay leaves or fenugreek leaves on top, stir well and bring to a gentle simmer.

Cover the pan loosely with a lid and leave to simmer for 1 hour, or until the lamb is tender. Remove the lid and stir the curry occasionally as it cooks. When the lamb is tender, stir in the double cream and increase the heat. Simmer the curry for about 10 minutes or until the sauce is thick, stirring very regularly. Serve with rice or bread.

Lovers of hot curry will devour this vindaloo. Have some cooling yoghurt at the ready and some good naan bread. Vindaloo originated in Goa, once a Portuguese colony, and the vinegar is a classic Portuguese trick to lift the flavours to another level. **Serves 6**

LAMB VINDALOO

1.3kg boneless lamb shoulder
100ml red wine vinegar
2 tbsp sunflower oil
2 tsp flaked sea salt
500g medium potatoes (preferably Maris Pipers)

Sauce

about 125ml sunflower oil
3 medium onions, finely sliced
1 medium onion, roughly chopped
6 plump garlic cloves, roughly chopped
3 long red chillies (do not deseed), roughly chopped
25g chunk of fresh root ginger, peeled and roughly chopped
1 tbsp English mustard powder
1 tbsp ground cumin
1 tbsp ground coriander
1 tbsp ground paprika
2 tsp ground turmeric
2 tsp cayenne pepper
1 tsp ground cinnamon
2 tsp flaked sea salt
2 bay leaves
500ml cold water

Trim the lamb, discarding any really hard lumps of fat and sinew. You need a bit of fat to add flavour and succulence to the meat. Cut the meat into chunks of about 4cm – you should end up with about 1kg of trimmed, prepared meat. Put the vinegar, oil and salt in a large non-metallic bowl, add the lamb and turn to coat the chunks in the marinade. Cover the bowl and chill for 2 hours.

To make the sauce, heat 3 tablespoons of the sunflower oil in a large non-stick frying pan. Add the sliced onions and cook very gently over a medium-low heat for 15 minutes until they are softened and lightly browned, stirring occasionally.

While the sliced onions are cooking, put the chopped onion, garlic, chillies, ginger, mustard powder, cumin, coriander, paprika, turmeric, cayenne pepper and cinnamon in a food processor and blend to make a purée. You may need to remove the lid and push the mixture down a couple of times with a spatula. Tip the purée into the fried onions, add 2 tablespoons of oil and cook for 5 minutes until thickened and beginning to colour and darken, stirring regularly. Scrape the mixture out of the pan into a large flameproof casserole dish.

Drain the lamb really well in a colander and keep the marinade. Return the frying pan to the heat and add 2 tablespoons of the remaining oil. Fry the lamb in 4 or 5 batches over a medium-high heat, turning the pieces occasionally until lightly browned. Add a little extra oil if necessary. Put each batch of lamb in the casserole dish with the curry sauce as soon as it's ready. Preheat the oven to 180°C/Fan 160°C/Gas 4.

Pour the reserved marinade and water into the casserole dish with the lamb. Add the salt and bay leaves and bring to a simmer. Cover the surface of the curry with a piece of baking parchment and pop a lid on top. Cook in the oven for 45 minutes.

Peel the potatoes and cut them into chunks of about 2.5cm. Take the casserole dish out of the oven and stir the potato chunks into the curry. Cover the surface with baking parchment and the lid and put the casserole back in the oven for another hour or until the lamb and potatoes are very tender. Season with a little extra salt if necessary and serve with rice or warm naan bread (see page 247) and perhaps some cooling yoghurt.

Dopiaza means something like 'double onions' and onions are certainly one of the main ingredients of this classic curry. They are often cooked in two different ways – in our recipe two of the onions are cut into wedges and cooked until just tender, while the rest are thinly sliced and fried until very soft. All in all, this is a wonderfully succulent, flavoursome dish that we both love. **Serves 4–5**

LAMB DOPIAZA

- 750g lamb leg meat, trimmed and cut into 3cm chunks
- 150g plain natural yoghurt
- 8 cardamom pods
- 2 tsp coriander seeds
- 2 tsp cumin seeds
- 6 medium onions
- 4 tbsp ghee or sunflower oil
- 4 garlic cloves, finely sliced
- 15g chunk of fresh root ginger, peeled and finely chopped
- 1 long red chilli, finely chopped (deseed first if you like)
- 1 tsp garam masala (see page 345 or use ready-made), plus a good pinch
- ½ tsp ground turmeric
- 2 tbsp tomato purée
- 300ml cold water
- freshly ground black pepper

Put the lamb in a large bowl and season with lots of black pepper. Add the yoghurt and stir well together. Put the cardamom pods in a pestle and mortar and bash them until the husks split. Tip them on to a board and peel off and chuck out the husks. Put the seeds in a dry frying pan and add the coriander and cumin seeds. Place the pan over a medium heat and toast for a minute or 2, stirring, until you can smell the aroma of the spices. Tip everything into the pestle and mortar and pound to make a powder, then set aside.

Peel all the onions and place them on a board. Cut them in half from tip to root then slice 4 of the onions very thinly. Cut each of the other 2 onions into 12 wedges. Heat a tablespoon of the ghee or oil in a large non-stick saucepan and fry the onion wedges over a high heat for about 5–6 minutes until lightly browned and just tender. Tip the onions on to a plate and return the pan to the heat.

Add the remaining ghee or oil and fry the finely sliced onions, garlic and ginger for 15 minutes, until very soft, stirring occasionally. Turn up the heat for the last 2–3 minutes and stir-fry over a high heat until the onions are tinged with brown. This will add lots of flavour to your curry, but make sure the onions don't burn.

Reduce the heat once more and stir in the chilli, ground mixed spices, the teaspoon of garam masala and the turmeric. Cook for a minute, then add the tomato purée and cook for a minute more. Stir the lamb and yoghurt into the pan and cook over a medium-high heat for 3–4 minutes until lightly coloured, turning often. Pour the water into the pan, cover tightly with a lid and leave to cook over a low heat for 1 hour; it should be simmering gently. Remove the lid every now and then and stir the curry. You may need to add a little extra water but this is meant to be a fairly dry curry.

After the hour is up, the lamb should be almost tender. Remove the lid, give the curry a good stir and continue simmering over a slightly higher heat for 15 minutes or until the sauce is well reduced and the lamb meltingly tender, stirring regularly. Stir in the reserved onion wedges and the pinch of garam masala and cook with the lamb and sauce for 1–2 minutes until piping hot, stirring constantly. Serve with some rice or bread.

T
ti
a
ar
or

W
as
be
ha
ar
su
ur

Ta
to
la
Se
fo
(s

SP
wi

Juicy lamb meatballs in a wonderful spicy sauce – what's not to like? **Serves 6**

LAMB KOFTA CURRY

1 medium onion, roughly chopped
2 long green chillies (do not deseed)
15g chunk of fresh root ginger, peeled and roughly chopped
4 garlic cloves, roughly chopped
1 tsp flaked sea salt
2 tsp garam masala (see page 345 or use ready-made)
¼ tsp hot chilli powder
1 tbsp tomato purée
600g lean minced lamb
3 heaped tbsp finely chopped fresh coriander leaves
freshly ground black pepper
thick plain yoghurt and fresh coriander, for serving (optional)

Sauce

3 tbsp ghee or sunflower oil
2 medium onions, roughly chopped
25g chunk of fresh root ginger, peeled and finely chopped
4 garlic cloves, finely chopped
½–1 tsp hot chilli powder
1 tbsp garam masala
4 ripe tomatoes, roughly chopped
1 tbsp tomato purée
1 tsp flaked sea salt
½ tsp caster sugar
500ml lamb stock (made with ½ lamb stock cube)
1 cinnamon stick
2 bay leaves
200ml water

To make the meatball mixture, put the onion, chillies, ginger, garlic, salt, garam masala, chilli powder and tomato purée in a food processor. Season with loads of freshly ground black pepper.

Blitz the ingredients into as smooth a paste as you can. You'll need to remove the lid of the food processor and push the mixture down with a spatula 2–3 times. Add the lamb and blitz once more. Transfer the mixture to a bowl and stir in the coriander. Cover the dish with cling film and chill for 1–3 hours or overnight to allow the mixture to stiffen and the meat to absorb all the wonderful spices.

To make the sauce, heat the ghee or oil in a large non-stick saucepan and gently fry the onions, ginger and garlic for about 10 minutes or until softened and lightly browned, stirring regularly. Add the chilli powder and garam masala and cook for 20–30 seconds, stirring constantly. Stir in the tomatoes and cook for 3–4 minutes over a high heat until they soften and release their juice, stirring constantly. Sprinkle with the salt and sugar and pour over the stock. Season with lots of ground black pepper, add the cinnamon and bay leaves and bring to a simmer. Cover the sauce loosely with a lid and cook for 20 minutes, stirring occasionally.

While the sauce is simmering, shape the meatballs. Take a small portion of mince mixture at a time and roll it into a smooth ball – a little smaller than a walnut in its shell. You should be able to make about 24 balls. If your mince becomes a little sticky, either roll with wet hands or dust your hands with plain flour as you roll.

Remove the pan with the sauce from the heat when the 20 minutes are up and discard the cinnamon and bay leaves – they should be easy to pick out with a fork or tongs. Blitz the sauce with a stick blender until as smooth as possible. Alternatively, leave the sauce to cool for a few minutes, then transfer to a food processor and blitz to make a purée.

Return the sauce to the heat and stir in the 200ml of water. Bring to a gentle simmer. Drop all the meatballs gently into the bubbling sauce and return to a simmer. Cook, uncovered, for a further 30–35 minutes or until the meatballs are tender and the sauce is thick, stirring regularly. If the sauce reduces too far or begins to stick on the bottom of the pan, add a little extra water and continue cooking. Adjust the seasoning to taste. Serve the meatballs topped with plain yoghurt and fresh coriander leaves if you like and accompany with some rice.

Spinach and lamb – this is magic in a pan and a real classic curry. One of our favourites, it's packed with flavour and is medium-hot but if you prefer a milder curry, remove the seeds from the chillies. **Serves 6**

TRADITIONAL LAMB SAAG

- 5 tbsp sunflower oil
- 4 large onions, sliced
- 10 cardamom pods
- 1 tbsp cumin seeds
- 2 tsp mustard seeds
- ½ cinnamon stick
- 2 long red chillies, sliced
- 6 large garlic cloves, roughly sliced
- 1 tbsp ground coriander
- 2 tsp ground turmeric
- 500g mature spinach leaves (not baby spinach), washed and drained
- 900g boneless lamb leg, cut into chunks of about 4cm
- 1 bay leaf
- 2 tbsp tomato purée
- 800ml cold water
- 1 tsp flaked sea salt, plus extra for seasoning the lamb
- freshly ground black pepper

Heat 3 tablespoons of the sunflower oil in a large non-stick frying pan. Cook the onions gently for 20 minutes until softened and golden brown, stirring regularly.

Place the cardamom pods in a pestle and mortar and pound lightly to split the pods. Tip them on to a board and open each pod, scraping the seeds back into the mortar. Add the cumin, mustard seeds and the cinnamon stick. Pound to form a fairly fine, dry powder.

When the onions are ready, transfer about half of them to a plate and set aside. Return the pan to the heat and stir in chillies and garlic and cook for 3 minutes, stirring. Add the pounded spices, ground coriander and turmeric. Cook for 2 minutes more, stirring constantly.

Break off any tough stalks from 300g of the spinach, drop the leaves into the pan and cook for 2–3 minutes, turning it with the onions until well wilted. Remove the pan from the heat, scrape everything into a heatproof bowl and leave to cool. Get rid of any tough stalks from the remaining spinach and tear the leaves in half. Cover and set aside.

Return the pan to the heat and add another tablespoon of oil. Season the lamb all over with salt and freshly ground black pepper. Fry the lamb over a medium-high heat in 2 or 3 batches until browned on all sides, adding more oil if necessary. As soon as a batch is browned, transfer it to a medium flameproof casserole dish while you fry the rest. Preheat the oven to 170°C/Fan 150°C/Gas 3½.

Transfer the spiced onions and spinach to a food processor and blitz to a thick green paste. Stir this into the casserole dish with the lamb and add the bay leaf, tomato purée and water. Season with the teaspoon of flaked sea salt, stir well and bring to a simmer.

Remove the casserole dish from the heat and cover the surface of the curry with some crumpled baking parchment. Pop a lid on top and cook the curry in the oven for 2½–3 hours or until the meat is very tender and the sauce is thick. Stir halfway though cooking if possible. Take the curry out of the oven and stir in the reserved onions and the rest of the spinach. Cover with the lid alone and return to the oven for a further 15–20 minutes or until the onions are hot and the spinach has wilted. Serve with freshly cooked rice or warm naan (see page 247).

Our homage to Jah, this dish is rich in treacle and spice – the flavours of the Caribbean. Traditionally, the curry is made with goat meat – you'll see curry goat on menus everywhere in the Caribbean – but you can get great results with lamb too. **Serves 6**

JAMAICAN LAMB CURRY

- 1.2kg lamb or young goat shoulder meat
- freshly squeezed juice of 2 limes
- 2 tsp dried thyme
- 2 tsp ground allspice
- 1 tsp ground cloves
- 1 tsp flaked sea salt
- 3 tbsp sunflower oil
- 2 medium onions, sliced
- 4 garlic cloves, thinly sliced
- 1 –2 scotch bonnet chillies, finely chopped (do not deseed)
- 2 tbsp medium curry powder
- 400g can of chopped tomatoes
- 2 tbsp black treacle
- 500ml cold water
- freshly ground black pepper

Trim the lamb or goat meat of any really hard fat and sinew and cut it into rough 3–4cm chunks. Put these in a medium flameproof casserole dish with the lime juice, thyme, allspice, cloves, salt and lots of ground black pepper. Mix well and leave to stand for 30 minutes.

Preheat the oven to 180°C/Fan 160°C/Gas 4. Heat the oil in a large non-stick frying pan and gently fry the onions and garlic for 5 minutes, while stirring, then stir in the chillies and curry powder. Cook for a further 2 minutes, stirring constantly.

Tip the spiced onions into the casserole dish with the meat, then fry together for about 3-4 minutes until the meat is lightly coloured, stirring. Add the tomatoes and treacle, then stir in the cold water and bring to a simmer. Cover with a lid and transfer the curry to the oven.

Cook for about 2 hours or until the meat is very tender and the sauce is thick, stirring halfway through the cooking time. If your meat is very fatty, you may need to spoon some fat off the surface of the curry before you serve it. Let the curry stand for 10 minutes before serving.

In true Jamaican style, we like to serve this curry with rice and peas (see page 266).

A great family dinner; a bit like mince and tatties with a kick. If your family prefers a milder curry, reduce the chilli powder to a pinch. **Serves 4–5**

KEEMA LAMB CURRY

- 2 tbsp sunflower oil
- 2 medium onions, finely chopped
- 3 garlic cloves, crushed
- 20g chunk of fresh root ginger, peeled and finely grated
- 2 tsp ground coriander
- 2 tsp ground cumin
- 2 tsp garam masala (see page 345 or use ready-made)
- ½ tsp hot chilli powder
- ½ tsp ground turmeric
- 500g minced lamb
- 400g can of chopped tomatoes
- 2 bay leaves
- 1 cinnamon stick
- 6 cloves
- 1 tsp caster sugar
- 1 tsp flaked sea salt
- 3 medium potatoes (about 475g)
- 300ml cold water
- 100g frozen peas

Heat the oil in a large non-stick frying pan or sauté pan and fry the onions, garlic and ginger for 5 minutes until softened and beginning to brown, stirring regularly. Sprinkle over all the spices and cook for 2 minutes more, stirring constantly.

Add the lamb and fry with the spiced onions for 6–8 minutes until lightly coloured. Use 2 wooden spoons or spatulas to break up the meat as it cooks – you want it in nice small pieces.

Stir in the tomatoes, bay leaves and cinnamon stick. Pinch the ends off the cloves and sprinkle them on to the lamb mixture, then throw away the stalks – this way you won't end up biting down on them when you come to eat your keema. Add the sugar and salt and bring to a gentle simmer. Cook for 10 minutes, stirring regularly.

While the lamb is bubbling away, peel the potatoes and cut them into rough 2cm chunks. Don't worry if they are a bit uneven. Add the potatoes to the pan with the lamb after the 10 minutes are up and stir in the water. Return to a simmer, cover loosely with a lid and cook for 15 minutes or until the potatoes are just tender. Remove the lid, turn up the heat and simmer for another 5 minutes or until the curry is fairly thick. Make sure to stir regularly especially towards the end of the cooking time.

When the potatoes are tender, stir in the frozen peas and cook for 2–3 minutes until hot. Serve the curry with naan bread, parathas or chapatis rather than rice if you like, and a nice selection of chutneys. Try making your own breads rather than using shop-bought – they are much easier than you might think. Check out our recipes on pages 245–253 of this book.

More Birmingham than Bombay, this is a great midweek treat that you can have ready to serve in less than 30 minutes. **Serves 2**

SIZZLING BEEF BALTI

- 4 tbsp sunflower oil
- 227g can of chopped tomatoes
- 2 garlic cloves, crushed
- 2 tsp ground cumin
- 1 tbsp garam masala (see page 345 or use ready-made)
- 1 tsp ground turmeric
- ½ tsp ground ginger
- scant 1/4 tsp cayenne pepper
- 1 tsp caster sugar
- 1 tsp flaked sea salt
- 200ml cold water
- 2 heaped tbsp finely chopped fresh coriander, plus extra to garnish
- 500g sirloin steak
- ½ medium onion, cut into 5 wedges
- ½ green pepper, deseeded and cut into 3cm chunks
- ½ yellow pepper, deseeded and cut into 3cm chunks
- 1 large ripe tomato, cut into 6 wedges
- freshly ground black pepper
- warm naan bread or freshly cooked rice, for serving

Place a large non-stick frying pan, sauté pan or wide-based saucepan over a medium-high heat. Add 2½ tablespoons of the oil, followed by the canned tomatoes, garlic, cumin, garam masala, turmeric, ginger, cayenne pepper, sugar and salt. Watch your hands as the tomatoes are added to the pan as the oil will splutter. Cook for 4 minutes, stirring constantly with a long handled wooden spoon as the oil separates from the tomatoes and the liquid evaporates away.

Pour in the water, add the coriander and bring to a simmer. Reduce the heat and cook the sauce gently for 15 minutes, stirring occasionally until it is well reduced and the tomatoes are very soft. The simmering should help mellow the spices but don't allow the sauce to reduce so far that it begins to stick.

While the sauce is simmering, trim the beef of any hard fat and slice the meat into thin strips from 1 short end, cutting diagonally along the length of the beef. The strips should be about 5mm thick. Toss them with ½ tablespoon of the sunflower oil and season well with freshly ground black pepper.

Just before the sauce is ready, heat the remaining 1 tablespoon of oil in a large non-stick frying pan or wok and stir-fry the onion and peppers for 3 minutes until they are just beginning to soften. Add the beef and tomato wedges and fry for 1 minute more, stirring until the beef is lightly browned. You may need to use 2 wooden spoons to keep the strips of beef separate as they fry.

Pour the sauce over the beef and vegetables and let them sizzle together for 20–30 seconds, while stirring. Bring the balti to the table in the pan and serve immediately with warm naan breads or rice.

Hot as Hades, but this is not so hot that it doesn't also have lots of flavour and a deliciously rich sauce. We love our beef phall, but then we do love a good hot curry. In our version, we use fresh red chillies, dried bird's-eye chillies for heat and paprika for colour. Deseed the chillies before chopping if you prefer more of a Madras-style beef curry – the heat is mainly in the inside of the chilli and the white membrane. Serve this with some yoghurt if you need to dampen down the fire. **Serves 4**

BEEF PHALL

Trim the beef of any hard fat and sinew, then cut the meat into rough 3cm chunks and season with ground black pepper. Place the long red chillies on a board and roughly chop 2 of them without deseeding. Split the other 2 from stalk to tip on 1 side without opening or removing the seeds and set them aside for later.

Put the fresh chopped chillies in a food processor with the onions, garlic, ginger and dried chillies, then blitz them to a purée as smooth as you can make it. You will need to remove the lid and push the mixture down a couple of times with a rubber spatula until you get the right consistency. Preheat the oven to 190°C/Fan 170°C/Gas 5.

Heat the oil in a large, flameproof casserole dish over a medium-high heat. Add the cumin and fenugreek seeds and cook for a few seconds, while stirring. Add the onion mixture and fry for 6–8 minutes, stirring constantly until the onions turn golden brown. Do this with an extractor fan on full blast as the chillies could make you sneeze!

Stir the paprika, garam masala and turmeric into the pan and cook them together for 30 seconds, stirring constantly. Add the beef and cook it with the spiced onion mixture for 2 minutes, stirring constantly with a wooden spoon until lightly coloured on all sides. If the spices begin to stick, add a little extra oil and give the base of the pan a good scrape before they have a chance to burn.

Next, add the tomatoes, water and whole chillies. Stir in the salt and bring to a simmer. Cover the casserole dish with a lid and carefully put it in the oven. Cook for 45 minutes, then remove the dish from the oven and stir the curry. Put it back into the oven and cook for another 30 minutes or until the beef is tender and the sauce has thickened.

TOP TIP

You can check the beef is tender by taking out a chunk, putting it on a plate and cutting through it with the side of a fork. If a fork can cut the meat, it's sure to be tender enough. If the beef is still a little tough, put it back in the oven for 15–30 minutes more, and be ready to add a little extra water if necessary.

800g braising steak (ideally chuck steak)
4 long red chillies
2 medium onions, roughly chopped
6 garlic cloves, roughly chopped
25g chunk of fresh root ginger, peeled and roughly chopped
10 dried extra-hot chillies (bird's-eye)
3 tbsp sunflower oil
2 tsp cumin seeds
1 tsp fenugreek seeds
1 tbsp paprika
1½ tbsp garam masala (see page 345 or use ready-made)
1 tsp ground turmeric
400g can of chopped tomatoes
400ml cold water
2 tsp flaked sea salt
freshly ground black pepper

Tender chunks of gently spiced beef in a fluffy saffron rice – this is a celebratory dish, a party on a plate, and a great way of feeding lots of people. Biryanis originated Persia, not India, and started as a simple meal of rice and meat baked in the oven. Later, a biryani became a more complex dish with lots of richly aromatic ingredients. **Serves 6**

EXTRA-SPECIAL BEEF BIRYANI

100ml full-fat milk
1 heaped tsp saffron threads
1kg braising steak, cut into bite-sized chunks
about 135ml sunflower oil
4 onions
4 garlic cloves
25g chunk of fresh root ginger, peeled and roughly chopped
2 fresh red chillies, deseeded and roughly chopped
500ml cold water
5 cloves
2 tsp cumin seeds
2 tsp coriander seeds
¼ piece of cinnamon stick
2½ tsp sea salt flakes, plus extra to season
12 cardamom pods
½ whole nutmeg, finely grated
200ml natural yoghurt
2 bay leaves
2 tsp caster sugar
325g basmati rice
50g butter
freshly ground black pepper

Pour the milk into a small saucepan, add the saffron threads and heat gently for 2 minutes without boiling. Remove from the heat and set aside for 2–3 hours, preferably overnight.

Trim the beef of any hard fat and cut it into bite-sized pieces. Heat 2 tablespoons of oil in a frying pan. Season the beef with salt and freshly ground black pepper and fry it in 2–3 batches over a medium-high heat until browned on all sides, adding more oil to the pan if necessary. Transfer the beef to a large saucepan that has a lid.

While the beef is frying, roughly chop 2 of the onions and put them in a food processor with the garlic, ginger and chillies. Add 50ml of the cold water and blend to a smooth paste.

Put the cloves, cumin, coriander, cinnamon, 1½ teaspoons of salt and seeds from the cardamom pods into a pestle and mortar. Grind until you have a fine powder. Grate the nutmeg into the spice mixture, then tip it all into the onion paste. Add plenty of freshly ground black pepper. Mix until all the ingredients are combined.

Add another 3 tablespoons of oil into the same frying pan that was used to cook the beef and fry the spiced onion paste over a medium heat for about 10 minutes until lightly browned, stirring often. Place the mixture into the pan with the beef. Stir in the yoghurt, the rest of the water and the bay leaves. Place the pan over a low heat and bring to a gentle simmer. Cover with a lid and simmer gently for 1½ hours or until the beef is tender, stirring occasionally.

Remove the lid from the pan and stir in the sugar. Increase the heat and simmer the sauce for 10 minutes, or until reduced and thick. Add a little more salt and pepper to taste.

Put the almonds for the garnish into a non-stick frying pan and toast them over a medium heat for 4–6 minutes. Stir the sultanas into the almonds, then tip them all into a heatproof bowl. Set aside to cool.

Cut the remaining 2 onions in half and slice them thinly. Pour 2 tablespoons of oil into a frying pan and fry the onions for 6–8 minutes over a fairly high heat until softened and golden-brown, stirring frequently. Set aside.

Preheat the oven to 180°C/Fan 160°C/Gas 4. Half-fill a large pan with water, add a teaspoon of salt and bring to the boil. Put the rice in a sieve and rinse under plenty of cold water. Stir the rice into the hot water and return to the boil. Cook for 5 minutes and drain well. Add the coriander and stir until well combined.

Transfer half the meat and sauce into a large ovenproof dish. Spoon over half of the part-cooked rice and drizzle with half the soaked saffron threads and milk. Top with half the fried onions. Repeat the layers once more. Dot with the butter. Cover the dish with 2 layers of tightly fitting foil and bake for 30 minutes.

To finish the garnish, hard boil the eggs for 9 minutes until firm and drain them in a sieve under running water until cool enough to handle. Peel the eggs and cut them into quarters. Remove the dish from the oven and discard the foil. Use a fork to lightly fluff the rice. Garnish with the freshly boiled eggs, then scatter with toasted almonds and sultanas. Add some chopped coriander and serve.

TOP TIP

If you like a bit more heat in your curry, don't worry about deseeding both the chillies.

Garnish

40g flaked almonds
50g sultanas
3 large eggs
fresh coriander leaves
4 tbsp chopped fresh coriander

We first tasted this dish at a roadside stall in Kerala after we'd come down from the Cardamom Hills. It has a delicious, slightly aniseed flavour and makes a lovely change to the usual saucy curries. Serve with Indian breads, especially Keralan parathas (see page 250) and pickles. If you don't want to prepare your own ground spices you could use 2 heaped teaspoons of garam masala and 2 teaspoons of fennel seeds instead. It won't taste quite the same but will be very delicious nonetheless. **Serves 4–5**

DRY KERALAN BEEF CURRY

- 2cm piece of cinnamon stick
- 4 cloves
- 2 tsp fennel seeds
- 4 extra-hot dried chillies (bird's-eye)
- 1 tbsp coriander seeds
- 1 tsp ground turmeric
- 2 tsp fine sea salt
- 800g chuck steak (braising beef) trimmed and cut into 2.5cm chunks
- 2 medium onions, halved and thinly sliced
- 25g chunk of fresh root ginger, peeled and finely grated
- 4 garlic cloves, finely sliced
- 1 long green chilli, deseeded and finely chopped
- 1 tbsp red or white wine vinegar
- 10 fresh or 15 dried curry leaves
- 350ml cold water
- 25g fresh or 15g dry shredded coconut strips (optional)
- 4 tbsp coconut oil or sunflower oil
- freshly ground black pepper

Put the cinnamon, cloves, fennel, chillies and coriander seeds in a spice grinder and grind them to a fine powder. You could also do this in a pestle and mortar but the cinnamon will be difficult to grind by hand, so add ½ teaspoon of ground cinnamon at the same time as the turmeric instead. Tip the spices into a large bowl and add the turmeric and salt. Stir well to mix. Add the beef, half the onion slices, ginger, garlic, chilli, vinegar and half the curry leaves, then season with lots of pepper and toss well. Cover the bowl and leave to marinate in the fridge for 1 hour.

Preheat the oven to 180°C/Fan 160°C/Gas 4. Transfer the beef mixture to a medium flameproof casserole dish and stir in the water. (Beef fry isn't traditionally simmered with water but because we cook the beef in the oven, the additional liquid helps to keep it succulent and you can evaporate it off later.) Bring to the boil over a high heat then cover the dish with a lid and transfer it to the oven. Cook for 1½–2 hours or until the beef is very tender.

Remove the lid and place the casserole dish back on the hob. Bring to the boil and cook until all the liquid has evaporated. This will take about 5 minutes. You'll need to stir it regularly as the drier the curry becomes, the more likely it is to stick. Remove from the heat. At this point, the beef can be cooled and popped into the fridge until just before you serve it, as the rest of the cooking is very quick.

Heat a large non-stick frying pan or wok and add the shredded coconut. Cook for 2–3 minutes or until toasted, stirring constantly. This step isn't essential but it will bring extra flavour to the curry.

Add the oil to the pan, then the reserved sliced onion and stir-fry for 3–4 minutes until golden brown. Add the beef mixture and the remaining curry leaves, reduce the heat slightly and stir-fry for 5–6 minutes until the meat is nicely browned and looks dry but glossy and rich. Serve with parathas, roti or rice and a selection of chutneys.

Before you cut and juice a lime, roll it on a board. This helps release the juice from the segments inside.

This is our version of a dish that we ate and enjoyed when travelling in Vietnam. It's not authentic but includes lots of the ingredients that are so characteristic of Vietnamese cookery, such as lemon grass. Fresh, fragrant and very tasty. **Serves 6**

VIETNAMESE PORK CURRY
with lemon grass

- 2 lemon grass stalks
- 1 medium onion, quartered
- 2 garlic cloves, halved
- 1 long red chilli, halved and roughly chopped
- 25g chunk of fresh root ginger, peeled and roughly chopped
- small bunch of fresh coriander, plus extra to garnish
- 1.5kg boneless rindless pork shoulder (buy thickly cut steaks if you like)
- 3 tbsp sunflower oil
- 4 tsp garam masala (see page 345 or use ready-made)
- 4 tsp ground cumin
- 1½ tsp turmeric
- 400ml can of coconut milk
- 400ml cold water
- 2 tbsp Thai fish sauce (nam pla)
- 1 large sweet potato (about 400g)
- juice of 1 lime (2½ tsp)
- flaked sea salt
- freshly ground black pepper

Trim the lemon grass at each end and remove the papery outer layers. Chop the lemon grass into thin slices – you need about 20g. Put the sliced lemon grass in a food processor and add the onion, garlic, chilli, ginger and coriander, then blitz to make a fine paste. You want to get the paste as fine as possible. You will need to remove the lid and push the mixture down 2–3 times with a rubber spatula until the right texture is reached. If you don't have a food processor, bash all the ingredients together with a pestle and mortar until they form a paste.

Cut the pork into rough 3cm chunks and season with salt and ground black pepper. Heat a tablespoon of the oil in a large non-stick frying pan and cook the pork in 2–3 batches over a fairly high heat until nicely browned, adding a little extra oil if necessary. Transfer the pork to a large flameproof casserole dish. Preheat the oven to 190°C/Fan 170°C/Gas 5.

Add the remaining oil, the paste, garam masala, cumin and turmeric to the frying pan. Fry over a medium heat for 3–4 minutes, stirring constantly, until the mixture smells fragrant and is beginning to colour. Pour the coconut milk into the frying pan and stir well.

Tip the mixture over the browned pork in the casserole dish. Add the water, stir in the fish sauce, season with lots of black pepper and bring to the boil. Remove the pan from the heat, cover with a lid and place in the centre of the oven to cook for 1 hour. Just before the hour is up, peel the sweet potato and cut it into rough 3cm chunks.

Take the curry out of the oven and remove the lid. Add the sweet potato, stir well and cover the surface with a crumpled sheet of baking parchment or greaseproof paper to prevent the sauce reducing too much. Return to the oven without a lid and cook for a further 45–60 minutes or until the pork is very tender and the sauce is fairly thick. Take the dish out of the oven and stir in the lime juice and a little more salt and pepper to taste. Sprinkle with chopped fresh coriander and serve with rice.

There are loads of versions of this wonderful dish of curry-flavoured noodles. Its origins are hazy but when done right it makes a fantastic lunch or supper. Here's our take on it, using marinated pork fillet and prawns. **Serves 4**

SINGAPORE NOODLES

- 300g pork fillet, trimmed of fat and sinew
- 3 tbsp dark soy sauce
- 2 tbsp dry sherry
- 2 tsp soft light brown sugar
- ½ tsp Chinese five-spice powder
- 3 tbsp sunflower oil
- 100g fine egg noodles (vermicelli egg noodles)
- 1 medium red onion, cut into thin wedges
- 1 red pepper, deseeded and sliced
- 100g shiitake mushrooms, wiped and sliced
- 2 garlic cloves, crushed
- 20g chunk of fresh root ginger, peeled and finely grated
- 2 tsp medium Madras curry powder
- 200g cold-water peeled prawns, thawed if frozen and then drained
- 10 spring onions, trimmed and sliced diagonally

Put the pork fillet in a bowl, pour over the soy sauce and sherry and stir in the sugar and five-spice powder. Leave to stand for 30 minutes, turning the pork in the marinade every 10 minutes. Preheat the oven to 200°C/Fan 180°C/Gas 6.

Drain the pork and set aside the marinade. Place the pork on a small foil-lined tray, drizzle with a tablespoon of the oil and put it in the oven to roast for 12 minutes. Remove the pork from the oven and leave it to stand. While the pork is in the oven, cook the noodles according to the packet instructions, then drain well in a sieve.

Place a large non-stick frying pan or a wok over a medium heat and add the remaining 2 tablespoons of the oil. Stir-fry the onion, red pepper and mushrooms for 5–6 minutes or until they are beginning to soften and lightly colour. Add the garlic and ginger and stir-fry for another minute, then sprinkle the curry powder into the pan and cook for 2 minutes more, stirring.

Cut the pork in half lengthways and then slice it into thin pieces. Add these to the hot pan along with the prawns and spring onions. Stir-fry for 1 minute, then add the drained noodles and reserved marinade. Toss together with chopsticks, or a couple of forks, for 2–3 minutes until everything is piping hot, then serve immediately.

This fab curry contains tender chunks of pork in a rich, slightly sticky, sweet but tangy sauce. It's great garnished with sliced spring onions and chopped lightly toasted peanuts or cashew nuts. **Serves 4**

STICKY PORK CURRY

- 800g boneless, rindless pork shoulder (buy as thickly cut steaks if you like)
- 3 tbsp Thai fish sauce (nam pla)
- 3 tbsp light soft brown sugar
- 3 tbsp fresh lemon juice
- 4 tbsp dark soy sauce
- 6 fresh kaffir lime leaves or 10 dried leaves
- 2 tbsp sunflower oil
- 300g shallots (10–12 smallish shallots), finely sliced
- 25g chunk of fresh root ginger, peeled and very finely chopped
- 4 garlic cloves, finely sliced
- 1 long red chilli, trimmed and finely sliced
- 2 tbsp good-quality massaman curry paste or Thai red curry paste
- 1.5 litres cold water
- 3 tbsp runny honey
- freshly ground black pepper

Trim the pork, but don't cut away all the fat as it will make the meat more succulent and add flavour to the curry. Cut the pork into 3cm chunks and put them in a large bowl, then add the fish sauce, sugar, lemon juice, soy sauce and lime leaves. Season with lots of ground black pepper. Toss everything together well and leave to stand for about 30 minutes.

When you are ready to cook, heat the oil in a large, non-stick deep frying pan or sauté pan – you need one that has a lid. Add the shallots and fry them over a medium-high heat for 5 minutes. Keep stirring regularly until they are lightly browned and beginning to crisp in places. Add the ginger, garlic and chilli, then fry for 2 minutes more, stirring constantly. Spoon the curry paste into the pan and fry for 1 minute, stirring constantly. Now stir in the pork and its marinade and cook together for 2–3 minutes, turning the pork until it is lightly coloured on all sides.

Pour the water into the pan and bring to a simmer. Cover the pan with a lid, reduce the heat and leave the curry to simmer gently for about 1 hour or until the pork is tender. Take off the lid 2–3 times during the cooking time and stir the curry. If the pork isn't quite tender after an hour, simmer for a short while longer.

Once the hour is up and the pork is tender, remove the lid, stir the honey into the pan and bring to the boil. Cook for 5–8 minutes or until the sauce is well reduced and coating the pork thickly. Keep stirring regularly, especially towards the end of the cooking time. The curry should look rich and glossy when you are finished. Serve with rice.

This is a lovely hot and spicy curry, a bit like a vindaloo, with a tangy sour flavour coming from the vinegar. You can use pork shoulder steaks if you like. **Serves 6**

PORK CURRY WITH A KICK

1.2kg boneless, rindless pork shoulder meat
5 tbsp sunflower oil
750ml cold water
1 heaped tsp flaked sea salt
2 tbsp soft light brown sugar

Marinade

4 long green chillies, trimmed
3 medium onions, 2 quartered and 1 sliced
6 garlic cloves
25g chunk of fresh root ginger, peeled and roughly chopped
10 extra-hot dried chillies (bird's-eye)
1 tsp ground turmeric
75ml red wine vinegar, plus 2 tsp
2 tsp cumin seeds
1 tsp coriander seeds
1 tsp fenugreek seeds
3–4cm piece of cinnamon stick
5 cloves
½ tsp black peppercorns

First make the marinade. Roughly chop 2 of the chillies, deseeding them first if you don't like very spicy food. Split the other 2 chillies from stalk to tip on 1 side without opening them or removing the seeds and set aside. Put the chopped chillies, quartered onions, garlic and ginger in a food processor. Add the dried chillies, turmeric and the 75ml of vinegar, then blitz the mixture to a thick paste.

Put the cumin, coriander and fenugreek seeds, cinnamon, cloves and peppercorns in a dry frying pan and toast them over a medium-high heat for 1 minute. Tip the toasted spices into a spice grinder and blend them to a powder. Add the spice powder to the onion paste and blitz for a few seconds until thoroughly combined.

Trim the pork, but don't cut away all the fat as it makes the meat more succulent and adds flavour to the curry. Cut the pork into 3cm chunks and put them in a large non-metallic bowl. Add the marinade and stir together well. Cover and leave to marinate in the fridge for 1–2 hours.

To make the curry, preheat the oven to 180°C/Fan 160°C/Gas 4. Heat 2 tablespoons of the sunflower oil in a large non-stick frying pan and cook the sliced onion over a medium-high heat for 6–8 minutes until softened and well browned, stirring regularly. Tip the onion into a large flameproof casserole dish. Put the casserole dish back on the heat, add 1 tablespoon of the remaining oil and fry the pork with its marinade for 3–4 minutes until lightly browned. Do this in 3 batches so you don't overcrowd the pan and add an extra tablespoon of oil to the pan between each batch. Stir the pork well with a wooden spoon as it cooks so the marinade doesn't get a chance to stick.

Once the last batch of pork has been added to the dish, put the frying pan back on the heat and add 300ml of the water. Bring to a simmer, stirring and scraping the bottom of the pan to lift any sediment, then pour the water over the pork in the dish. Add the remaining water, reserved split chillies, salt and sugar and bring everything to a simmer. Cover with a lid, put it in the oven and cook for 1 hour. Once the hour is up, take the casserole out of the oven and spoon off the fat that will have risen to the surface. Put the casserole on the hob over a medium heat and simmer the pork for 8–10 minutes, stirring regularly until the sauce has reduced by a third and the meat is tender. Stir in the remaining 2 teaspoons of vinegar to accentuate the flavours.

There's lots of argument about the origins of this much-loved South African street food classic. Basically, it's a spicy curry served in a hollowed-out loaf of bread that acts as both the bowl and cutlery. It can be made with veg and beans, lamb or chicken – no bunnies involved. Everyone has their own favourite recipe – there's even an annual bunny chow festival – but this is our version. **Serves 4 very generously, or 6 if you want to put the bunny chow in large crusty rolls instead**

SOUTH AFRICAN BUNNY CHOW

- 450g lamb neck fillets
- 3 tbsp sunflower oil
- 2 medium onions, halved and sliced
- 4 garlic cloves, crushed
- 15g chunk of fresh root ginger, peeled and finely grated
- 2 tbsp medium curry powder
- 1 bird's-eye chilli, trimmed and finely sliced or ¼ tsp cayenne pepper (optional)
- 1 cinnamon stick
- 1 star anise
- 6 cardamom pods, crushed
- 12 dry curry leaves
- 400g can of chopped tomatoes
- 450ml lamb stock (made with 1 lamb stock cube)
- 1 tsp flaked sea salt, plus extra to season
- 2 medium potatoes (about 415g)
- 400g can of haricot or cannellini beans, drained and rinsed
- 2 small fresh white sandwich loaves (unsliced)
- freshly ground black pepper
- grated carrot and fresh coriander, to garnish

Trim the lamb of any large fatty pieces and cut it into 2.5cm chunks. Season all over with salt and pepper. Heat the oil in a large non-stick saucepan or flame-proof casserole dish and gently fry the onions, garlic and ginger for 10 minutes until softened and lightly coloured.

Add the curry powder, chilli or cayenne, if using, cinnamon, star anise, cardamom pods and curry leaves to the pan and cook for 2 minutes more, stirring. Add the lamb to the pan, increase the heat a little and fry for 3–4 minutes, turning every now and then until lightly coloured.

Tip the tomatoes into the pan, add the stock and salt and bring to a simmer. Cover with a lid and leave to cook over a low heat for 45 minutes, stirring occasionally. The curry should simmer gently without boiling. Peel the potatoes and cut them into 2cm cubes. Put them in a large bowl and cover with cold water to stop them turning brown.

After the 45 minutes is up, drain the potatoes. Remove the lid from the pan and take the star anise and cinnamon stick out of the curry. Add the potatoes and beans to the lamb. Bring the curry back to a simmer, cover and cook for a further 30 minutes or until the lamb and potatoes are very tender and the sauce is thick. You need lots of sauce as the bread will soak it up quickly, so add a little extra water if you think it needs it. Add a little extra salt and pepper to taste.

Cut the loaves of bread in half right through the middle and use a knife to cut out the inner soft bread, leaving the crust completely intact. Try to keep the bread that you remove in 1 piece if you can. It's a matter of cutting all around the edge, then grabbing the inner bread with your hands and pulling.

Place each bread half on a plate, cut side up. Spoon the hot curry into the bread and garnish with grated carrot and fresh coriander. Serve with the scooped-out pieces of bread for dipping and pinching up bits of the curry– you're not supposed to use cutlery with this curry!

Vegetable Curries

Vegetable curries are in no way second best and the alchemy of flavour and spices means that they stand as great dishes in their own right. Much of south India is vegetarian so their veg curries are superb. **Serves 4 as a main course or 6–8 as an accompaniment**

VEGETABLE COCONUT CURRY

300g aubergine
200g small button mushrooms, wiped
6 tbsp ghee or sunflower oil
2 large onions, sliced
4 garlic cloves, finely chopped
25g chunk of fresh root ginger, finely chopped
500g sweet potatoes
1 tbsp garam masala (see page 345 or use ready-made)
1 tsp ground turmeric
1 tsp cumin seeds
15 dry curry leaves
3 whole green chillies, split lengthways
300ml vegetable stock (made with 1 vegetable stock cube)
150ml coconut milk
400g can of chopped tomatoes
2 tsp caster sugar
300g small cauliflower florets (about ½ small cauliflower)
150g frozen peas
small bunch of fresh coriander, leaves chopped
flaked sea salt
freshly ground black pepper

Cut the aubergine into rough 2cm chunks and slice the mushrooms in half if large. Heat 3 tablespoons of the ghee or oil in a large non-stick sauté pan or wide-based saucepan. Add the aubergine and mushrooms and stir-fry them for 4–5 minutes or until lightly browned. Tip everything into a heatproof bowl and set aside.

Put the pan back on the heat and add the remaining ghee or oil. Fry the onions with the garlic and ginger over a low heat for 10 minutes until softened but not coloured. Meanwhile, peel the sweet potatoes and cut them into rough 2cm chunks.

Stir in the garam masala, turmeric, cumin and curry leaves and cook for 2 minutes more, stirring constantly. Tip the aubergine chunks and mushrooms back into the pan and add the sweet potatoes and chillies. Cook for 3 minutes, stirring regularly.

Stir in the stock, coconut milk, tomatoes and sugar, then cover the pan and bring to a gentle simmer. Cook for 5 minutes, then add the cauliflower, making sure it is well covered by liquid, and cook for 10 minutes more, stirring once or twice. Add the peas and simmer uncovered for 5–10 minutes or until all the vegetables are just tender and the sauce is thick, stirring occasionally.

Season with a little salt and freshly ground black pepper if necessary, then tip into a warmed serving dish and scatter with freshly chopped coriander before serving.

This is one of our very favourite veg curries and something we first cooked while watching elephants bathe at sunset. It combines a juicy mix of spinach, tomatoes and spices with fried cubes of paneer – a kind of set cottage cheese that's used in many Indian vegetarian dishes. The crunchy semolina coating is a special Hairy Biker touch. **Serves 4**

CRUNCHY PALAK PANEER

- 3 tbsp ghee or sunflower oil
- 2 medium onions, finely chopped
- 20g chunk of fresh root ginger, finely grated
- 3 garlic cloves, finely chopped
- 1 tsp ground cumin
- 1 tsp ground coriander
- 1 tsp ground turmeric
- 1 whole green chilli, split lengthways
- 1 tsp flaked sea salt, plus extra for seasoning
- 400g can of chopped tomatoes
- 1 tsp caster sugar
- 400g young spinach leaves, washed and drained
- freshly ground black pepper

Paneer

- 1 tsp garam masala (see page 345 or use ready-made)
- 3 tbsp semolina
- 220g paneer
- 3–4 tbsp sunflower oil
- squeeze of fresh lemon juice, about 1 tsp

Heat the ghee or oil in a large non-stick saucepan. Gently fry the onions with the ginger and garlic for 6–8 minutes until they are soft and very lightly coloured, stirring regularly.

Add all the dry spices, the whole chilli and teaspoon of salt and fry for another minute, stirring. Tip the chopped tomatoes into the pan and add the sugar. Bring to a gentle simmer and cook for 20 minutes, stirring regularly until the sauce is well reduced. Season with a little extra salt and some black pepper if necessary.

While the sauce is cooking, combine the garam masala and semolina in a large mixing bowl. Cut the paneer into pieces about the size of a stock cube (about 1.5cm square) and add them to the bowl. Toss everything together until all the cubes are lightly coated.

Add enough of the sunflower oil to cover the base of a large non-stick frying pan and place it over a medium heat. Fry the cubes of paneer for 4–5 minutes, turning occasionally, until they are browned and crisp on all sides.

Stir the spinach into the pan with the spiced tomato sauce and cook for 2–3 minutes, stirring until the leaves are well wilted. Tip the sauce and spinach into a warmed serving dish and gently toss with the paneer. Add a squeeze of lemon juice to sharpen the flavour and serve at once.

One of the most popular of all vegetarian curries, mutter paneer is a roadside classic that we enjoyed all over India. It's a stand-alone dish with wonderful hits of flavour. **Serves 3–4**

MUTTER PANEER

- 4 tbsp sunflower oil
- 2 tsp cumin seeds
- 1 tsp black mustard seeds
- 1 tsp fenugreek seeds
- 2 medium onions, halved and finely sliced
- 4 garlic cloves, finely sliced
- 15g chunk of fresh root ginger, peeled and finely grated
- 1 long green chilli, trimmed and finely chopped (do not deseed)
- 2 tsp ground coriander
- ¼ tsp hot chilli powder
- 400g can of chopped tomatoes
- 150ml plain natural yoghurt
- ½ tsp fine sea salt
- 225g paneer, drained and cut into 2cm cubes
- 150g frozen peas
- 100ml cold water
- handful of chopped coriander (optional)
- freshly ground black pepper

Heat a tablespoon of the sunflower oil in a large non-stick saucepan. Fry the cumin, mustard and fenugreek seeds over a medium-high heat for a few seconds until the mustard seeds begin to pop, stirring constantly. Don't let them burn.

Add the onions to the pan and fry for 5 minutes, stirring regularly, until softened and well browned. Add another tablespoon of oil, the garlic, ginger and green chilli and cook for 1 minute more, stirring. Sprinkle over the ground coriander and chilli powder and cook for 1 minute, stirring constantly.

Tip the tomatoes into the pan, add the yoghurt and salt and season with lots of ground black pepper. Bring to the boil, while stirring, then reduce the heat and leave the sauce to simmer gently for 10–12 minutes. Keep stirring regularly until the sauce is thick and intense.

While the sauce is simmering, prepare the paneer. Place a small non-stick frying pan over a medium-high heat. Add the remaining 2 tablespoons of oil, then the paneer. Fry for about 5 minutes, turning regularly until the cubes are lightly browned all over. Watch out for splashes as the fat does spit a bit as the paneer comes close to the end of the frying time. Put the paneer pieces on a plate lined with kitchen paper and let it drain.

When the curry sauce is ready, stir in the peas and then the paneer. Add about 100ml of cold water to make the curry a bit looser – it should be reasonably saucy. Bring it back to a simmer and cook for 2–3 minutes or until the peas are hot. Serve with parathas or naan bread and some pickles. Garnish with chopped coriander too, if you like.

Some channa masala recipes call for just a few minutes of simmering, but we've found that letting the chickpeas bubble away in the richly spiced tomatoes for 40 minutes mellows all the spices and creates a rich unctuous sauce. This dish should be slightly sour, so add a little extra lemon juice if necessary. Fresh coriander is our touch – we love the fragrance it gives to the final dish – but leave it out if you prefer. **Serves 4–6**

CHANNA MASALA

- 2 tbsp sunflower oil
- 2 medium onions, halved and finely sliced
- 4 garlic cloves, finely chopped
- 15g chunk of fresh root ginger, peeled and finely grated
- 1 long green chilli, finely chopped (deseed if you like)
- 1 tsp cumin seeds
- 1 tbsp ground coriander
- 1 tsp ground cumin
- 2 tsp paprika
- 1 tsp ground turmeric
- 1½ tsp garam masala (see page 345 or ready-made)
- ¼ tsp cayenne pepper
- 400g can of chopped tomatoes
- ¼ tsp fine sea salt, plus extra to season
- 750ml cold water
- 2 x 400g cans of chickpeas
- 2–3 tbsp fresh lemon juice
- 2 tsp caster sugar
- handful of chopped coriander (optional)
- freshly ground black pepper

Heat the oil in a large non-stick sauté pan or frying pan. Add the sliced onions and fry them for 5 minutes, stirring occasionally until softened. Increase the heat a little and cook the onions for 1–2 minutes more until lightly browned, stirring.

Add the garlic, ginger, chilli and cumin seeds to the pan and fry together for 2 minutes, stirring constantly. Sprinkle over the ground coriander, ground cumin, paprika, turmeric, garam masala and cayenne pepper and stir over a low heat for 2 minutes. Don't let the spices burn or the curry will be bitter. Flop the tomatoes into the pan and stir in the salt and the water. Bring to the boil.

Tip the chickpeas into a sieve and rinse them well under running water. Add them to the spiced onion sauce and bring it to a gentle simmer, stirring. Leave to simmer gently for about 40 minutes, stirring regularly, until the sauce is thick and the spices have mellowed. If the sauce becomes too thick before the 40 minutes is up, add a little extra water and continue cooking.

Season with salt and black pepper and add the lemon juice and sugar to taste. You want the flavour to be slightly sour but rich. Continue to cook for 2 minutes more, then stir in the coriander, if using, and serve.

Canned are fine sometimes, but we find that fresh, ripe, juicy tomatoes make the world of difference to a curry.

People say there are as many versions of sambar as there are households in India. Here is our version of this soupy vegetable curry but you can make it more liquid if you prefer. Sambar is great on its own or as a side dish to grilled meat. We like to make a big batch and freeze some for another day. **Serves 6**

SAMBAR

Dhal

2 tbsp sunflower oil
½ medium red onion, chopped
4 shallots or 1 small brown onion, finely chopped
2 garlic cloves, finely chopped
1 large ripe vine tomato, roughly chopped
100g toor dhal (see page 361)
½ tsp ground turmeric
1 tsp flaked sea salt
850ml cold water

Vegetables

1 medium aubergine (about 250g)
1 large potato (about 285g), peeled
2 tbsp sunflower oil
½ tsp black mustard seeds
½ tsp fenugreek seeds
1 tsp cumin seeds
1 small dried red chilli, slit lengthways
1 long green chilli, slit lengthways
10 fresh curry leaves
2 large ripe fresh tomatoes, chopped
½ medium red onion, chopped
½ tsp asafoetida
½ tsp ground turmeric
1 tsp ground coriander
1 tsp hot chilli powder
1 heaped tsp tamarind paste
100ml cold water
freshly chopped coriander, to garnish

Start by making the dhal. Heat the oil in a medium saucepan and gently fry the red onion, shallots or brown onion, garlic and tomato for 5 minutes until softened, stirring regularly.

Add the dhal, turmeric and salt, then stir in the water and bring to the boil. Reduce the heat slightly and simmer for 35 minutes or until the dhal is very soft and mushy, stirring occasionally.

Next, prepare the vegetables. Cut the aubergine and potato into 1.5cm cubes. Heat the oil in a large non-stick saucepan and add the mustard seeds. As soon as they begin to pop, stir in the fenugreek, cumin, dried red chilli, green chilli and curry leaves. Cook for 1 minute, stirring constantly over a medium heat.

Add the chopped tomatoes, red onion, asafoetida, turmeric, coriander and chilli powder. Fry for 2–3 minutes more, stirring constantly and watching to make sure the spices don't burn.

Scatter the aubergine and potato cubes into the pan and cook for 10 minutes, stirring regularly. You want the aubergine cubes to get lightly browned, but if they begin to stick, add a little more oil or a couple of tablespoons of water to get them going again.

Tip the cooked dhal into the pan with the veg and bring to a gentle simmer. Cook for 3–5 minutes more or until all the vegetables are softened without falling apart, stirring regularly.

Mix the tamarind with the water until smooth and pour the mixture into the pan. Continue cooking for a further 2–3 minutes, stirring regularly until all the flavours are well blended. The sambar should look fairly soupy when you've finished. Serve in bowls and sprinkle with fresh coriander.

This is a dry vegetable curry that goes beautifully with saucy or rich curries. We think it's like the bubble and squeak of the curry world and it's fantastic. We like to include a small amount of urad dhal to add a little crunch to the dish – this is a rather special dhal, popular in southern India, and well worth seeking out. **Serves 4–6**

MIXED VEGETABLE THORAN

- 375g green or savoy cabbage (about ½ cabbage)
- 2 medium carrots
- 1 medium onion
- 3 tbsp desiccated coconut
- 2 tbsp cold water
- 2 tbsp sunflower oil
- 1 tsp black mustard seeds
- ½ tsp cumin seeds
- ½ tsp urad dhal (optional)
- 4 fresh curry leaves or 8 dried curry leaves
- ½ tsp dried chilli flakes
- ½ tsp flaked sea salt
- ¼ tsp ground turmeric

Remove any damaged or tough outer leaves from the cabbage. Place the cabbage on a board and cut out the central white stem part. Finely shred the cabbage and put it in a large mixing bowl.

Peel the carrots, then, watching out for your fingertips, grate them in a vertical position on a box grater so you end up with long strips. Cut the onion in half and slice it finely, then toss the carrot and onion together with the cabbage. Put the coconut in a small bowl, pour over the water and leave to soak.

Heat the oil in a large non-stick frying pan or wok. Add the mustard and cumin seeds, the urad dhal, if using and the curry leaves. As soon as the mustard seeds begin to crackle and pop, stir in the prepared vegetables, chilli flakes, salt and turmeric.

Stir-fry over a high heat for 2 minutes. Add the coconut and its water and stir-fry for a further minute until the vegetables are only just tender – they should maintain some bite. Add a little extra salt if necessary and serve hot.

Everyone loves a pad Thai with its great textures of soft noodles, crispy bean sprouts and nuts, all brought together with egg. Just get everything measured out and ready before you start, as you need to be able to cook this dish quickly over a high heat. This is a veggie version with tofu but you can use prawns or chicken instead. **Serves 4**

PAD THAI

300–400g firm tofu
about 400ml sunflower oil
175g wide, flat rice noodles (about 5mm wide)
3 tbsp sunflower or groundnut oil, plus 1 tsp
1 medium red onion, halved and cut into 12 slender wedges
2 garlic cloves, finely chopped
½ tsp dried chilli flakes
2 large eggs, well beaten
2½ tbsp Thai fish sauce (nam pla)
juice of 1 lime (about 2 tbsp)
1 tbsp soft brown sugar
50g roasted unsalted peanuts, roughly chopped
6 spring onions, trimmed and thinly sliced
100g bean sprouts, rinsed

Press the tofu on to folded kitchen paper, turning it every now and again and replacing the paper as needed until you are pretty sure you have soaked up as much of the excess liquid as possible. Put the tofu on a board and cut it into cubes of about 2cm.

Pour the sunflower oil into a medium wide-based saucepan. It's best to use a saucepan rather than a frying pan as the oil can spit once the tofu is added. A sauté pan would also do the job. Place the oil over a medium heat and as soon as it is hot, add the tofu pieces. DO NOT ALLOW THE OIL TO OVERHEAT. DO NOT LEAVE HOT OIL UNATTENDED.

Fry the tofu for about 4 minutes until golden brown, turning it once or twice. Watch out for splashes and use a long-handled slotted spoon or tongs for turning. Remove the tofu when it's crisp and drain it on folded kitchen paper.

Half fill a large saucepan with water and bring it to the boil. Add the noodles in 3–4 batches, stirring well after each addition. Bring the water back to the boil and cook the noodles for 3–4 minutes until just tender. You may need to use a fork to stir the noodles as they cook. Drain them in a colander and toss them with the teaspoon of oil to stop the strands sticking together, then put to one side.

Pour the 3 tablespoons of oil into a large wok or non-stick frying pan and stir-fry the onion over a medium heat for 2 minutes. Add the chopped garlic and chilli flakes and cook for 30 seconds more. Pour in the beaten eggs and stir-fry for a few seconds until they begin to scramble. Immediately add the noodles, fried tofu, fish sauce, lime juice and sugar. Turn the heat up to its highest setting and stir-fry everything together for 2 minutes. Toss with chopsticks or use 2 wooden spoons as you stir-fry to make sure all the ingredients are thoroughly hot.

Add the peanuts, spring onions and bean sprouts. Stir-fry for 2–3 minutes more until the egg becomes lightly browned. Divide the pad Thai between warmed plates or bowls and serve immediately.

A fabulously hot but aromatic curry, this contains a mix of dry and fresh chillies and is one serious feast for the curry veteran – beginners beware. Cut down on the chilli if you don't like your food highly spiced. It's well worth finding fresh curry leaves for this if possible. **Serves 4 as a main meal with rice or 6 as an accompaniment**

KIDNEY BEAN CURRY

- 3 tbsp sunflower oil
- 1 tsp yellow mustard seeds
- 1 tsp cumin seeds
- 1 tsp fennel seeds
- 2 dried long red hot chillies
- 10 fresh curry leaves or 15 dried curry leaves
- ½ medium onion, finely chopped
- 20g chunk of fresh root ginger, peeled and finely grated
- 1 long green chilli, trimmed and finely chopped (deseed first if you like)
- 3 garlic cloves, thinly sliced
- 2 tsp garam masala (see page 345 or use ready-made)
- ½ tsp ground turmeric
- 227g can of chopped tomatoes
- good pinch of asafoetida
- 1 tsp caster sugar
- 1 tsp flaked sea salt
- 200ml cold water
- 2 x 400g cans of red kidney beans, drained and rinsed

Heat the oil in a large, deep non-stick frying pan or a sauté pan and add the mustard, cumin and fennel seeds. Add the dried chillies and the curry leaves and cook for a few seconds over a medium heat until the mustard seeds begin to pop.

Add the onion, ginger, fresh chilli and garlic and continue cooking for another 3–4 minutes until the onions are beginning to soften. Add the garam masala and the turmeric and cook for 2 minutes more, stirring constantly. Make sure the heat isn't too high – you don't want the spices to burn or they will taste extremely bitter.

Tip the tomatoes into the pan and sprinkle with the asafoetida. Add the sugar and salt, stir in the water and bring to a simmer. Add the beans and cook over a medium heat for 10 minutes, stirring regularly. Serve with rice as a veggie meal or as an accompaniment to other curries.

Serve this lovely simple dish on its own with some bread for an easy comforting supper. Goes well with grilled meat or other curries too. **Serves 4–6**

LENTIL AND VEGETABLE CURRY

- 200g dry split red lentils
- 3 tbsp sunflower oil
- 1 medium onion, halved and finely sliced
- ½ medium butternut squash (about 550g), peeled, deseeded and cut into 2cm chunks
- 2 medium carrots, peeled and cut into 5mm diagonal slices
- 3 garlic cloves, crushed
- 15g chunk of fresh root ginger, peeled and finely grated
- 1 long green chilli, deseeded and finely chopped
- 1 tsp garam masala (see page 345 or use ready-made)
- 1 tsp fenugreek seeds
- ¼ tsp cayenne pepper
- ½ tsp ground turmeric
- good pinch of asafoetida (optional)
- 1 litre cold water
- 1 tsp fine sea salt, plus extra to season
- 100g green beans, trimmed and cut into short lengths
- 3 fresh ripe tomatoes, quartered
- freshly ground black pepper

Put the lentils in a sieve and rinse them well under cold water, then drain. Place a large non-stick saucepan or flameproof casserole dish over a medium-high heat. Add the oil and then the onion and fry for about 5 minutes until the onion is pale golden brown, stirring constantly. Do not allow the onion to burn.

Stir in the squash, carrots, garlic, ginger, chilli, garam masala, fenugreek, cayenne pepper, turmeric and asafoetida, if using. Cook together for 1 minute, stirring constantly, but don't allow the spices to burn or they will make your curry taste bitter.

Tip the lentils into the pan with the spiced onion mixture and pour over the water. Stir well and bring to the boil, then skim off any foam that rises to surface with a spoon and throw it away. Add the teaspoon of salt, stir well and reduce the heat to low.

Cover loosely with a lid and leave to simmer gently for 20 minutes or until the lentils are almost tender, stirring occasionally. Stir in the beans and cook for 3 minutes more, stirring regularly. Add the tomatoes and cook for 3–5 minutes, stirring until the tomatoes are softened, but still holding their shape, and the lentils are very tender.

As the curry thickens, it bubbles like lava, so watch out for splashes and turn down the heat a little if necessary. This curry will continue to thicken after it has been taken off the hob. If making in advance, you may need to add a little extra water when you come to reheat it. Season to taste with salt and freshly ground black pepper.

Okay, we know this isn't a vegetable curry, but we love curried eggs and we had to have them in the book somewhere. They do make a great lunch for vegetarians – or for anyone. **Serves 4**

CURRIED EGGS

- 3 tbsp sunflower oil
- 3 medium onions, halved and sliced
- 4 garlic cloves, finely chopped
- 25g chunk of fresh root ginger, peeled and finely chopped
- 1 plump green chilli, deseeded and roughly chopped
- 2 tsp cumin seeds
- 2 tsp ground coriander
- 1 tsp ground turmeric
- ¼ tsp cayenne pepper (optional)
- ½ tsp garam masala (see page 345 or use ready-made)
- pinch of asafoetida (optional)
- 300g canned chopped tomatoes
- 1 tsp flaked sea salt
- 2 tbsp mango chutney
- 200ml cold water
- 4 tbsp double cream
- 8 large eggs (fridge cold)
- freshly ground black pepper

Heat the oil in a large non-stick saucepan and add the onions, garlic, ginger and chilli. Cover and cook over a low heat for 15 minutes or until the onions are very soft, removing the lid and stirring them occasionally. Uncover the pan, turn up the heat and cook for 6–8 minutes more, stirring constantly until the onions are a nice rich brown. This will add lots of flavour to your sauce, but watch the onions carefully to make sure they don't burn.

Sprinkle over the cumin seeds, coriander, turmeric, cayenne, if using, garam masala and asafoetida. Cook for 2 minutes, stirring constantly, then add the tomatoes, salt, chutney and water into the pan. Season with lots of black pepper and bring to a gentle simmer, then cook for 10 minutes, stirring regularly.

Remove the pan from the heat and blitz the onion mixture with a stick blender until you have a smooth sauce. You can also do this in a food processor, but leave the sauce to cool for a while first. Pour the sauce into a large non-stick sauté pan or frying pan and then stir in the double cream.

Half fill a large saucepan with water and bring it to the boil over a high heat. Gently add the eggs and bring the water back to the boil. Cook the eggs for 8 minutes, then drain them in a sieve under running water until the shells feel cool enough to handle. Crack the shells and carefully peel the eggs.

Warm the sauce through gently, stirring constantly. When the sauce is beginning to bubble gently, add the eggs and heat them for 2–3 minutes. Keep stirring and spooning the hot sauce over the eggs. You may need to add a little water if the sauce begins to spit a little – it will bubble and burble like lava if too thick. Serve the eggs and sauce hot, with some freshly boiled rice.

Curry for a Crowd

Rich and spicy, rendang is an Indonesian dish that's traditionally served at festivals and special occasions – perfect for a party then. We use the plump red chillies for this, but if you have the hotter long red chillies you will need to deseed two of them before chopping. **Serves 14–16**

BEEF RENDANG

- 4 lemon grass stalks
- 5 medium red onions, quartered
- 12 garlic cloves
- 50g chunk of fresh root ginger, peeled and roughly chopped
- 75g chunk of galangal, peeled and roughly chopped (or about 3 tbsp galangal paste)
- 5 plump red chillies, roughly chopped (do not deseed)
- 4 tbsp sunflower oil
- 1 tbsp ground cumin
- 2 tbsp ground coriander
- 2 tsp ground turmeric
- 3kg beef chuck steak (or any braising beef), trimmed and cut into 3cm cubes
- 2 x 400ml cans of coconut milk
- 400ml cold water
- 6 kaffir lime leaves (fresh or dried)
- 2 cinnamon sticks
- 2 tbsp soft light brown sugar or palm sugar
- 1 tbsp tamarind paste or freshly squeezed juice of 1 lime
- 3 tbsp dark soy sauce
- 1 tbsp flaked sea salt
- toasted coconut flakes, for serving (optional)

Peel off the dry outer layers of each lemon grass stalk and slice the inner whiter part into 1cm pieces. Put them in a food processor, add the onions, garlic, ginger, galangal and chillies and blend to make as fine a paste as possible. You may need to remove the lid and push the mixture down a couple of times with a rubber spatula until the right consistency is reached.

Heat the sunflower oil in a large flameproof casserole dish and fry the onion paste gently for 3–4 minutes, stirring constantly. Add the cumin, coriander and turmeric and cook for 2 minutes more.

Add the beef to the casserole dish and toss it with the onion paste and spices. Cook for 5 minutes, stirring constantly until the meat is very lightly coloured all over. Pour in the coconut milk, then add the water, lime leaves, cinnamon sticks, sugar, tamarind paste or lime juice, soy sauce and salt.

Bring to a simmer, then turn down the heat and leave the beef to simmer gently for about 2½ hours, uncovered, or until the meat is meltingly tender and the coconut milk has reduced to a very thick, rich sauce. Stir the beef occasionally at the beginning of the cooking time, then more often as the coconut milk reduces. You don't want the sauce to stick.

This dish is even better made the day before you eat it, so if you're doing this, cook the beef for 15 minutes less and cool it quickly in a large, shallow dish. Cover and keep in the fridge for 1–2 days before serving. When you want to eat, slowly reheat the rendang in a large casserole dish until piping hot, stirring just enough to distribute the heat but not so much that the meat breaks up.

Spoon the curry into a couple of warm serving dishes and sprinkle with the toasted coconut, if using. Serve with jasmine rice and Asian greens (see page 239). Warn your guests to watch out for the lime leaves and cinnamon sticks and not to eat them.

Rogan josh is one of the all-time favourite curries. The slow cooking of the finely sliced onions is essential to the flavour of the sauce so don't be tempted to skip that, and it's worth seeking out kashmiri chilli powder to give the authentic rich red colour. **Serves 18–20**

LAMB ROGAN JOSH

- 8 medium onions
- 6–7 tbsp sunflower oil or ghee
- 2kg boneless lamb leg meat
- 3 tsp flaked sea salt, plus extra to season
- 3 plump red chillies (about 30g total weight)
- 75g chunk of fresh root ginger, peeled and roughly chopped
- 12 garlic cloves
- 2 tbsp kashmiri chilli powder
- 3 tbsp garam masala (see page 345 or use ready-made)
- 1 tbsp ground coriander
- 1 tbsp fennel seeds
- 1 tbsp cumin seeds
- 1 tsp ground turmeric
- 1 tsp asafoetida (optional)
- 4 x 400g cans of chopped tomatoes
- 1.3 litres cold water
- 4 bay leaves
- 2 cinnamon sticks
- bunch of fresh coriander, roughly chopped including the stalks
- 300ml plain natural yogurt
- 1.9kg medium potatoes, (preferably Maris Pipers)
- 450g young spinach leaves
- freshly ground black pepper

Peel the onions, cut them in half, then slice them thinly. You want them fine enough to 'melt' into the sauce as they cook. You can blitz them in a food processor but the sauce won't be quite as good.

Heat 4 tablespoons of the oil or ghee in a large non-stick sauté pan or wide-based saucepan. Add the onions and cook them over a medium heat for 30–35 minutes or until well softened and golden brown. You'll need to stir every few minutes, especially towards the end of the cooking time, or the onions could stick, but it's well worth cooking them to a good brown colour as this will give the curry lots of flavour.

While the onions are cooking, and in between stirs, trim the lamb meat and chuck away any fatty bits or sinew. Cut the lamb meat into rough 3cm chunks and season with 2 teaspoons of salt and lots of ground black pepper. Toss well together and set aside.

Trim off and discard the stalks from the chillies. Cut each chilli in half and remove the seeds and membrane if you don't like your curries too hot. Chop the chillies roughly and put them in a food processor, then add the ginger, garlic and a teaspoon of the salt. Blitz the mixture until very finely chopped, removing the lid and pushing the mixture down a couple of times with a spatula until it is as fine as you can get it.

Tip the chilli mixture into the pan with the golden onions and cook together for 5 minutes, stirring with a wooden spoon. Sprinkle the chilli powder, garam masala, coriander, fennel and cumin seeds, ground turmeric and asafoetida on top and stir well. Cook for a further 3 minutes, stirring. Scrape the chilli paste into a very large flameproof casserole dish. Add the canned tomatoes, 1 litre of the water, bay leaves, cinnamon sticks and the coriander. Stir well and set aside. Preheat the oven to 180°C/Fan 160°C/Gas 4.

Take the non-stick pan you used for the onions and put it back on the heat. Add a tablespoon of the remaining oil. Brown the lamb in 4 batches over a high heat, adding a little more oil between each batch. The lamb should be coloured all over.

continued overleaf…

LAMB ROGAN JOSH CONTINUED...

As soon as each batch of meat is ready, tip it into the casserole dish with the tomatoes. Stir in the yoghurt and place the dish over a high heat, then bring to a simmer and cover with a lid. Cook in the oven for 1 hour.

While the lamb is cooking, peel the potatoes and cut them into rough 2.5cm chunks. Put these in a large bowl and cover them with cold water to prevent them from turning brown.

Remove the casserole dish from the oven when the hour is up. Using a large ladle, very carefully transfer half the lamb and sauce into another large casserole dish to make room for the potatoes.

Divide the potatoes, coriander and the remaining 300ml of water between the 2 casserole dishes. Put the lids on and put the casseroles in the oven for a further 50–60 minutes or until the lamb and potatoes are tender and the sauce is thick. Stir halfway through the cooking time to ensure the potatoes cook completely. You might need to cook one casserole at a time unless you have a double oven.

Just before the curry is ready, quarter fill a large saucepan with water and bring it to the boil. Add the spinach, a large handful at a time, and cook for 30 seconds until wilted, while stirring. Drain thoroughly in a colander. Divide the spinach leaves between the hot curries and stir them in lightly. Adjust the seasoning to taste and sprinkle with the reserved coriander leaves just before serving. If cooking the curries one at a time, you can warm the first up over a low heat on the hob just before the second curry comes out of the oven. Stir the curry regularly to prevent it sticking.

If you're going to serve the curry a day or so later, leave it to cool, then put it in the fridge and keep chilled until ready to reheat. Reheat the curry in a preheated oven at 190°C/Fan 170°C/Gas 5 for 40–60 minutes until it's bubbling and hot throughout. You can also reheat it on the hob which will take 25–35 minutes. If reheating the curry on the hob, it is important to stir it regularly so it doesn't begin to stick, but try not to break up the meat. Add a little extra water if the sauce thickens too much.

This bhuna-style curry is a real crowd pleaser and you can use a ready-made medium curry paste to make it extra easy. We've used boneless chicken thighs because they are more forgiving than chicken breasts and can be reheated without becoming tough. They'll also help give your curry lots of flavour. This is a great curry to make ahead, so either pop it into the fridge up to two days before serving or freeze it for up to two months. Be sure to defrost it thoroughly before reheating. **Serves 14–16**

CHICKEN CURRY FOR A CROWD

- 5 tbsp sunflower oil or ghee
- 6 medium onions, halved and thinly sliced
- 24 boneless, skinless chicken thighs
- 8 garlic cloves, crushed
- 50g chunk of fresh root ginger, peeled and finely grated
- 250g medium curry paste
- 4 x 400g cans of chopped tomatoes
- 300ml cold water
- 1 chicken stock cube
- 2 tbsp mango chutney
- large bunch of fresh coriander, leaves roughly chopped
- flaked sea salt
- freshly ground black pepper

Heat the oil in a very large saucepan or a flameproof casserole dish, preferably non-stick. Add the onions and cook them over a medium-high heat for about 10 minutes until softened, stirring regularly. While the onions are cooking, put the chicken thighs on a board and trim off the fat. Cut each thigh into 4 pieces, season with a little salt and pepper, then set aside.

Whack up the heat and cook the onions for 6–8 minutes more or until they are a rich golden brown, stirring constantly. Add the garlic and ginger and cook for another minute, while stirring. Add the chicken pieces and fry them for 5 minutes, turning often until they are no longer pink. Stir in the curry paste and cook it with the chicken for 2–3 minutes, stirring until it covers the chicken all over and gently sizzles. Tip the tomatoes into the pan, add the water, crumble over the stock cube and stir in the chutney. Bring to a simmer, stirring regularly.

Cover the pan loosely with a lid and simmer gently for about 1¼ hours or until the chicken is tender and the sauce is nicely reduced but still plentiful enough to soak into rice or be scooped up with warm bread. Stir the curry occasionally and more regularly as it comes towards the end of the cooking time as you don't want it to stick. If you are making the curry ahead of time, it's best to reduce the simmering time to about 50 minutes, as the chicken will be cooked again when you reheat it.

Remove the pan from the heat and skim off and discard any fat that might have risen to the surface with a spoon – some ready-made curry pastes are quite oily. If serving straight away, stir in most of the coriander, saving a few leaves for the garnish, and ladle the curry into a couple of warmed serving dishes. Garnish with the rest of the coriander.

If serving the curry a day or so later, leave the curry to cool, then cover and chill until ready to eat. Reheat the curry in a preheated oven at 190°C/Fan 170°C/Gas 5 for 40–60 minutes until it's bubbling and hot throughout. You can also reheat it on the hob which will take 25–35 minutes. If reheating the curry on the hob, it is important to stir it regularly so it doesn't begin to stick, but try not to break up the chicken. Add a little extra water if the sauce thickens too much.

Ladies' fingers, bhindi, okra – call it what you will, I love it and it's great in a curry.

Rich, creamy and with a mild-medium heat, this is a good saucy curry, which reheats beautifully, so make a day ahead if it helps. Cool thoroughly and keep chilled in the fridge. Take it out of the fridge about 30 minutes before reheating. Reheat slowly on the hob until piping hot, stirring regularly so it doesn't get a chance to stick. **Serves 18**

CREAMY KASHMIRI CHICKEN CURRY

- 10 cardamom pods
- 6 tbsp ghee (or 4 tbsp butter and 2 tbsp sunflower oil)
- 6 medium onions, halved and finely sliced
- 8 garlic cloves, sliced
- 75g chunk of fresh root ginger, peeled and finely chopped
- 3 tbsp ground cumin
- 3 tbsp ground coriander
- 2 tsp ground turmeric
- 1 tbsp kashmiri chilli powder (or 1 tsp hot chilli powder and 2 tsp paprika)
- 75g ground almonds
- 2 x 400g cans of chopped tomatoes
- 600ml cold water
- 1 tbsp caster sugar
- 2 tsp flaked sea salt, plus extra to season
- 2–3 tbsp sunflower oil
- 36 boneless, skinless chicken thighs
- 2 bay leaves
- 1 cinnamon stick
- 150ml double cream
- freshly ground black pepper
- 2 tbsp toasted flaked almonds and some freshly chopped coriander, to garnish (optional)

Lightly crush the cardamom pods in a pestle and mortar, then tip them on to a board and split them open. Remove the seeds and chuck out the husks, then put the cardamom seeds back in the pestle and mortar and pound them to a powder. Set aside.

Melt the ghee (or butter and oil) in a large non-stick saucepan and add the onions, garlic and ginger. Cover and cook over a low heat for 15 minutes, stirring occasionally until very soft. Remove the lid and cook the onions over a high heat for 6–8 minutes, stirring constantly until they are nicely browned. Don't allow the onion mixture to burn.

Stir the cardamom, cumin, coriander, turmeric and kashmiri chilli powder into the pan with the onions and cook the spices for 2 minutes, stirring constantly. Stir in the almonds, tomatoes, water, sugar, salt, then bring to a gentle simmer and cook for 10 minutes, stirring regularly. Remove the pan from the heat and blitz the sauce with a stick blender until smooth. Set aside.

Trim the chicken thighs of any obvious fatty bits – we find a good pair of kitchen scissors works better than a knife. Cut the chicken thighs in half and season with a little salt and lots of black pepper. Heat 2 tablespoons of the oil in a very large flameproof casserole dish and fry the chicken in 2 batches over a medium-high heat for 3–4 minutes until lightly coloured on all sides. Put the first batch in a mixing bowl while you fry the second lot. Add a little more oil between the batches if you need to.

Put the first batch of chicken and any resting juices back into the casserole dish with the rest of the chicken and add the puréed onion mixture over the top. Add the bay leaves and cinnamon stick. Cover the dish loosely with a lid and bring to a gentle simmer, then cook for 25 minutes, stirring regularly. Add the cream, stir well and return to a simmer, uncovered. Cook for 5 minutes more or until the chicken is tender, stirring regularly. Garnish with toasted flaked almonds and some roughly chopped coriander if you like.

This is a perfect party dish, as you can do most of the work in advance and the final preparation on the day itself will only take about 15 minutes. Eggs are optional, but they make the dish a bit more special, and we like to scatter toasted flaked almonds on top just before serving. A biryani is a good buffet dish too. **Serves 8**

VEGETABLE BIRYANI

- 3 tbsp ghee or sunflower oil
- 250g small chestnut mushrooms, wiped and quartered
- 2 medium onions, halved and finely sliced
- 2 tbsp garam masala (see page 345 or use ready-made)
- 1 tsp black mustard seeds
- 3 plump green chillies, finely chopped
- 4 garlic cloves, finely chopped
- 20g chunk of fresh root ginger, peeled and finely chopped
- 1 tsp fine sea salt
- 3 medium potatoes (500g), cut into 2cm chunks
- 4 small carrots (about 275g), peeled and cut into 1cm diagonal slices
- 400g can of chopped tomatoes
- 400ml cold water
- ½ small cauliflower (about 300g), cut into florets
- 125g green beans, trimmed and cut into 3cm lengths
- 4 large eggs
- handful of fresh coriander leaves, roughly chopped

Heat the ghee or sunflower oil in a large non-stick saucepan and fry the mushrooms over a high heat for 2–3 minutes, stirring regularly until they are golden brown. Add the onions and cook for 5–6 minutes more or until they are golden.

Turn the heat down to medium and stir in the garam masala, mustard seeds, chillies, garlic, ginger and salt. Cook for a minute, stirring constantly. If the spices begin to stick, add an extra tablespoon of ghee or sunflower oil and keep stirring.

Add the potatoes, carrots, tomatoes and water. Bring to a simmer and cook for 12–14 minutes, stirring occasionally until the vegetables are starting to get tender and the sauce is beginning to thicken. Stir in the cauliflower florets and green beans, cover with a lid and cook for 8–10 minutes more or until all the vegetables are just tender. Remove the lid every now and again to stir the vegetables and add a little extra water if necessary. You want the curry to be fairly saucy but not at all watery.

Mix the milk and saffron in a small bowl and leave to infuse for about 10 minutes. Preheat the oven to 190°C/Fan 170°C/Gas 5. About 10 minutes before the vegetables are due to be ready, prepare the rice. Pour the water into a medium saucepan and crumble in the stock cube. Bring the water to the boil, stirring to dissolve the stock cube. Rinse the rice in a sieve under cold water, then tip it into the pan.

Add the cardamom, curry leaves and cinnamon stick. Bring the water back to the boil and cook for 2½ minutes or until the rice is just partly cooked, stirring occasionally. Remove the pan from the heat, drain the rice thoroughly in a sieve and tip it back into the pan. Stir the peas into the rice. Stir the yoghurt into the saffron-infused milk.

Spoon half the cooked vegetable curry into a large, shallow ovenproof dish or flameproof casserole dish – it will need to hold about 3 litres. Scatter half of the rice over the vegetables and drizzle with half of the saffron-infused milk. Spoon the remaining vegetable curry on top and finish with the rest of the rice.

Pour the rest of the yoghurt and saffron mixture over the top and dot with small knobs of the butter. Cover the dish tightly with lightly buttered foil and cook the biryani in the oven for 45 minutes or until the rice is tender and everything is steaming hot. The steam from the vegetable curry should finish cooking the rice.

To finish the garnish, hard boil the eggs for 9 minutes until firm and drain them in a sieve under running water until cool enough to handle. Peel the eggs and cut them into quarters. Remove the dish from the oven and take off the foil. Use a fork to lightly fluff the rice, then garnish with the freshly boiled eggs. Sprinkle with roughly chopped coriander or small coriander sprigs and serve with chapatis (see page 245), raita (see page 285) and a selection of chutneys.

Topping

5 tbsp milk
good pinch of saffron
4 tbsp plain natural yoghurt
50g butter,
plus extra for greasing

Rice

500ml cold water
1 vegetable stock cube
400g basmati rice
10 cardamom pods, crushed
20 fresh curry leaves
1 cinnamon stick,
broken in half
200g frozen peas

Side Dishes

Deliciously spicy masala potatoes make a great vegetable accompaniment for a curry or can be used as a stuffing for parathas (see page 253) or dosas (see page 38). There are loads of different versions of the recipe, but this is our take. We think it's well worth getting hold of some asafoetida. It's a very potent spice but when used sparingly it gives a unique savoury character to any dish and it makes the humble potato something special. **Serves 4–6**

MASALA POTATOES

Half fill a medium pan with water and bring it to the boil. Peel the potatoes and cut them into chunks of about 2.5cm. Drop the potatoes carefully into the pan, bring the water back to a fast simmer and cook for 8–10 minutes or until just tender. Drain the potatoes in a colander in the sink and leave them to stand while you prepare the spice mix.

While the potatoes are draining, heat 2 tablespoons of the sunflower oil in a large non-stick frying pan or sauté pan and fry the cumin and mustard seeds for a few seconds until they begin to pop. Add the onion and chilli and cook for 2 minutes over a medium heat, stirring constantly.

Add the remaining oil and the drained potatoes, then sprinkle over the turmeric, coriander, asafoetida and salt. Stir-fry for 2–3 minutes more, turning the potatoes in the spices until they are lightly coated and beginning to soften around the edges. Sprinkle with the lemon juice, toss together and serve hot.

- 650g potatoes, preferably Maris Pipers
- 3 tbsp sunflower oil
- 1 tsp cumin seeds
- 1 tsp yellow mustard seeds
- ½ medium onion, finely sliced
- 1 plump green chilli, trimmed and finely chopped (deseed first if you prefer)
- ¼ tsp ground turmeric
- 1 tsp ground coriander
- pinch of asafoetida
- 1 tsp flaked sea salt
- 2 tsp fresh lemon juice

This potato and spinach recipe makes a brilliant side dish to serve with any meat or chicken curry. We use proper mature spinach, as it has more flavour than the baby leaves. Serve this instead of rice sometimes – you don't always have to have rice with a curry. **Serves 4–6**

SAAG ALOO

- 650g medium potatoes, preferably Maris Pipers
- 1 tsp fine sea salt
- 250g spinach leaves
- 4 tbsp ghee or sunflower oil
- 1 tsp black mustard seeds
- 2 tsp cumin seeds
- 2 medium onions, halved and sliced
- 4 garlic cloves, finely sliced
- 10g chunk of fresh root ginger, peeled and finely chopped
- 2 long green chillies, finely chopped (deseed first if you like)
- 1 tbsp garam masala (see page 345 or use ready-made)
- freshly ground black pepper

Peel the potatoes and cut them into 2.5cm cubes. Put them in a large saucepan and cover them with cold water. Add ½ teaspoon of the salt and bring the water to the boil. Reduce the heat slightly and simmer the potatoes for 6–8 minutes until they are tender but still holding their shape. Drain the potatoes in a colander and set aside.

While the potatoes are cooking, wash the spinach leaves well and pat them dry on a clean tea towel. Remove any damaged parts and cut out the tough central stems. Shred the leaves roughly and set them aside.

Heat the ghee or oil in a large non-stick frying pan or in a sauté pan, and add the mustard seeds and cumin. As soon as the mustard seeds begin to pop, add the onions. Cook them with the spices for about 5 minutes over a medium heat until they are softened, stirring regularly. Increase the heat and cook for a further 2–3 minutes until the onions are nicely browned, stirring constantly.

Add the garlic, ginger and chilli, then cook for 2 minutes more, while stirring. Stir in the garam masala, remaining salt, and the potatoes and spinach leaves. Add the spinach in handfuls, allowing each lot to soften before adding the next. Cook for a further 4–5 minutes, stirring until the spinach has softened and the potatoes are hot and lightly coated in the spices. Season with freshly ground black pepper and serve.

There's barely a curry
in this book that doesn't
feature onions, so hone
your chopping skills
and look like a pro.

We think this famous Indian vegetable dish is one of the best ways to enjoy cauliflower. It's simple to make and goes beautifully with a meat curry, such as lamb pasanda or lamb dhansak. **Serves 4–6**

ALOO GOBI

2 tbsp sunflower oil or ghee
1 medium onion, finely chopped
20g chunk of fresh root ginger, peeled and finely grated
1½ tsp black mustard seeds
5 curry leaves
½ tsp ground turmeric
½ tsp fenugreek seeds
½ tsp hot chilli powder
2 green chillies, slit lengthways
250g fresh ripe tomatoes, roughly chopped
400g potatoes, preferably Maris Pipers, peeled
½ tsp caster sugar
1½ tsp flaked sea salt
400ml cold water
1 small cauliflower

Heat the oil or ghee, in a large non-stick saucepan. Add the chopped onion and cook it over a low heat for 5 minutes until softened, stirring regularly. Add the ginger, mustard seeds, curry leaves, turmeric, fenugreek seeds, chilli powder and chillies. Cook for a minute or until the mustard seeds begin to pop, then add the chopped tomatoes and cook for another 5 minutes, stirring constantly.

Cut the potatoes into chunks of about 2cm and add them to the pan. Stir in the caster sugar and salt and cook for a couple of minutes, continuing to stir. Pour the water into the pan and bring to the boil, then reduce the heat slightly and simmer for 5 minutes.

While the potatoes are cooking, prepare the cauliflower. Remove all the outer leaves and chuck them away. Cut the cauliflower into small florets – you'll need about 450g of prepared weight.

Stir the cauliflower into the potato and spice mixture and bring it back to a simmer. Cook for 15 minutes, stirring occasionally until the potatoes and cauliflower are tender and most of the liquid has evaporated, then serve.

Aubergines and tomatoes are perfect partners, as we know from many Mediterranean dishes. They work equally well in this curry that's tasty, tangy and terribly addictive! **Serves 6**

AUBERGINE AND TOMATO CURRY

3 smallish aubergines (each about 275g)
5 tbsp sunflower oil
2 medium onions, halved and finely sliced
4 garlic cloves, finely sliced
2 tsp garam masala (see page 345 or use ready-made)
¼–½ tsp hot chilli powder (depending on how hot you like your curry)
400g can of chopped tomatoes
300ml cold water
1 tsp caster sugar
½ tsp flaked sea salt, plus extra to season
1 bay leaf
1 tbsp freshly squeezed lemon juice
handful of fresh coriander, roughly chopped
freshly ground black pepper

Trim the aubergines and cut them into slices about 1.5cm thick. Put them in a large bowl and season with lots of black pepper. Pour over 3 tablespoons of the oil and toss well. Place a large non-stick frying pan or sauté pan over a high heat – you'll need a pan with a lid. Fry the aubergines in 3 batches for just 1–2 minutes on each side until nicely browned but not cooked through. Drain the slices on a tray lined with kitchen paper.

Return the pan to a medium heat after the last batch of aubergines is fried. Pour another tablespoon of oil into the pan. Add the onions to the pan and fry for 10 minutes, stirring regularly until softened and golden brown. Add the remaining oil and garlic and cook for 2 minutes more, stirring constantly. Sprinkle the garam masala and chilli powder into the pan and cook with the onions for 1 minute, stirring constantly.

Tip the tomatoes into the pan. Add the water, sugar, salt and bay leaf and bring to a simmer. Cook for 10 minutes, stirring regularly until the sauce is fairly thick. Return the aubergines to the pan and turn to coat them in the sauce. Cover with a lid and cook over a medium heat for 10 minutes, removing the lid and stirring every now and again until the aubergines are tender and hot and the sauce is thick and glossy.

Remove from the heat and stir in the lemon juice. Season with a little more salt if necessary and scatter with chopped coriander. For a delicious veggie lunch, serve the curry with rice, yoghurt and some home-made pickles if you like.

A lovely Afghan dish, this meltingly luscious aubergine stew is served on yoghurt spiked with mint and coriander. Perfect with home-made flatbread. **Serves 4 as a light meal or 6 as a side dish**

AFGHAN AUBERGINES *with yoghurt*

Heat 2 tablespoons of the oil in a large non-stick sauté pan or deep frying pan. Gently fry the sliced onions for 10 minutes until softened, stirring regularly. Increase the heat a little and cook for a further 4–5 minutes until golden brown, stirring constantly.

Take half the onions out of the pan and put them to one side. Put the pan back on the heat, add the sliced garlic, red chilli, cumin seeds, coriander, turmeric and chilli powder and cook for 2 minutes more, while stirring. Roughly chop 2 of the tomatoes and add them to the pan, then season with the salt and lots of freshly ground black pepper. Add a splash of the just-boiled water and bring to a simmer, stirring constantly until the tomatoes begin to soften, then add the tomato purée and the remaining water and bring back to a simmer. Cook for 10 minutes, stirring regularly until the sauce is thick, then remove the pan from the heat.

While the sauce is simmering, trim the ends off the aubergines and cut them into 1.5cm slices. Put these in a bowl and toss with the remaining 3 tablespoons of olive oil, then season with a couple of pinches of salt and lots of freshly ground black pepper. Heat a large non-stick frying pan and fry the aubergine slices in 3 batches, turning them once until nicely browned on both sides. They shouldn't be cooked right through to the middle, but it is important that they have a good colour. Drain the slices on a tray lined with kitchen paper. If the aubergine gets a little dry and isn't frying properly, toss it with some extra oil.

Arrange the aubergine slices over the tomato sauce, overlapping where necessary. Slice the reserved tomatoes and place them on top, then finish with the rest of the sautéed onions. Season with black pepper. Cover the pan with a lightly fitting lid and place it over a low heat. Cook for 30 minutes, giving the pan a little shake every now and then to stop the sauce sticking. Mix the yoghurt with the 2 tablespoons of cold water, the crushed garlic, mint and half the coriander. Put this mixture on to your plates and spread thickly with the back of a dessert spoon. Divide the hot aubergines and tomato sauce between the plates.

Scatter the rest of the coriander over the top and serve. This is especially delicious served warm but you can also serve it at room temperature, placing the aubergines on the yoghurt once cooled.

- 5–6 tbsp olive oil
- 4 medium onions, halved and fairly thinly sliced
- 6 garlic cloves, finely sliced
- 1 long red chilli, trimmed and thinly sliced
- 1 tsp cumin seeds
- 2 tsp ground coriander
- 1 tsp ground turmeric
- ½ tsp hot chilli powder
- 4 ripe medium tomatoes, skinned
- 1 tsp flaked sea salt, plus extra to season
- 250ml just-boiled water
- 2 tbsp tomato purée
- 2 small to medium aubergines (about 550g total weight)
- 300g Greek-style yoghurt
- 2 tbsp cold water
- 1 garlic clove, crushed
- 2 tbsp finely chopped fresh mint leaves
- small bunch of fresh coriander, leaves roughly chopped
- freshly ground black pepper

Okra, or bhindi, has an unusual texture which isn't to everyone's taste but we love it. The secret of success with this recipe is a hot pan. Cook the okra fast and hot to enjoy it at its best. **Serves 6**

SI'S BHINDI BHAJI

- 3 tbsp ghee or sunflower oil
- 1 medium onion, finely chopped
- 300g okra, well washed and drained
- ½ tsp flaked sea salt
- ½ tsp turmeric
- 1 tsp black mustard seeds
- 1 tsp ground coriander
- 1 tsp ground cumin
- 10 curry leaves
- 2 plump red chillies, finely chopped (do not deseed)
- 2 large ripe tomatoes, roughly chopped
- ¼ small lemon, for squeezing

Heat 2 tablespoons of the ghee or oil in a large non-stick frying pan and fry the onion for 4–5 minutes until softened, stirring regularly. Trim the stalk ends off the okra without going too far down.

Turn up the heat under the pan, add another tablespoon of ghee or oil and stir-fry the okra for 2 minutes.

Mix the salt, turmeric, mustard seeds, coriander, cumin and curry leaves in a small bowl, then sprinkle the mixture over the okra in the pan. Add the chopped chillies and continue stir-frying for a further 3 minutes or until the okra is just beginning to soften and looks lightly crusted with the spices.

Tip the chopped tomatoes into the pan and stir-fry for 1–2 minutes more until they have just softened and are becoming juicy. Remove the pan from the heat and season the okra with a squeeze of lemon. Serve immediately while it's good and hot.

This is one of the best ways of enjoying your green beans that we know. A touch of chilli, curry leaves and coconut makes a dish fit for a king – or a kingy! **Serves 4**

GREEN BEANS WITH COCONUT

400g green beans, trimmed and halved
3 tbsp ghee or sunflower oil
1 tsp yellow mustard seeds
½ tsp dried chilli flakes
2 long green chillies, trimmed and finely chopped
10 fresh curry leaves
50g medium-grated fresh coconut or 50g desiccated coconut
1 tsp fine sea salt, plus extra for seasoning
¼ tsp ground turmeric
1 tsp garam masala (see page 345 or use ready-made)
200ml coconut milk (optional)

Half fill a large saucepan with water and bring it to the boil. Add the green beans, stir once and bring the water back to the boil. Cook for 2 minutes, then drain the beans in a colander and refresh them under running water until cold. Leave them to drain while you get on with preparing the spices.

Heat the ghee or oil in a large non-stick frying pan or sauté pan and as soon as it's hot, add the mustard seeds, chilli flakes, green chillies and curry leaves. Fry them over a medium-high heat for 2 minutes, stirring constantly.

Add the coconut to the pan and cook it with the spices for a further 2–4 minutes until lightly toasted, stirring regularly. Sprinkle over the salt, turmeric and garam masala and fry for a few seconds before adding the beans.

Cook the beans with the coconut and spices for 2 minutes, while stirring, then pour over the coconut milk, if using, and bring to the boil. Cook for 2–3 minutes more, or until the sauce is well reduced and coating the beans lightly. Adjust the seasoning to taste and serve.

Dhal is an important part of an Indian meal and there are a multitude of variations, made from different kinds of beans, peas and lentils. We like to spice up our basic dhal with this mix of fried onions and infused oil – it's fantastic. **Serves 4**

GREAT BASIC DHAL

200g moong dhal
1.1 litres water
½ medium onion, finely sliced
15g chunk of fresh root ginger, peeled and finely grated
3 garlic cloves, crushed
2 plump green chillies, finely chopped
good pinch of asafoetida
½ tsp cayenne pepper
¼ tsp turmeric
1 tsp fine sea salt
freshly squeezed juice of ½ lemon

Topping
2 tbsp sunflower oil or ghee
½ medium onion, very finely sliced
½ tsp black mustard seeds
½ tsp cumin seeds
10–15 dried or fresh curry leaves
1 tsp garam masala (see page 345 or use ready-made)

Put the dhal in a sieve and rinse it well under cold water. Tip it into a large heavy-based saucepan or flameproof casserole dish and pour in the 1.1 litre of water to cover. Bring to the boil, then skim off any foam that rises to surface.

Stir in the onion, ginger, garlic, chillies, asafoetida, cayenne pepper and turmeric. Stir well and reduce the heat to low. Cover the pan loosely with a lid and leave the dhal to simmer gently for 60–90 minutes or until the dhal is very tender and thick. It should have the texture of a thick soup. Stir fairly regularly, more often towards the end of the cooking time as the dhal thickens, adding extra water if necessary. When the dhal is ready, remove it from the heat and season with the salt and lemon juice to taste. Pour the dhal into a warmed serving dish.

For the topping, place a small frying pan over a medium-high heat. Add the oil or ghee, then the onion. Fry the onion slices for 2–3 minutes until they are crisp and brown, stirring constantly. Watch that the onion doesn't burn.

Stir the mustard and cumin seeds and garam masala into the frying pan with the onion and cook for just a few seconds until the mustard seeds begin to pop. Crumble the curry leaves in your hands and stir them into the spices. Working quickly, pour the infused oil and spices over the dhal, then stir lightly just before serving.

A classic dish that's always welcome on our table – a kind of pease pudding with attitude! **Serves 4–6**

ALL-IN-ONE SPLIT PEA DHAL

- 3 tbsp sunflower oil or ghee
- 1 medium onion, halved and finely sliced
- 3 garlic cloves, crushed
- 15g chunk of fresh root ginger, peeled and finely grated
- 1 tsp garam masala (see page 345 or use ready-made)
- ¼ tsp cayenne pepper
- ½ tsp ground turmeric
- good pinch of asafoetida (optional)
- 300g yellow split peas
- 1.2 litres water
- 1 tsp fine sea salt, plus extra to season
- freshly ground black pepper

Place a large non-stick saucepan over a medium-high heat. Add the oil or ghee and then the onion. Fry for 2–3 minutes until the onion is pale golden brown, stirring constantly – don't let it burn. Stir in the garlic, ginger, garam masala, cayenne pepper, turmeric and asafoetida, if using. Cook together for 2 minutes over a low heat, stirring constantly.

Put the split peas in a sieve and rinse them well under cold water, then drain. Tip them into the pan with the spiced onion mixture, pour over the water and bring to the boil. Skim off any foam that rises to the surface with a spoon and discard. Add the teaspoon of salt, stir well and reduce the heat to low.

Cover loosely with a lid and leave to simmer gently for 60–75 minutes or until the peas are very tender and thick, stirring occasionally with a long-handled wooden spoon. The dhal should have the texture of a thick soup. Keep stirring fairly regularly, especially towards the end as the mixture thickens. As dhal thickens, it bubbles like lava, so watch out for splashes. Season to taste with salt and freshly ground black pepper, then serve hot.

TOP TIP

If your split peas still aren't tender enough after 1¼ hours, add a little extra water if necessary and continue cooking for a while longer. If you have a mixed batch of peas, you may find that some cook quicker and become softer than others. This will give your dhal a more chunky texture. Some older pulses never seem to soften, however long you cook them, so don't waste your time at the hob, get rid of them and start again with a new batch.

This is a rich, creamy and comforting dish, with the tadka adding a bit of pizzazz. Adding a mixture of spice-enhanced oil or ghee like this, the tadka, is also known as 'tempering' the dhal and is a popular technique in Indian cooking. **Serves 6**

MASOOR (SPLIT RED LENTIL) DHAL

300g split red lentils
1 tsp ground turmeric
1 tsp garam masala (see page 345 or use ready-made)
1 litre cold water
2 tbsp sunflower oil or ghee
1 medium onion, finely sliced
15g chunk of fresh root ginger, peeled and finely grated
2 garlic cloves, finely sliced
2 ripe medium tomatoes, finely chopped
1 plump green chilli, split lengthways
½ tsp fine sea salt, plus extra for seasoning
freshly ground black pepper

Tadka

2 tbsp sunflower oil or ghee
½ tsp cumin seeds
½ tsp black mustard seeds
½ tsp dried chilli flakes
pinch of asafoetida

Put the lentils in a sieve and rinse them under cold water. Drain well, then tip them into a large saucepan and add the turmeric, garam masala and water. Bring to the boil, then reduce the heat and leave to simmer gently for 20 minutes, stirring occasionally. Skim off and discard any foam that rises to the surface of the pan when the water first begins to boil.

While the lentils are cooking, heat 2 tablespoons of sunflower oil or ghee in a large non-stick frying pan and fry the onion gently for 5 minutes until softened, stirring regularly. Turn up the heat and cook for 2 minutes more or until pale golden brown, stirring constantly. Reduce the heat, add the ginger and garlic, then cook for 2 minutes, while stirring. Add the chopped tomatoes, chilli and salt and cook over a medium heat for 5 minutes, stirring regularly until the tomatoes are very soft.

Stir the onion and tomato mixture into the lentils once their 20 minutes of cooking time is up. Cook together for a further 10–15 minutes or until the lentils are completely soft. The dhal will thicken as it cooks, so you may need to add a little extra water. Don't forget to stir regularly as the lentils cook. Remove from the heat and season with more salt and a little pepper to taste; you may find it doesn't need any.

To make the tadka, heat the oil or ghee in a small non-stick pan and fry the cumin and mustard seeds and chilli flakes for just 15 seconds, stirring constantly over a medium heat – don't let them burn. Remove from the heat, sprinkle over the asafoetida and stir well. Spoon the dhal into a warmed serving dish, pour over the tadka and serve.

Mooli is a kind of radish. It's much larger than the little red jobs we know and love and it can grow to 40cm long or more. Try it grated in this light and fragrant salad, adding the flavoured oil (tadka) if you fancy a little extra kick. **Serves 4–6**

MARVELLOUS MOOLI SALAD

400g mooli radish
15g chunk of fresh root ginger, peeled and finely chopped
1 long green chilli, finely chopped
2 tbsp finely chopped coriander leaves
1 tbsp fresh lime juice
½ tsp flaked sea salt

Tadka (optional)

1 tbsp sunflower oil
½ tsp cumin seeds
½ tsp yellow mustard seeds
5 fresh curry leaves
pinch of asafoetida

Peel the mooli and cut it into pieces of about 10cm long. Place a box grater (the kind you grate cheese on) on a board and grate the mooli into long strips on the coarsest side. If you hold the mooli vertically, you will get longer strips, which look great on the plate. Watch your fingers!

Place the mooli in a large bowl and add the ginger, chilli, coriander and lime juice. Sprinkle with the salt and toss together.

To make the tadka, heat the oil in a small frying pan and add the cumin seeds, mustard seeds, curry leaves and asafoetida. Cook over a high heat until the mustard seeds begin to pop. Remove from the heat, shake it over the salad and toss well.

Serve this as a starter or as refreshing accompaniment to a hot curry.

This is a zingy fresh-tasting salad that will liven up any meal. You can prepare the oranges, pomegranate, onions and chilli ahead of time if you like and toss them together lightly, but leave the coriander until last so the leaves don't get a chance to wilt. **Serves 4–6**

RED ONION, ORANGE AND POMEGRANATE SALAD

2 large oranges
1 pomegranate
1 medium red onion
1 long red chilli
large bunch of fresh coriander
1 tsp extra virgin olive oil
pinch of flaked sea salt
freshly ground black pepper

Slice the ends off the orange and place it on a chopping board, cut side down. Using a small sharp knife, cut off the peel and pith, working your way around the orange. Next, cut between the membranes to release the segments. Put the segments in a salad bowl but do not add any juice that might have oozed on to your board.

Cut the pomegranate in half and tap it hard on a chopping board to shake out the seeds. Use a teaspoon to dislodge any stubborn seeds, avoiding the white pith. Scrape the seeds into the bowl with the orange segments.

Peel the onion and cut it in half from root to tip. Finely slice both halves and add the slices to the bowl with the oranges. Very finely slice the chilli. If you want your salad a little less spicy, cut the chilli in half lengthways and scrape out the seeds and membrane before slicing. The slices will be semi-circles rather than rings but that's fine.

Trim the coriander and tear or chop the leaves very roughly, then add them to the bowl with the oranges. Pour the oil over the top and season the salad with a good pinch of sea salt and lots of ground black pepper. Toss lightly together and serve at once before the leaves have a chance to wilt.

A spot of tangy ginger, chilli and soy sauce does wonders for pak choi, sometimes known as Chinese cabbage. The stems and leaves have different cooking times so are best cooked separately as in this simple, but tasty recipe. **Serves 4**

ASIAN GREENS WITH GINGER

3 heads of pak choi, rinsed
15g chunk of fresh root ginger
1 plump red chilli
1 tbsp sunflower oil
1 tsp sesame seeds
1 tsp cornflour
2 tbsp cold water
2 tbsp dark soy sauce
2 tbsp cream sherry or mirin
2 tsp caster sugar

Trim about 1cm off the root of each pak choi and throw them out, then cut the pale greeny-white parts into 3cm-wide slices. The leaves can stay whole as they will be added to the stir-fry later – they cook very quickly. Peel the ginger, place it on a board and cut it into wafer-thin slices. Trim and finely chop the chilli, deseeding first if you like.

Heat the oil in a large non-stick frying pan or wok. Add the sesame seeds and sizzle for 30-60 seconds until they're beginning to turn golden, stirring constantly. Add the slices of pak choi and the ginger and chilli, then fry over a medium-high heat for 3 minutes or until just tender, stirring regularly.

While the pak choi is cooking, put the cornflour in a bowl and stir in 1 tablespoon of the water. Mix to make a thin paste, then add the remaining water, soy sauce, sherry or mirin and caster sugar.

Add the pak choi leaves to the pan and the cornflour and soy mixture. Stir-fry together for 30–60 seconds more, until the leaves begin to wilt and the sauce looks glossy. Transfer the pak choi to a warmed serving dish with a slotted spoon and pour the sauce over the top. Serve hot.

Make life really easy for yourself and buy bags of ready-shredded kale for this recipe. The tasty mushrooms match its flavour extremely well and the toasted sesame seeds make the perfect finishing touch. Serve this stir-fry with any of the Thai-style curries. **Serves 4–5**

STIR-FRIED MUSHROOMS AND GREENS

- 2 tbsp sesame seeds
- 1 tbsp toasted sesame oil
- 1 tbsp sunflower oil
- 150g shiitake mushrooms, wiped and sliced
- 150g mangetout, trimmed
- 150g young curly kale, thickly shredded
- 1–2 tsp dried chilli flakes, according to taste
- 2 tsp dark soy sauce
- freshly ground black pepper

Place a large non-stick frying pan or wok over a high heat. Add the sesame seeds and stir-fry for 1–1½ minutes, stirring them every now and then until they're golden brown. Watch them carefully so they don't get a chance to burn. Tip the toasted seeds on to a plate and leave to cool.

Put the pan back on the heat, add the oils and the mushrooms and stir-fry for 2 minutes until the mushrooms have softened and are just beginning to brown. Add the mangetout and stir-fry for 1 minute more.

Add the kale to the pan, sprinkle the chilli flakes over the top and stir-fry for a further minute until the kale softens. Sprinkle the toasted sesame seeds over the top, then pour in the soy sauce, season with ground black pepper and cook for 20–30 seconds more, stirring constantly. Serve.

Breads & Rice

These are the classic Indian breads, sometimes also called rotis, and very easy to prepare. They're delicious with all sorts of curries and dips. For best results, buy some atta flour (see page 360) which is available from Asian grocers and online. **Makes 8**

CHAPATIS

225g wholewheat atta flour, plus extra flour for rolling
2½ tbsp sunflower oil
1 tsp fine sea salt
150ml warm water (75ml just-boiled and 75ml cold)

Put the flour in a large bowl and stir in the salt. Rub in the sunflower oil until the dough starts to come together and feels like damp sand in your hands. Stir in the water and knead it into the dry ingredients with your hands until the dough feels smooth and elastic.

Turn the dough on to a lightly floured board and knead it for another minute. Divide the dough into 8 portions and then roll them into smooth balls.

Sprinkle the work surface with a little more flour and roll out 1 of the balls very thinly. It needs to be about 20cm in diameter and no thicker than a 2 pence coin. Turn the dough regularly so it becomes a nice even shape. If it begins to stick, simply sprinkle it with a little more flour.

Place a large non-stick frying pan or tava pan over a medium-high heat and once it is hot, add the chapati. Cook it for 2½ minutes, turning half way through the cooking time and pressing with a metal spatula so that it cooks evenly. The chapati should be lightly browned in places and look fairly dry without being crisp. If it looks dark or damp, continue cooking it for a few seconds more.

Put the chapati on a plate, then cover it with a piece of foil and a clean tea towel to help keep it warm. Continue rolling and cooking the rest of the chapatis in the same way, sliding the cooked ones under the foil and adding them to the pile. Serve the chapatis warm with yoghurt, pickles or curry.

TOP TIP

If you can't get any atta flour, make the chapatis with a mixture of 125g plain flour and 100g fine wholemeal flour. Measure out the water and then take out 2 tablespoons (30ml) before mixing, as this flour will absorb the liquid differently.

Who would have thought that making naan bread could be so easy, but it is. The secret is to have a really hot oven and cook the breads on a furiously hot surface. We've discovered that a good baking tray can make great naans – much better than you might think from a domestic kitchen. So, have a go and you'll never want to buy the ready-made ones again. **Makes 6**

NAAN BREAD

- 600g plain flour, plus extra for rolling
- 2 tsp baking powder
- ½ tsp bicarbonate of soda
- 2 tbsp caster sugar
- 2 heaped tsp fine sea salt
- 1 tsp nigella seeds (optional)
- 1 medium egg, beaten
- 300ml semi-skimmed milk
- 2 tbsp sunflower oil
- 25g melted ghee or butter, for brushing

Put the flour, baking powder, bicarbonate of soda, sugar, salt and nigella needs, if using, in a food processor and blitz them quickly until lightly mixed. Break the egg into a bowl and whisk in the milk and oil.

With the motor running, slowly add the milk mixture to the flour and blend for about 20 seconds or until the dough comes together into a rough ball. It will be very soft and fairly sticky. You can also mix the dough by hand, adding the liquid gradually to the dry ingredients. Remove the blade and turn the dough out on to a well-floured surface. Place a large baking tray in the oven and preheat to its hottest setting. This could be as high as 280°C/Fan 260°/Gas 9, but don't worry if it's a bit less.

Break the dough into 6 portions and roll them into balls. Taking 1 ball at a time, roll it out on the floured surface into a tear-drop shape with a slightly pointed end. The dough will need to be no more than 4mm thick or it will be too scone-like when baked.

Pull the oven shelf out a little and place the naan bread quickly, but very carefully, on the baking tray and push the shelf back into the oven. Cook the naan for about 2½ minutes or until it is puffed up and lightly browned in places. Melt the butter or ghee in a small saucepan.

Take the naan out of the oven with tongs and place it on a warmed serving dish or board, then brush it lightly with a little melted butter or ghee. Cover with foil and a clean tea towel to keep warm and continue cooking the other naan breads in the same way. Serve them warm.

TOP TIP

For really authentic-looking naan breads, with the blackened patches that you get when they're cooked in a tandoor, try this tip. Place a large non-stick frying pan over a high heat. As soon as each naan is out of the oven and before brushing it with butter, place it in the pan for 8–10 seconds, until toasted in places, then turn and toast on the other side. Watch your timings carefully as the naan will brown very quickly.

Once you've got the hang of the basic naan recipe, try some variations such as these delicious stuffed versions. Though we say it ourselves, they are unbelievably good. **Makes 6**

KEEMA NAAN

- 400g lean minced lamb
- ½ medium onion, very finely chopped
- 1 plump green chilli, very finely chopped (deseed first if you like)
- 15g chunk of fresh root ginger, peeled and very finely chopped
- 4 garlic cloves, very finely chopped
- 1 tsp flaked sea salt
- 2 tsp garam masala (see page 345 or use ready-made)
- ¼ tsp cayenne pepper
- 3 tbsp tomato purée
- freshly ground black pepper

Put the lamb, onion, chilli, ginger and garlic in a large non-stick frying pan. Cook over a medium-high heat for 4–5 minutes until the lamb is coloured all over and any liquid that comes out of the meat has evaporated. You'll need to stir constantly to break up the meat.

Add the salt, garam masala and cayenne pepper. Season with black pepper and cook for 3 minutes more, stirring constantly. Stir in the tomato purée and cook for 2–3 minutes until the mince comes together and looks thick and paste-like. Remove from the heat and leave to cool, then divide into 6 portions.

Make the naan bread dough as on page 247 and divide it into 6 balls. Roll out one of the balls on a lightly floured surface into a circle of about 14cm in diameter. Take a sixth of the lamb mixture and spoon it into the centre of the dough. Bring up all the sides around the filling and pinch them together to make a purse containing the spiced mince. Turn over with the joins underneath and gently roll it out into a round about 5mm thick.

Bake the keema naan on the preheated baking tray (see basic recipe on page 247) for 3–3½ minutes until puffed up and browned in places. Keep warm while you make the remaining naans in the same way.

PESHWARI NAAN

- 50g desiccated coconut
- 100g coconut powder
- 100g ground almonds
- 50g flaked almonds
- 50g sultanas
- 3 tbsp golden caster sugar
- 6–7 tbsp cold water

In a medium bowl, mix the coconut, coconut powder, ground and flaked almonds, sultanas and sugar. Pour over the cold water and bring everything together with your fingers to form a moist clumpy mixture.

Make the naan bread dough as before (see page 247) and divide it into 6 balls. Roll a ball out on a lightly floured surface into an oval about 9mm thick. Place a sixth of the coconut mixture in the centre, then fold the dough in half lengthways to enclose the filling. Pinch the sides together to seal.

Roll the naan out into a large oval shape about 7mm thick. Bake it on the preheated baking tray for 3½–4 minutes until risen and browned in places, then remove from the oven and brush with butter as before.

We first ate these in Kerala and they are different from anything we'd ever had before. They're made with white flour and the buttery layers break up deliciously when you tear them – great for mopping up a juicy curry sauce. The process might look a bit fiddly at first, but you soon get the knack. **Makes 4**

KERALAN PARATHAS

- 500g plain white flour, plus extra for rolling
- 2 eggs, beaten
- 1 tsp sugar
- 1 tsp salt
- 2 tbsp condensed milk
- 150ml full-fat milk
- 110g butter, melted
- 2 tbsp sunflower oil

Put the flour, eggs, sugar, salt and condensed milk in a food processor fitted with a dough blade and blitz until well combined.

With the processor on, gradually add the full-fat milk in a thin stream, until the mixture comes together as a soft dough. Wrap the dough in cling film and leave it to chill in the fridge for at least an hour.

Turn the dough out on to a lightly floured work surface. Take a small piece of dough and roll it out into a ball about the size of a golf ball.

Using a rolling pin, roll the ball out into a disc about the thickness of a £1 coin, then brush it with some of the melted butter.

Start folding the dough into pleats about 2.5cm wide, like a concertina, keeping the pleats tight. When you've pleated the whole disc, shape it into a coil and tuck the outer end into the centre so it holds together.

Turn it over and flatten it with your hand, then sprinkle the top with a little flour and roll it out again to about 15cm in diameter. It will be thicker this time because of the buttery layers. Set the paratha aside and repeat the process until you've used all the dough.

Heat a little of the sunflower oil in a frying pan over a medium heat. Add a paratha and fry for 1–2 minutes on each side or until crisp and golden-brown on the outside and soft and flaky on the inside. Keep the paratha warm while you cook the rest, then serve with our Keralan king prawn curry (see page 110). If you like, you can make a whole batch, wrap them in foil, then warm them up in the oven.

These are so good and not hard to make. Atta flour can be bought from Asian grocers and online, but if you can't get any, use 225g strong white flour mixed with 225g fine wholemeal flour, which must be ground very finely. Use 250ml warm water instead of 300ml to mix the dough. **Makes 8**

VEGETABLE-STUFFED PARATHAS

450g wholewheat atta flour, plus extra for rolling
2 tsp fine sea salt
5 tbsp sunflower oil, plus 1 tsp
300ml warm water (150ml just-boiled and 150ml cold)
50g ghee or butter, melted

Vegetable stuffing
100g wedge of savoy or green cabbage, tough outer leaves removed
1 medium carrot
½ medium onion
2 tbsp desiccated coconut
2 tbsp cold water
1 tbsp sunflower oil
½ tsp black mustard seeds
½ tsp cumin seeds
¼ tsp dried chilli flakes
½ tsp flaked sea salt
¼ tsp ground turmeric

To make the vegetable stuffing, place the cabbage on a board and cut out the central white stem part. Finely shred the cabbage and put it in a large mixing bowl. Peel the carrot. Taking care of your fingertips, grate the carrot in a vertical position on a box grater so you end up with long strips. Cut the onion in half and slice finely, then add the carrot and onion to the bowl with the cabbage and toss. Put the coconut in a small bowl and pour over the water, then leave to soak.

Heat the oil in a large non-stick frying pan or wok. Add the mustard and cumin seeds. As soon as the mustard seeds begin to crackle and pop, stir in the prepared vegetables, chilli flakes, salt and turmeric and stir-fry over a high heat for 1-2 minutes. Add the coconut and its water and stir-fry for 30 seconds until the vegetables are only just tender. Add a little extra salt if necessary and remove from the heat.

To make the parathas, put the flour in a large bowl and stir in the salt. Rub in the oil until the dough starts to come together and feels like damp sand in your hand. Next, stir in the water and knead into the dry ingredients until the dough feels smooth and elastic. Pour the teaspoon of oil into the bowl and continue to knead the dough for a minute more to make it even smoother. Divide the dough into 8 portions and roll them into balls. Flatten the balls until they are about 5mm thick and place them on a lightly floured surface. Spoon about an eighth of the filling into the centre of a disc. Bring up all the sides around the filling and pinch together to make a purse containing the vegetable mixture.

Turn over, with the joins underneath and roll for a few seconds, then flip over and roll again. Continue flipping and rolling until the paratha is about 3mm thick and about 18cm in diameter. Flour the board as you roll if necessary and don't worry if the vegetables start to poke through a little. Make the rest of the parathas in the same way. Melt the ghee or butter in a small pan and have a pastry brush ready.

Heat a medium non-stick frying pan over a high heat. Take a paratha and brush one side with melted butter. Place it in the hot pan, butter side down. Cook for 1½ minutes, then brush the top side with melted butter and turn over. Cook for a further 1½ minutes on the other side until nicely browned and cooked through. Put the cooked paratha on a tray and cover with foil and a dry tea towel. Cook the rest in the same way and serve as soon as possible.

We just love these delicious puffs of crisp dough and they work a treat with some of the curries in this book, such as the prawn dish on page 49, or to add a clever twist to any meal. For best results, you'll need some atta flour (see page 360) which you can find in Asian grocers and some supermarkets. If you can't find any, make the puri dough with a mixture of 100g strong white flour and 100g fine wholemeal flour instead, but reduce the amount of water by about 2 tablespoons. **Makes 12**

PUFFY PURIS

- 200g wholewheat atta flour, plus extra for rolling
- ½ tsp fine sea salt
- 4 tsp sunflower oil, plus ¼ tsp
- 150ml water (75ml just-boiled and 75ml cold)
- about 1 litre sunflower oil, for frying

Put the flour and salt in a large bowl and make a well in the centre. Pour the 4 teaspoons of oil into the flour and rub together with your fingertips until the flour comes together in a loose clump. It should look like slightly damp sand. Add the water to the flour, a couple of tablespoons at a time, mixing well between each addition. Bring the mixture together to form a dough that's wet and sticky but still quite firm. Knead the dough in the bowl until it's smooth and no longer sticky, then add the remaining ¼ teaspoon of oil and knead again for 30 seconds. Take a pea-sized piece of the dough and set it aside.

Divide the dough into 12 portions and roll them into small balls. Take a ball and flatten it into a disc. Sprinkle a little flour on to the work surface and, using a rolling pin, roll the disc into a 12cm circle about the thickness of a 2 pence coin. It is important that it has an even thickness, so take it slowly, lifting and turning the pastry frequently. Put the disc on a very lightly floured tray and repeat to make 11 more.

Pour about a litre of oil in a large saucepan or deep sauté pan – it should be about 4cm deep. Heat the oil to 190°C, using a cooking thermometer to check the temperature. DO NOT OVERHEAT. DO NOT LEAVE HOT OIL UNATTENDED. You can also take half the reserved tiny ball of dough and drop it into the oil. If it rises to the surface immediately the oil is hot enough to fry the puris. It is important that the oil is the right temperature or the puris won't puff up as they fry.

Brush any excess flour off a puri and using a heatproof slotted spoon, lower it into the hot oil. Push it under, paddling it gently with the bowl of the spoon so it remains submerged. As the puri begins to puff up, work the spoon around it to encourage the hot oil to create enough steam inside the disc to puff. Cook for 8–10 seconds once completely puffed, then carefully turn it over and fry on the other side for a further 8–10 seconds.

Lift the puri out of the hot oil and drain well on kitchen paper. Continue frying the rest puris in the same way, but make sure the oil remains at up to 190°C, so the puris puff up properly and don't become greasy. Be ready to increase or reduce the heat accordingly. Serve warm with any of the curries or with a range of pickles and chutneys.

All good bread starts
with careful measuring
of the ingredients.

If you've ever had trouble cooking plain basmati rice in the past, follow our simple recipe and you will make light, fluffy rice every time. Lots of recipes for basmati rice rely on the absorption method, using little water and cooking the rice at a very low temperature in a covered pan. We've tried lots of different methods for the perfect rice and we think that this absorption method was most likely developed in countries without a ready supply of clean water and where fuel for cooking is scarce or expensive. It's great when you want to cook the rice with spices or vegetables but not necessary for plainly cooked rice.

Our recipe cooks the rice in plenty of boiling water over a high heat. You can keep a good eye on it – some rice does vary in cooking time – and only drain it when it is ready. This method is also the best when you are cooking for a crowd, but make sure you cook the rice in a huge pan, so you can use plenty of water. If cooking rice for a large number, reduce the initial cooking time by a couple of minutes to compensate for the time taken for the water to return to boiling once the rice is added. **Serves 5–6**

THE PERFECT BASMATI RICE

cold water
¼ tsp fine sea salt
300g white basmati rice

Half fill a large saucepan with water, stir in the salt and bring the water to the boil. Put the rice in a fine sieve and rinse it under plenty of cold water. (We don't usually soak the rice, but some manufacturers recommend soaking the rice in a bowl of cold water for 30 minutes before using.) Tip the rinsed and drained rice into the boiling water and wait for the water to return to the boil.

Stir once, then boil the rice for 10 minutes. Stir a couple of times during the boiling process to ensure that the rice grains remain separated. You'll know the rice is boiling as the water will be bubbling furiously, with large bubbles of steam rising rapidly to the surface.

Thirty seconds before the 10 minutes is up, test the rice. Take a few grains out with a fork and when they are cool enough, taste – tip the grains on to a cold plate so they cool quickly. They should be slightly chalky, which indicates that the rice isn't quite cooked through but this is just how you want it. If the rice is overcooked, the grains will start to break up. If the grains feel very hard when you bite them, increase the cooking time a little.

Carefully, but quickly, drain the rice in the sieve over the sink and then tip it straight back into the hot saucepan off the heat. Cover the top of the pan with a clean tea towel and leave it to stand for 5 minutes. The tea towel will absorb excess moisture and help stop the rice sticking. Remove the tea towel and fluff up the rice with a fork. Serve hot.

TOP TIP

This recipe serves 5–6, but you can prepare more or less rice in exactly the same way.

Basmati rice is best for the perfect pilau. Follow our recipe and you can't go wrong, but don't be tempted to miss out the final stage of leaving the rice to stand for five minutes before serving. It makes all the difference. **Serves 5–6**

PILAU RICE

- ½ tsp coriander seeds
- 6 cardamom pods
- 1 tsp cumin seeds
- 8 cloves
- 1 cinnamon stick, broken in half
- 2 bay leaves
- 75g butter
- 1 small onion, finely chopped
- 1 garlic clove, finely chopped
- ½ tsp ground turmeric
- ½ tsp black mustard seeds
- 300g white basmati rice, rinsed and drained
- 500ml chicken or vegetable stock (fresh or made with 1 stock cube)
- pinch of flaked sea salt
- freshly ground black pepper

Put the coriander seeds in a pestle and mortar and pound them until you have a coarse powder. Add the cardamom pods and pound until the husks split and the seeds are lightly crushed. Add the cumin seeds, cloves, cinnamon stick and bay leaves, then pound everything very lightly for a few seconds to mix together.

Melt 40g of the butter in a non-stick sauté pan or wide-based saucepan over a medium heat. Add the onion and garlic and fry for about 5 minutes until softened, stirring regularly. Sprinkle the turmeric and mustards seeds, plus all the spices and bay leaves from the pestle and mortar, into the pan and fry gently for 2 minutes, while stirring.

Stir the rice into the onion mixture until it is coated in the buttery spices, then pour the stock into the pan. Add a pinch of salt and a good grind of black pepper, then stir well and bring to the boil. Give a final stir and then cover the pan with a tight fitting lid – block any air vents with a piece of softened bread. Reduce the heat to its very lowest setting and cook the rice for 15 minutes.

While the rice is cooking, cut the rest of the butter into small pieces. Remove the lid of the pan and dot the butter over the hot rice. Allow the butter to melt for a few seconds, then quickly fluff up the rice with a fork, taking care not to break up the grains.

Replace the lid and allow the rice to stand for 5 minutes before serving. Watch you don't eat the cardamom, cinnamon or whole cloves!

This goes a treat with any meat or chicken curry and is also excellent with a vegetable curry to complete a veggie meal. **Serves 4–6**

MUSHROOM RICE

- 4 black peppercorns
- 6 cardamom pods
- 1 tsp cumin seeds
- 6 fresh curry leaves
- 4 cloves
- ½ cinnamon stick
- ½ tsp black mustard seeds
- 75g butter
- 1 small onion, finely sliced
- 250g chestnut or closed-cup mushrooms, wiped and sliced
- 1 garlic clove, finely sliced
- 10g chunk of fresh root ginger, peeled and finely chopped
- 250g white basmati rice, rinsed and drained
- 450ml cold water
- 1 tsp flaked sea salt

Put the black peppercorns in a pestle and mortar and pound them to make a coarse powder. Add the cardamom pods and pound again until the husks of the pods split and the seeds are lightly crushed. Add the cumin seeds, curry leaves, cloves and cinnamon stick and pound very lightly for a few seconds to mix all the spices.

Melt half the butter in a non-stick sauté pan or wide-based saucepan over a medium heat. Add the onion, mushrooms, garlic and ginger, then fry for about 5 minutes until softened, stirring regularly. Sprinkle all the pounded spices into the pan, add the mustard seeds and fry gently for 2 minutes, stirring.

Stir the rice into the spiced onions and pour over the water. Add the salt and bring to the boil, then give a final stir and cover the pan very tightly with a lid. Block any air vents with a piece of softened bread. Reduce the heat to its very lowest setting and cook for 15 minutes.

While the rice is cooking, cut the remaining butter into small pieces. Remove the lid of the pan and dot the butter over the hot rice. Allow the butter to melt for a few seconds, then quickly fluff up the rice with a fork, taking care not to break up the grains. Serve at once. Watch out for the cardamom, cinnamon and whole cloves when you're eating!

This is a fantastic rice recipe with added crunch from the dhals and nuts. It's a really good dish that makes any meal that extra bit special, but we think it goes particularly well with a fish curry or with lamb saag. Great with chicken madras too. **Serves 4–5**

LEMON RICE
with cashews and peanuts

- 2 tbsp sunflower oil
- 1 tsp black mustard seeds
- 1 tsp ground turmeric
- 1 tsp urad dhal (optional)
- 1 tsp chana dhal (optional)
- ¼ tsp asafoetida
- ½ small onion, very finely chopped
- 1 long green chilli, finely chopped (deseed first if you like)
- 10g chunk of fresh root ginger, peeled and finely chopped
- 10 fresh curry leaves
- 50g roasted unsalted peanuts
- 50g roasted unsalted cashew nuts
- 550g cooked and cooled white basmati rice
- freshly squeezed juice of 1 large lemon
- finely grated zest of ½ large unwaxed or well-scrubbed lemon
- flaked sea salt
- freshly ground black pepper

Heat the oil in a large non-stick sauté pan or wok. Add the mustard seeds, turmeric, urad and chana dhals, if using, and the asafoetida. Fry the spices over a medium heat for 1 minute, stirring constantly until the mustard seeds begin to pop.

Add the onion, green chilli, ginger, curry leaves and all the nuts. Stir-fry for a further 2–3 minutes until the nuts are lightly toasted and the onion has softened.

Tip the rice into the pan and stir-fry for 3–4 minutes until piping hot. Pour over the lemon juice and stir in the lemon zest. Toss everything together well and season with more salt and some freshly ground black pepper if necessary. Serve hot.

TOP TIP

To cook rice for this recipe, follow the instructions on page 258, using 200g of rinsed and drained rice. Rinse the rice in the sieve under lots of cold water as soon as it is cooked and leave out the resting period. The rice will continue to cook when it is reheated with the other ingredients.

This easy-to-make rice dish is the classic accompaniment to Jamaican lamb or goat curry. **Serves 6**

SIMPLE RICE AND PEAS

- 6 spring onions
- 400g can of red kidney beans
- 200ml coconut milk
- 450ml cold water
- 300g easy-cook long-grain rice
- 2 garlic cloves, crushed
- 3 bushy sprigs of fresh thyme
- ½ scotch bonnet chilli
- 1 tsp flaked sea salt

Trim the spring onions and slice them thinly, keeping the green and white parts separate. Tip the kidney beans into a sieve and rinse them well under cold water. Pour the coconut milk and water into a large saucepan and bring it to the boil.

Add the rice, kidney beans, white parts of the spring onions, garlic, thyme, chilli and salt to the pan, then stir well and bring it back to the boil. Cover the pan with a lid and cook for 10–12 minutes over a low heat until the rice is tender and all the liquid has been absorbed. Check the rice is cooked and give it a good stir just before the cooking time is up – add a little extra water if necessary.

Remove the pan from the heat, remove the chilli and stir in the remaining sliced spring onions. Serve hot.

A lightly spiced rice, this has a lovely coconuty taste without being sweet and is perfect with almost any curry. Look out for coconut milk powder – it's different from basic coconut powder, which is finely ground desiccated coconut, and it makes a good coconut milk standby when made up with water. **Serves 5–6**

COCONUT RICE

¼ tsp fine sea salt, plus extra to season
50g coconut milk powder
250g white basmati rice
100g desiccated coconut
3 tbsp sunflower or groundnut oil
2 or 3 shallots (100g) or ½ small onion, finely chopped
½ tsp black mustard seeds
½ tsp yellow mustard seeds
½ tsp cumin seeds
½ tsp nigella seeds
5 dried curry leaves, crumbled
1 garlic clove, finely chopped
1 long green chilli, deseeded and finely chopped

Half fill a large saucepan with water, stir in the salt and coconut milk powder and bring to the boil. Put the rice in a fine sieve and rinse it under plenty of cold water. Tip the rice into the boiling water and wait for it to return to the boil. Stir once, then boil the rice for 10 minutes. Stir the rice a couple of times during the boiling process to ensure that the grains remain separate.

Carefully, but quickly, drain the rice in the sieve over the sink, then tip it out of the sieve and straight back into the hot saucepan off the hob. Cover the top of the pan with a clean tea towel and leave it to stand for 5 minutes. Remove the tea towel and fluff up the rice with a fork.

Place a large non-stick frying pan over a high heat, add the desiccated coconut and cook for 1–2 minutes, stirring occasionally until lightly toasted. Tip it on to a plate.

Put the frying pan back on a medium heat and add the oil and shallots. Fry the shallots for 2–3 minutes until they are pale golden brown, stirring constantly. Add all the mustard seeds, cumin seeds, nigella and crumbled curry leaves, then cook for 30 seconds, stirring. Add the garlic and chilli and cook for 30 seconds more, stirring all the time.

Reduce the heat to low, scatter the cooked rice into the pan and add the toasted desiccated coconut. Cook together with the spiced shallots for 1–2 minutes, tossing and stirring the rice until it's thoroughly combined with all the other ingredients, then serve.

Pickles

& Chutneys

Glossy, golden and delicious, this favourite chutney is easy to put together and has a good kick of chilli. It's best made with mangoes that are good and firm. Great with a curry, but let's not forget its uses with a Cheddar cheese sandwich! **Makes 2 x 500ml jars**

THE VERY BEST MANGO CHUTNEY

6 garlic cloves
30g chunk of fresh root ginger, peeled and roughly chopped
2 large very firm mangoes, about 1.2kg total weight
600g demerara sugar
500ml white wine vinegar
2 tsp fine sea salt
1 long red chilli, finely chopped (deseeded if you like)

Spices

2 cinnamon sticks
2 star anise
6 cardamom pods
4 dried extra-hot chillies (bird's-eye)
2 tsp cumin seeds
2 tsp coriander seeds
1 heaped tsp nigella seeds
10 cloves
10 black peppercorns

Place all the spices in a small frying pan. Warm them over a medium heat, stirring occasionally, for a couple of minutes or until lightly toasted. You'll know they are ready when you can smell the wonderful aroma, but don't let them burn. Remove the pan from the heat.

Take out the cinnamon sticks and star anise and put them aside, then tip the rest of the spices into a pestle and mortar. Pound until the spices are lightly bruised and the cardamom pods and coriander seeds are crushed. Tip the spices into a large saucepan and return the cinnamon and star anise to the mix. Peel the garlic cloves and pound them in a pestle and mortar with the ginger to make a paste. Add this to the spices but do not stir.

Peel the mangoes, then place them on a board and cut carefully either side of the large flat central stone. Cut the mango flesh into long strips, which should measure about 1cm x 6cm and look a little like shoestring French fries. Cut off the flesh around the stone and slice it in the same way, then add all the mango to the pan with the spices. Add the sugar, vinegar, salt and chopped red chilli, then stir well until all the ingredients are nicely mixed. Cover the pan with a lid and leave to stand overnight in a cool place – no need to put this in the fridge.

The next day, remove the lid from the pan and you'll find that the sugar will have dissolved into the vinegar. Put the pan on the hob and bring the liquid to the boil. Reduce the heat and leave the chutney to simmer gently for 60–70 minutes or until the mixture looks thick and very glossy. Stir occasionally, especially towards the end of the cooking time.

Remove the pan from the heat and leave the chutney to stand for 10 minutes before potting it into 2 warmed and sterilised jars. Cover tightly and label when cold. Store the mango chutney in a cool, dark place for at least 2 weeks before eating. This will give the vinegar a chance to mellow. Use the chutney within 6 months and keep it in the fridge once opened.

TOP TIP

To sterilise jars and lids, wash them very well and leave them upturned on a rack to dry. Place the jars on a tray and put them in a preheated oven at 180°C/Fan 160°C/Gas 4 for 10 minutes. Leave until they are cool enough to handle but still warm.

Rich and tangy with more than a hint of heat, this is a truly luscious chutney that is so easy to make that you'll never go back to shop-bought again. Traditional Indian lime pickle is made from raw limes steeped in lime juice and salt and left in the sun for a few weeks. You don't get much sun up north where we live, so we've cheated a bit and made our pickle on the hob. We think you'll agree that it's well worth the effort. You'll need an electric spice grinder for this recipe. **Makes 2 x 400ml jars**

LIME PICKLE

12 limes
1 tsp cumin seeds
1 tsp coriander seeds
1 tsp fenugreek seeds
2 tsp black mustard seeds
10 dried extra-hot chillies (bird's-eye)
3 tbsp sunflower oil
1 tsp ground turmeric
150ml distilled malt vinegar
150g caster sugar
4 tsp flaked sea salt

Wash the limes well and dry them with a clean tea towel. Place the limes on a board, cut 4 of them in half and squeeze out the juice. You should end up with 150ml. Put the lime skins, pith and all, in a food processor and chop them fairly finely. The pieces need to be about 5mm in diameter. Remove the lid and push the mixture down a couple of times with a rubber spatula. Cut the rest of the limes in half across the equator, then cut each half into 8 wedges – or 6 if small.

Place a small frying pan over a medium heat and toast the cumin, coriander, fenugreek and 1 teaspoon of the mustard seeds for 2–3 minutes until lightly toasted. You'll know when they are ready because they will give off a fragrant aroma. Toss them gently as you toast. Stir the chillies into the pan, then remove from the heat and leave for 5 minutes. Put all the toasted spices and chillies in a spice grinder and grind them to a powder.

Heat the oil in a large saucepan and stir in the freshly ground spices, turmeric and remaining mustard seeds. Cook for 2 minutes, stirring constantly, over a medium-high heat. Before the spices get a chance to burn, add all the limes to the saucepan and stir in the lime juice, vinegar, sugar and salt.

Set the pan over a medium-low heat. Bring to a gentle simmer, then cook for 1 hour, stirring occasionally, until the limes are very soft and the sauce is thick. You'll need to stir regularly towards the end of the cooking time as you don't want the pickle to stick, so watch it carefully. While the pickle is cooking, wash and sterilise your jars (see page 270).

Spoon the hot pickle into the warm jars and leave to cool before covering with lids or sealing the jars if using Kilners. Leave in a cool dark place for at least a week before opening if you can bear to wait that long. Spoon into little bowls to serve with poppadums or curry.

Use the pickle within 3 months and keep it in the fridge once opened.

This is a lovely fresh relish that we ate in Kerala and now love to make at home. It's great served with some poppadums to scoop up luscious mouthfuls. **Serves 6**

FRESH ONION AND TOMATO RELISH

1 small red onion
2 fresh ripe tomatoes (about 275g)
small bunch of fresh coriander
1 tbsp fresh lemon or lime juice
pinch of caster sugar
flaked sea salt
freshly ground black pepper

Peel the onion and cut it in half from top to root. Cut the onion into slices of about 5mm – they shouldn't be too chunky as you need to be able to scoop them up with a piece of poppadum. Put the slices in a serving bowl.

Roughly chop the tomatoes and add them to the onion. Trim the coriander, roughly chop the leaves and add them to the bowl with the onions and tomatoes. Season with lemon or lime juice, a pinch of caster sugar and salt and a few twists of freshly ground black pepper, then serve.

We're used to chutneys that are stewed up in a big pan with vinegar and sugar, but Indian chutneys can be much fresher and lighter. This one is great with hot curries, as the cooling coconut tempers the spices. There's only a hint of chilli and you can leave the seeds out if you prefer an even milder taste. Also, this is dead easy to make, as we use desiccated coconut instead of fresh. **Serves 6–8**

COCONUT AND CORIANDER CHUTNEY

150g desiccated coconut
½ tsp flaked sea salt
1 long green chilli, finely chopped (deseed if you like)
10g chunk of fresh root ginger, peeled and finely grated
2 tsp caster sugar
freshly squeezed juice of 1 lime
175ml cold water
small bunch of fresh coriander, leaves fairly finely chopped

Put the coconut and salt in a bowl and stir in the chilli, ginger, sugar, lime juice and water. Set aside for 10 minutes so the coconut can absorb the liquid and swell.

Stir the coriander into the coconut mixture, then spoon the chutney into a serving bowl and serve. You can make this ahead of time if you like. Just cover the bowl with cling film and keep the chutney in the fridge for 2–3 days.

This is the richest, stickiest chutney and it's sweet, spicy and hot. A great all-rounder to have in your fridge, this is good with cold cuts as well as curry. **Makes 2 x 500ml jars**

AUBERGINE (BRINJAL) PICKLE

- 2 large aubergines (about 600g)
- 4 tsp fine sea salt
- 7 tbsp sunflower oil
- 2 medium onions, halved and sliced
- 25g chunk of fresh root ginger, peeled and finely grated
- 4 garlic cloves, crushed
- 2 tsp cumin seeds
- 2 tsp fenugreek seeds
- 2 tsp yellow mustard seeds
- 1 heaped tsp coriander seeds
- 8 curry leaves
- ¼ of a cinnamon stick
- 1 long dried red chilli or 3 dried extra-hot chillies (bird's-eye)
- 1 tsp ground turmeric
- 250g soft dark brown sugar
- 300ml malt vinegar

Trim the aubergines and cut them into rough 2cm chunks. Spread these out on a tray lined with kitchen paper and sprinkle with 2 teaspoons of the salt. Leave for 30 minutes, then rinse the chunks in a colander under running water and drain them well. Heat 2 tablespoons of the oil in a large non-stick frying pan and fry the aubergines in 2 batches over a high heat for 2–3 minutes until lightly browned but not softened. Add another 2 tablespoons of oil between each batch as the aubergines will soak it up. Tip the aubergines into a large saucepan as soon as it is golden.

Heat another tablespoon of oil in the same frying pan and fry the onions for 6–8 minutes until lightly browned, stirring regularly. Add the ginger and garlic and cook for 2 minutes more, while stirring, then add everything to the pan with the aubergines.

Place a small frying pan over a medium heat and add the cumin seeds, fenugreek, 1 teaspoon of the mustard seeds and the coriander seeds. Toast for 1–2 minutes until you can smell the spicy aromas, then take the pan off the heat and add the curry leaves, cinnamon and chilli. Toss all the spices together and leave to cool for 5 minutes. Grind them to a powder in a spice grinder.

Heat the remaining 2 tablespoons of oil in the same pan used to toast the spices. Lightly crush the reserved teaspoon of mustard seeds in a pestle and mortar and add them to the pan. Cook for a few seconds, stirring constantly. Immediately add the freshly powdered spices and ground turmeric. Cook for 1 minute, stirring constantly over a low heat.

Scrape all the spices into the pan with the aubergines and onions. You may need to use a rubber spatula to ensure you get every last bit. Add the sugar, vinegar and remaining 2 teaspoons of salt. Bring to a simmer over a low heat and cook for 1 hour, uncovered, stirring regularly with a wooden spoon until thick. The pickle should bubble gently during this time, but don't let it go mad. Meanwhile, sterilise your jars (see page 270).

Spoon the hot pickle into the warm jars and leave to cool before covering with lids. Store this pickle in the fridge and try to keep it for at least a month before opening. Eat within 3 months.

This is a real humdinger of a pickle. It's quick to make, doesn't need maturing and can be eaten warm with Indian-style breads – especially good with our puris (see page 255). We advise cooking it in a well-ventilated room with your extractor fan on full as the chilli aroma can get to your throat and make you cough. **Serves 4–6**

HOT CHILLI PICKLE

2 medium carrots
2 long green chillies
2 long red chillies
1½ tbsp sunflower oil
1 heaped tsp black mustard seeds
1 heaped tsp cumin seeds
¼ tsp ground turmeric
½ tsp flaked sea salt
4 tbsp cold water

Peel the carrots and cut them into batons of about 6cm long. Trim the chillies, slice them lengthways and discard only the seeds – don't remove the white cores. Cut the chillies in half lengthways once more and then in half widthways.

Heat the oil in a small frying pan or wok and add the mustard and cumin seeds. Fry them for a minute or 2 until the mustard seeds begin to pop. Add the carrots and chillies and stir-fry for about 30 seconds, then sprinkle the turmeric and salt into the pan.

Stir well and stir-fry for a further 30 seconds. Turn down the heat a little, add the cold water to the pan and stir everything well again. Continue to cook for 3–4 minutes or until the carrots are just tender and all of the water has evaporated, stirring regularly. Tip the pickle into a heatproof serving bowl and serve warm.

These two cooling sauces are perfect with some of the hot curries and brilliant with poppadums, chapatis or naan. **Serves 6**

CUCUMBER RAITA

Peel the cucumber and coarsely grate it on to a board. Take a handful of the grated cucumber and squeeze out the excess juice over a sink. Put the cucumber in a bowl and repeat the squeezing process with the rest.

Season the cucumber with the salt and stir in the yoghurt and mint, then cover and keep in the fridge until ready to serve. This sauce should keep for up 2 days in the fridge but you'll need to give it a good stir before serving.

- ½ cucumber
- pinch of flaked sea salt
- 150g plain natural yoghurt
- 1 tbsp finely chopped fresh mint leaves

FRESH CORIANDER CHUTNEY

Trim the coriander, but leave at least 5cm of the stalks attached because these will increase the flavour. Wash the coriander well and shake off any drips, then plonk it in a food processor.

Rinse the bunch of mint and strip the leaves off the stalks – you should end up with about 30 leaves. Put the leaves in the food processor with the coriander, then add the chillies, ginger, spring onions, lemon juice, sugar, salt, yoghurt and water.

Blend to make a bright green purée. You'll need to remove the lid and push the mixture down several times with a rubber spatula until you achieve the right consistency. Spoon the chutney into a serving bowl or cover and chill in the fridge. It will keep well for 3 days, but stir well before using.

- large bunch of coriander (about 80g)
- small handful of fresh mint (about 5g)
- 2 plump green chillies, halved and deseeded
- 10g chunk of fresh root ginger, peeled and roughly chopped
- 4 spring onions, trimmed and cut into short lengths
- 1 tbsp fresh lemon juice
- 2 tsp caster sugar
- ¼ tsp fine sea salt
- 3 tbsp plain natural yoghurt
- 3 tbsp cold water

A dollop or two of yoghurt is a beautifully cooling accompaniment to a curry and you can make your own for about half the price of shop-bought. What's more, you can have it just the way you like it – for example, swap some of the milk for single cream to make a richer yogurt; we'd suggest up to 200ml for extra creamy. For really thick yoghurt, strain it for a few hours, or if you leave it straining overnight it will become like a thick cream cheese. **Makes about 1 litre**

HOME-MADE YOGHURT

900ml full-fat milk
75g plain natural live yogurt

Pour the milk into a large saucepan and bring it just to the point of boiling. Watch the milk carefully because it could boil over – one reason to use a nice big pan. As soon as the milk begins to boil, reduce the heat (or switch to another ring if using an electric hob) so the temperature drops quickly.

Simmer the milk very gently for 2 minutes, stirring occasionally with a wooden spoon. Remove from the heat and leave the milk to cool in the pan for 30 minutes.

Pour the milk into a large bowl and stir in the yoghurt. Cover the bowl with cling film and place it in a warm airing cupboard overnight.

The next day, take the yoghurt out of the cupboard – it should look and feel deliciously thick. Cover it and chill in the fridge for a few hours before using.

If you want to make strained yoghurt, line a sieve with a square of muslin and place it over a bowl. Spoon the freshly made yoghurt into the muslin, cover loosely and place it in the fridge to strain for 2–6 hours. During this time, the liquid will drain out of the yoghurt and into the bowl and the yoghurt will become much firmer – a bit like cream cheese. Make sure the bowl is deep enough for the bottom of the sieve to remain above the liquid – as much as 500ml could drain off.

At the end of the straining time, scrape the yoghurt off the muslin with a spoon or spatula into a bowl. Cover with cling film and keep chilled. It should keep for up to 2 days in the fridge.

Our curry book would not be complete without us doffing our caps to the chip shop curry sauce. We've all grown up with it and we all love it. Exactly what was in this sauce was always a mystery, but we've managed to come up with a version and it's mega. **Serves 6**

CHIP SHOP CURRY SAUCE

- 3 tbsp sunflower oil
- 2 medium onions, roughly chopped
- 15g chunk of fresh root ginger, peeled and roughly chopped
- 4 garlic cloves, sliced
- 1 heaped tbsp mild curry powder
- ½ tsp ground turmeric
- ¼ tsp ground star anise
- 25g plain flour
- 400ml chicken or vegetable stock (made with 1 stock cube)
- 2 tsp tomato purée
- freshly ground black pepper

Heat the oil in a large non-stick saucepan and gently fry the onions for 10 minutes until well softened, stirring occasionally. Increase the heat a little and cook for 2–3 minutes more, while stirring, until the onions are golden.

Turn down the heat again, add the ginger and garlic and cook gently for 3 minutes, stirring regularly. Stir in the curry powder, turmeric, star anise and a few twists of black pepper, then cook for 2 minutes – keep stirring.

Sprinkle over the plain flour and stir well. Gradually add the chicken or vegetable stock, stirring constantly until it is all incorporated. Add the tomato purée and bring to a simmer, then cook for 5 minutes, stirring occasionally, until the sauce is thick.

Remove the pan from the heat and blitz the sauce with a stick blender until it is very smooth. If you don't have a stick blender, let the mixture cool for a few minutes and blend in a food processor until smooth, then tip it back into the saucepan. Cover the surface of the curry sauce with cling film to prevent a skin forming and set it aside.

When you are ready to serve, remove the cling film from the curry sauce and place the pan over a low heat. Slowly bring the sauce to a gentle simmer, stirring constantly, and continue to simmer and stir for a couple of minutes. Serve with freshly cooked chips.

This sauce can be cooled and then stored in the fridge for a couple of days or frozen for 1 month without spoiling.

Sweet Dishes

Curries are deeply savoury so it's nice to follow them with something sweet. Pears and spice make a great team – add a bit of honey and you have a cracking pud. We like William or Packham pears for this, but any firm variety is fine. **Serves 4**

SPICED POACHED PEARS

- 4 medium to large oranges
- 75g runny honey
- finely grated zest of ½ unwaxed or well-scrubbed lemon
- ½ tsp ground ginger
- ½ cinnamon stick
- 1 star anise
- 1 vanilla pod
- 4 firm medium pears
- 10g flaked almonds
- vanilla ice cream, single cream or crème fraiche, for serving

Wash 1 of the oranges well to remove any waxy coating and cut off 2 wide strips of zest with a vegetable peeler. Cut all the oranges in half and squeeze out the juice. You should end up with about 450ml. Put the orange juice, orange zest strips, honey, lemon zest, ginger, cinnamon and star anise in a large nonstick saucepan.

Put the vanilla pod on a board and cut it in half lengthways and then widthways. Add the vanilla to the pan and place it over a medium heat. Bring to the boil, stirring constantly, then remove from the heat.

Peel the pears, leaving the stalks intact. Cut out the fuzzy brown bit on the base of each pear where the flower once was – do this with the tip of a small knife. Place the pears in the hot syrup in the pan, but don't worry if it doesn't cover them completely, as you will turn the pears as they cook.

Return the pan to the heat and cover with a lid. Gently simmer the pears for 20–30 minutes according to their ripeness and size. Remove the lid every now again and turn the pears in the syrup so they have a chance to cook fully. They should be tender but not at all mushy at the end of the cooking time. You can test the pears by piercing them with a knife – it should slide fairly easily into the middle.

Remove the pears with a slotted spoon and place them on dessert plates. Return the pan to the heat and continue simmering the sauce until it has reduced to about 150ml. While the sauce is simmering, scatter the almonds into a small frying pan and toast them over a medium heat for 2 minutes or until golden brown, turning them a couple of times. Spoon the spiced syrup over the pears and add a small piece of vanilla to each plate. Sprinkle with the toasted almonds and serve with cream, crème fraiche or vanilla ice cream.

These pears are also delicious served cold, so you could make them in advance and then cover with cling film and chill. They will keep in the fridge for at least a day without spoiling.

A revelation! This is the perfect light dessert after any curry and can be served in shot glasses if you are looking for a palate cleanser between courses. It's a gorgeous pink colour and the flavour reminds us of those rhubarb and custard flavoured boiled sweets, only much, much better. You don't need forced rhubarb to get the vibrant pink colour – normal greeny-pink rhubarb is fine. **Serves 6**

RHUBARB AND VANILLA FREEZE

800g rhubarb stalks (without leaves)
200ml cold water
200g caster sugar
1 vanilla pod

Switch your freezer to its fast-freeze setting if it has one. Trim the ends off the rhubarb stalks and wash them well, then place the rhubarb on a board and cut the stalks into lengths of about 3.5cm. Place these in a large saucepan and add the water and sugar.

Cut the vanilla pod in half lengthways and scrape out the seeds into the same pan. Drop the pod into the pan too. Place the pan on the hob and bring to a very gentle simmer, then cover it with a lid and continue to simmer gently for 15 minutes until the rhubarb is very soft.

Place a fine sieve over a large bowl. Gently tip the softened rhubarb and its liquid into the sieve and leave to stand for about an hour to allow all the pink juice to drop through. Very gently press the rhubarb with the back of a spoon to release a little more of the juice, but take care not to press it too hard as you don't want any of the greenish pulp to end up in the bowl.

Pour the juice into a fairly shallow freezer-proof container, then cover and freeze for 2 hours. Remove the lid and stir the rhubarb syrup with a fork to break up the ice crystals that should be forming around the edges. Cover and put the container back in the freezer for another hour.

Repeat the process twice more, leaving the rhubarb mixture in the freezer for about an hour each time before 'forking'. After the final forking, freeze until solid. Don't forget to turn off the fast-freeze function. You can freeze this for up to 1 month.

Take the pud out of the freezer about 10 minutes before you want to eat and serve 1–2 scoops per person depending on how greedy they are!

Coconut and mango make a lovely tropical couple. You can serve this little delight warm or cold, but we prefer it warm, as the rice can go a bit stodgy as it cools. **Serves 6**

COCONUT STICKY RICE *with mangoes*

- 275g Thai sticky rice (glutinous rice)
- 400ml can of coconut milk
- 3 tbsp caster sugar, preferably golden caster sugar
- good pinch of flaked sea salt
- 2 ripe mangoes

Put the rice in a bowl and cover with cold water, then leave it to stand and swell for about 3 hours. Line a steamer basket with a piece of muslin, place it in the sink and pour the rice and water on top. Leave to drain for a couple of minutes.

Place the steamer basket over a steamer pan filled with water to a depth of about 5cm. Cover the pan with a lid and bring to the boil, then reduce the heat slightly and steam the rice for 15 minutes. Remove the lid and stir the rice. Sprinkle with 3 tablespoons of cold water, then cover again and return to a simmer. Steam for a further 10–15 minutes until the rice is tender and translucent.

While the rice is steaming, pour the coconut milk into a saucepan and add the sugar and salt. Heat together gently, stirring constantly, but do not allow to boil. Remove the pan from the heat.

When the rice is ready, take it off the heat and tip it into a bowl. Stir in about two-thirds of the warm coconut milk until it coats the grains of rice generously. Cover and leave to stand for 10 minutes. Place the saucepan with the remaining coconut milk back on the heat and bring to a simmer. Cook for a couple of minutes until the milk is reduced by about a third and has thickened slightly, stirring, then remove the pan from the heat.

Spoon the sticky rice on to plates, then pour over the remaining sauce and serve immediately with some slices of mango.

These are the perfect refreshers after a hot curry. If you don't have an ice cream maker, pour the lemon and lime or mango mixture into a freezer-proof container, cover and freeze for 2 hours. Remove from the freezer and scrape with a fork to break up the ice crystals. Cover and return to the freezer for another hour. You will need to repeat the process every hour for the next 3 hours to make the sorbet as smooth and ice free as possible. **Both serve 6**

LEMON AND LIME SORBET

- 300g caster sugar
- finely grated zest of 2 well-scrubbed limes
- 300ml cold water
- 150ml freshly squeezed lime juice (about 6 fresh limes)
- 150ml freshly squeezed lemon juice (about 4 fresh lemons)
- lime slices, to decorate (optional)

Switch your freezer to its fast-freeze setting if it has one. Put the sugar and lime zest in a pan with the 300ml of water and slowly bring to the boil, stirring occasionally. Boil for 5 minutes, then remove the pan from the heat. Strain the juices through a fine sieve into a bowl, then strain the sugar syrup into the same bowl and stir well. Leave to cool.

Pour the mixture into an ice cream maker and churn until it has a soft sorbet-like consistency. This may take over an hour. Tip into a freezer-proof container, cover and freeze for at least 4 hours before serving. When you're ready to serve, take the sorbet out of the freezer and leave it at room temperature for 10 minutes. Scoop the sorbet into glass tumblers or bowls and decorate with slices of lime if you like.

EASIEST-EVER MANGO SORBET

- 2 x 425g cans of mango slices in syrup
- freshly squeezed juice of ½ lemon

Switch your freezer to its fast-freeze setting if it has one. Tip the mango slices and syrup into a food processor, then add the lemon juice and blend to a purée. Press this mixture through a fine sieve into a bowl to remove any tough fibres.

Tip the pulp into an ice cream maker and churn until the mixture has a soft, sorbet-like consistency – this may take up to an hour. Transfer it to a freezer-proof container, cover and freeze for at least 4 hours before serving. When you're ready to serve, take the sorbet out of the freezer and leave at room temperature for 10 minutes. Serve scoops of the sorbet in tumblers or pretty bowls.

Irresistible – everyone loves a bit of fruit. This can be made a day ahead and then finished off with some sliced bananas just before serving. Best not to add them any earlier or they go brown and soggy, which is not a pretty sight. Mint leaves make the perfect garnish. **Serves 10–12**

TROPICAL FRUIT SALAD

- 1 small ripe pineapple
- 1 large ripe mango
- 2 large wrinkly passion fruit
- 4 kiwi fruit
- 2 x 425g cans of lychees in syrup
- 25–30 small fresh mint leaves
- 2 medium bananas

Place the pineapple on a board and cut off the leaves and skin. Pick out any prickly 'eyes' with the tip of a knife. Cut the pineapple in quarters lengthways and then remove the inner core. This has a slightly different, more fibrous texture than the juicy flesh and you should be able to cut it out in 1 long triangle from each quarter. Cut the pineapple quarters into 1cm slices and put these in a large serving dish.

Cut the mango in half either side of the large flat stone. Using a serving spoon, scoop the mango flesh away from the skin and place it on a board, then cut the flesh into long slices. Remove the skin from the sides of the stones and carefully strip off the remaining mango flesh, then add it to the rest.

Cut the passion fruit in half, scoop out the seeds and pulp and drop these into the bowl with the other fruit. Peel the kiwi fruit and cut them in half lengthways before slicing fairly thickly. Tip the lychees and all their syrup into the bowl, then add the mint leaves and stir well. Cover the bowl with cling film and chill the fruit until 10 minutes before serving.

Peel and slice the bananas diagonally. Add these to the salad, toss everything together lightly and serve.

We do love a meringue. Adding pistachios gives this version a tantalisingly exotic touch we think and we hope you agree. They're a doddle to make and a treat to eat so get whisking. **Serves 6**

PISTACHIO MERINGUES *with raspberries*

Meringues

1 tsp sunflower oil, for greasing
35g shelled, unsalted pistachio nuts
3 large egg whites
150g caster sugar

Raspberry cream

300ml double cream
15g caster sugar
1 tsp rose water (optional)
300g fresh raspberries

Preheat the oven to 150°C/Fan 130°C/Gas 2. Lightly oil a large baking tray and line it with baking parchment. Put 25g of the pistachio nuts in a spice grinder or food processor and blitz them to fine crumbs.

To make the meringue, put the egg whites in a large bowl and whisk with an electric whisk until stiff but not dry. They are ready when you can turn the bowl upside down without the egg white sliding out.

Gradually whisk in the sugar, just a tablespoon at a time, whisking for a few seconds between each addition. Tip the ground nuts into the bowl and, using a large serving spoon, fold them in very lightly – just a couple of turns – so the pistachios streak through the meringue.

Using a couple of dessertspoons, spoon 12 meringues on to the baking parchment, spacing them well apart. Roughly chop the remaining whole pistachios and scatter them over the meringues. Place the tray in the centre of the oven and turn the oven temperature down to 120°C/Fan 100°C/Gas ½. Bake the meringues for 2 hours until dry – turn the oven down more if they begin to colour. At the end of the cooking time, turn the oven off, but leave the meringues to cool in the oven for several hours until crisp. They should remain a little gooey in the centre.

Whip the cream with the caster sugar and rose water, if using, into soft billowing clouds. We use an electric whisk for this job but a large balloon whisk is fine if you are feeling energetic. Pile the meringues, large spoonfuls of the softly whipped cream and the fresh raspberries into a glass dish to serve. You can also assemble individual servings of this dish if you prefer.

Coconut ice cream makes us think of holidays and waving palm trees. It's tricky getting a good coconut flavour, but we've found a good glug of coconut liqueur makes all the difference. Serve this ice cream with our fabulous chocolate sauce for a treat that's even better than a Bounty bar. **Serves 6–8**

COCONUT ICE CREAM
with rich chocolate sauce

400ml can of coconut milk
150ml double cream
25g desiccated coconut
3 large egg yolks
25g caster sugar
3 tbsp cornflour
100ml coconut liqueur, such as Malibu

Rich chocolate sauce
100g plain dark chocolate
100ml double cream
50ml semi-skimmed milk

Switch your freezer to the fast-freeze setting if it has one. Put the coconut milk, double cream and desiccated coconut into a medium non-stick saucepan. Place the pan over a low heat and bring to a gentle simmer, stirring regularly. Watch carefully so the mixture doesn't have a chance to boil over. Remove the pan from the heat as soon as the mixture comes to a simmer.

Put the egg yolks, sugar and cornflour in a large heatproof bowl and beat with a metal whisk until pale and creamy. Pour the warm coconut cream over the egg mixture, whisking constantly.

Tip everything back into the saucepan and cook over a low heat for 3–4 minutes, stirring constantly with a wooden spoon until the custard is thickened and creamy – it should lightly coat the back of your spoon. Don't let it overheat, though. Remove the pan from the heat, pour the custard into a heatproof bowl and stir in the coconut liqueur. Cover the surface with cling film to prevent a skin forming and leave to cool.

Transfer the mixture to a freezer-proof container, then cover and freeze for 2 hours. Remove the lid and stir the ice cream with a fork to break up the ice crystals which should be forming around the edges. Cover and return the ice cream to the freezer for a further hour. Repeat the process twice more, leaving the ice cream in the freezer for about an hour each time before 'forking'.

Remove the ice cream from the freezer about 10 minutes before serving to allow it to soften. Serve 1–2 scoops per person with the chocolate sauce or some slices of ripe mango.

To make the chocolate sauce, put the chocolate on a board and chop it finely. You'll need to use a large knife and a sturdy board. Or, if you prefer, put the chocolate in a food processor and pulse until chopped. Pour the cream and milk into a saucepan and bring slowly to the boil, while stirring. Remove from the heat. Tip the chocolate into the pan with the cream and stir vigorously until the chocolate melts. Serve immediately while it's still warm.

Fragrant and luscious, mangoes are our favourite tropical fruit and we could eat them until the parrots come home. This recipes sets off their sweet flavour and meaty texture to great effect. **Serves 6 generously but will stretch to 8 smaller servings**

MANGO RIPPLE FOOL

2 large, very ripe mangoes (about 1kg total weight)
1 lime, well scrubbed
25g caster sugar, plus 1 tsp
300ml double cream
150g half-fat crème fraiche

Cut the mangoes in half either side of the large flat stones. Using a serving spoon, scoop the mango flesh away from the skin and put it in a food processor or blender. Remove the skin from the sides of the stones and carefully strip off the remaining mango flesh, then add it to the rest.

Finely grate the lime zest and put it into a small bowl. Stir in the teaspoon of caster sugar, cover the bowl with cling film and set aside. Squeeze the lime juice and pour it over the mango in the food processor. Add the remaining sugar and blitz to a smooth purée. You may need to remove the lid and push the mixture down a couple of times with a rubber spatula until you achieve the right consistency.

Pour the cream into a large bowl and whip until it forms fairly firm peaks. Stir in the crème fraiche and then about three-quarters of the mango purée until well combined. The mixture should feel fairly thick but light at this point.

Pour the remaining mango purée on top of the creamy mixture and stir with a large metal spoon just once so that the fruit purée is very loosely rippled through the cream. Gently spoon the fool into 6 stemmed wine glasses or tumblers. It should marble thickly as you spoon it and every glass will look a little different.

Place the glasses on a tray, cover with cling film and chill for at least 1 hour before serving. Remove the cling film and sprinkle each fool with a little of the lime sugar just before serving.

TOP TIP

Some people don't like the fibrous bits in mango. If you like your mango fool completely smooth, you can pass the mango purée through a fine sieve to remove any fibres before adding it to the cream.

This is our take on the popular Chinese pud and, without wanting to blow our own trumpets, we think it's pretty fantastic. We know the recipe looks long, and it does take a while to do, but if you have a sweet tooth like us you're going to be in heaven. Just be really careful, though, with the hot oil and the even hotter caramel. Works with chunks of apple too. **Serves 4**

TOFFEE BANANAS

2 large ripe but firm bananas
about 1 litre sunflower oil, for deep-frying
12 ice cubes
2 tbsp sesame seeds
vanilla ice cream, for serving

Batter

175g gluten- and wheat-free self-raising flour blend (such as Doves Farm)
300ml chilled fizzy water

Caramel

200g caster sugar
4 tbsp cold water

To make the batter, put the flour into a medium bowl and gradually whisk in the water until you have a smooth mixture with the consistency of thick double cream. Set the bowl aside. Peel the bananas and cut each one into 4 diagonal pieces. Drop the banana pieces into the batter and turn them with a wooden spoon until they are all thickly coated.

Pour the oil into a medium-large saucepan and set over a medium heat. Place a cooking thermometer in the oil and heat to 190°C. DO NOT ALLOW THE OIL TO OVERHEAT. DO NOT LEAVE HOT OIL UNATTENDED.

Take a banana piece with tongs and shake it lightly over the bowl for a few seconds to lose a little of the excess batter, then lower it gently into the hot oil. As soon as you have added 1 piece of banana, repeat the process with 3 more and cook all 4 together for 3–4 minutes until they are pale golden brown and crisp. Use metal tongs to turn them 3–4 times as they fry. As the banana pieces begin to cook, they will bob up to the surface of the oil and will be easier to see and to turn. They won't be as golden as a traditional batter.

Lift the crisp bananas out of the hot oil with a slotted spoon and drain on a large plate or tray lined with kitchen paper. Repeat the process to make another 4 deep-fried banana pieces. Watch the temperature of the oil carefully and be ready to reduce it or reheat it between batches.

Once all the bananas are fried, you can begin to make the caramel. Put the sugar and water in a small saucepan and place it over a low heat for about 3 minutes, stirring occasionally until the sugar dissolves and the syrup looks clear. Increase the heat so the syrup begins to bubble furiously, but do not stir, simply swirl the pan every now and then, taking care not to splash the hot caramel.

continued overleaf...

TOFFEE BANANAS CONTINUED...

Half fill a large bowl with cold water and add the ice cubes. Put this to one side to use for rapidly chilling the bananas once they've been dipped in the caramel. Place a cooling rack set over a small baking tray next to the water. Put an empty plate close by and the sesame seeds in a small bowl beside it.

Watch the caramel carefully and when it turns golden brown, after 6–8 minutes, remove it from the heat – it will continue to cook away from the hob. DO NOT BE TEMPTED TO TOUCH OR TASTE THE CARAMEL. IT WILL BE EXTREMELY HOT. Take the caramel to where the bowls of iced water and sesame seeds are waiting. Lift 1 piece of battered banana at a time with a fork and dip it into the caramel. If you hold the handle of the saucepan, you can tilt the caramel to one side when you add the banana.

Turn the banana to lightly coat it in the hot caramel, then lift it out with the fork. Holding the banana over the plate, sprinkle it lightly with a good pinch of the sesame seeds, then drop it immediately into the iced water. Count to 5, then remove it and put it on the rack. Take a second piece of banana and follow the same process of dipping in caramel and sprinkling with the seeds.

Working as if you are on a production line – but doing all the work yourself unless you can grab someone to help dip or sprinkle – continue coating the bananas with caramel and sprinkling with sesame seeds. You need to work quickly but safely, as you don't want the bananas to cool too much while they are waiting to be dipped or served.

The caramel should stay liquid enough for all the banana pieces, but you can always put it back on the hob if it begins to cool and thicken. These are best eaten as soon as they are ready if you want the bananas nice and hot inside with a cracking caramel crust. Delicious served with vanilla ice cream.

You need a really sweet, ripe pineapple for this recipe and it will taste extra good in our deliciously crisp batter, which is very easy to make once you know how. The cinnamon sugar is not traditional but we think it's a perfect match. Serve with coconut ice cream for the ultimate pina colada vibe. **Serves 6**

PINEAPPLE FRITTERS

1 small ripe, juicy pineapple (about 1kg)
about 800ml–1 litre sunflower oil, for deep-frying
1 tbsp caster sugar, for sprinkling
½ tsp ground cinnamon
well-chilled cream or ice cream, for serving (see page 306 for our coconut ice cream)

Batter

175g gluten- and wheat-free self-raising flour blend
1 tbsp caster sugar
300ml semi-skimmed milk
½ tsp vanilla extract

Place the pineapple on a board and carefully cut off the leaves and skin. Pick out any prickly 'eyes' with the tip of a knife. Using a thin, sharp knife, very carefully tunnel a hole of about 3cm in diameter through the pineapple and remove the central core. This has a slightly different, more fibrous, texture than the rest of the flesh. Cut the pineapple into 6 rings – each will be about 1.5cm thick – and put them on a plate.

To make the batter, put the flour and sugar into a medium bowl and gradually whisk in the milk until the mixture is smooth and has the consistency of thick double cream. Whisk in the vanilla extract.

Pour the oil into a medium-large saucepan and set it over a medium heat. Place a cooking thermometer in the oil and heat to 180°C. DO NOT ALLOW THE OIL TO OVERHEAT. DO NOT LEAVE HOT OIL UNATTENDED. Mix the sugar and cinnamon together in a small bowl while you wait for the oil to heat. Take a pineapple ring and drop it into the batter, then turn with a wooden spoon until it is thickly coated.

Lift the ring out of the batter with a fork poked through its hole so you don't scrape off the batter. Lower the ring gently into the hot oil and remove the fork. As soon as you have added 1 pineapple ring, repeat the dipping and frying process with another, pushing the first ring to the side first to make some space and stop them sticking together.

Cook both pineapple rings together for 3–4 minutes until golden brown and very crisp, turning them with metal tongs 3 or 4 times as they fry. As they begin to cook, the rings will bob up to the surface of the oil and will be easier to see and to turn. Try not to break the batter as you turn the fritters.

Lift the crisp fritters out of the hot oil with a slotted spoon or clean tongs and drain them on a large plate or tray lined with kitchen paper. Repeat the process to make another 4 fritters. Watch the temperature of the oil carefully and be ready to reduce it or reheat it between batches. Sprinkle the hot fritters with the cinnamon sugar and serve with lots of chilled cream or ice cream.

If a mango is properly ripe, it's easy to scoop the flesh out of the skin with a spoon.

These are deliciously rich and very filling so can be stretched to feed six quite easily, particularly after a big curry meal – unless they're real chocoholics, of course. The delicate chilli flavour marries beautifully with the creamy rich, smooth chocolate and they're no trouble to make. These make a fitting finale to any meal, so don't just keep them for after a curry! **Serves 4–6**

CHILLI CHOCOLATE POTS

- 200g plain dark chilli chocolate
- 200ml double cream
- 50ml semi-skimmed milk
- extra-thick double cream or crème fraiche, for serving

Put the chocolate on a sturdy board and chop it finely with a good strong knife. Or, if you prefer, put the chocolate in a food processor and pulse until chopped. Pour the cream and milk into a saucepan and bring slowly to the boil, while stirring. Remove the pan from the heat.

Tip the chocolate into the pan with the cream and stir vigorously until the chocolate melts. Pour the mixture into 4 or 6 small espresso coffee cups, ramekins or heatproof glass tumblers and leave to cool. Cover with cling film and chill for at least 2 hours before serving.

If you leave your pots for longer, you may find they stiffen just a bit too much, so it's worth taking them out of the fridge about 30 minutes before you want to eat. Add a dollop of double cream or crème fraiche on top just before serving.

TOP TIP

You can make these puddings with plain dark chocolate if you don't have any of the chilli variety. Just stir a pinch of hot chilli powder into the double cream and milk before adding the chocolate.

The traditional method of making kulfi means simmering a pan of milk for about an hour until it is very thick and well reduced. This is quite tricky to do, as the milk can burn all too easily if you don't watch it very carefully. We've come up with this much quicker version that tastes just as good and is much simpler to prepare. It's the perfect dessert after a spicy curry, as the cool, rose flavour is refreshing yet tastes luxurious too. **Makes 6**

PISTACHIO AND ROSE KULFI

- 50g shelled, unsalted pistachio nuts
- 25g flaked almonds
- 150ml full-fat milk
- 50g caster sugar
- 1 x 410ml can of evaporated milk
- 1 x 170ml can of evaporated milk
- 200ml double cream
- 1 tsp rose water (for flavouring food)
- few drops of green food colouring (optional)
- fresh rose petals, to decorate (optional)

Switch your freezer to the fast-freeze setting if it has one. Put 25g of the pistachio nuts and the flaked almonds in a spice grinder and blitz them to a powder. Roughly chop the remaining nuts and set them aside for decorating the kulfi.

Pour the milk into a saucepan and stir in the ground nuts and sugar. Heat through gently until the sugar dissolves, stirring constantly, but don't let the milk boil. Remove the pan from the heat and stir in the evaporated milk, double cream and rose water. Add a little green food colouring if you like, just enough to give the mixture a pretty pastel green colour. Leave to cool.

When the mixture is cool, have a quick taste to check the rose water is fragrant enough and if not, add a little more. Pour the mixture into 6 plastic cups – the kind used for parties – and put them on a small baking tray. Cover with cling film and pop them in the freezer.

As the kulfi begins to freeze, give it a stir with a fork every hour after the first 2 hours in the freezer to break up the ice crystals. After about 5 hours, the kulfi will be very stiff and almost too thick to stir. At this point, cover the cups tightly with foil and freeze them until solid. You can freeze them for up to 2 weeks.

When ready to serve, take the kulfi out of the freezer and leave to stand for 10 minutes, then turn them out on to small plates. Sprinkle the kulfi with the reserved chopped pistachios and rose petals if you have some and serve.

This is our version of a traditional Indian dessert made of strained yoghurt, inspired by those we ate during our travels in the Cardamom Hills in southern India. We like to spike our shrikhand with fragrant cardamom and saffron and add lots of seedless grapes to bring a lovely freshness that cuts through the creaminess. **Serves 4–5**

SHRIKHAND *with grapes*

- 1 litre plain natural yoghurt (see our recipe for home-made yoghurt on page 287)
- 16 cardamom pods (or use ½ tsp ground cardamom)
- 2 tbsp full-fat milk
- pinch of saffron threads
- 50g caster sugar
- pinch of grated nutmeg
- 250g seedless grapes, red or green or a mixture, halved
- 10g flaked almonds
- 10g shelled unsalted pistachios

Line a sieve with a square of muslin and place it over a bowl. Spoon the yoghurt into the muslin, cover it loosely and place the bowl in the fridge for 3–6 hours. During this time, the liquid will drain out of the yoghurt into the bowl and the yoghurt will become much firmer – a bit like cream cheese.

When you're ready to make the shrikhand, put the cardamom pods, if using, in a pestle and mortar and bash them to release the seeds. Remove the papery husks and grind the seeds into a powder.

Heat the milk in a small pan for a few seconds and stir in the saffron, then leave to stand for 10 minutes. Take the strained yoghurt out of the muslin and put it in a large mixing bowl. Throw out the whey.

Add the sugar to the yoghurt, just a tablespoon at a time, beating well with a wooden spoon between each addition. Stir in the saffron milk, ground cardamom and nutmeg, then add the grapes. Cover and chill for at least 3 hours before serving.

Scatter the almonds into a dry frying pan and toast them over a medium heat for 2–3 minutes until lightly browned, stirring often. Tip them on to a plate and leave to cool. Cut the pistachios very carefully into long strips – watch out as they do ping about a bit – and don't worry if they are not perfect. Set them aside.

Stir the chilled shrikhand well and spoon it into bowls. Scatter the almonds and pistachios on top and serve.

We've even managed to get chilli into a pud! This might seem quite filling after a curry but its gingery gorgeousness could be just the ticket after one of the lighter dishes, such as a fish curry, on a cold winter's night. Any excuse – we just love that fab toffee sauce! **Serves 8**

STICKY CHILLI GINGER SPONGE
with toffee sauce

125g butter, plus extra for greasing
125g soft dark brown sugar
125g black treacle
125g golden syrup
275g self-raising flour
1 tsp bicarbonate of soda
4 tsp ground ginger
1 tsp ground allspice
4 stem ginger balls in syrup (about 75g), drained and coarsely grated
1½ long red chillies, deseeded and finely chopped
2 large eggs
200ml semi-skimmed milk
vanilla ice cream, crème fraiche or chilled single cream, to serve

Toffee sauce

3 stem ginger balls in syrup (about 55g), drained
200ml double cream
100g dark brown soft sugar
75g butter

Preheat the oven to 180°C/Fan 160°C/Gas 4. Butter a 2-litre shallow ovenproof dish – a lasagne dish is ideal. Put the butter, sugar, treacle and syrup in a medium saucepan and melt together over a low heat, stirring regularly until the sugar dissolves. Increase the heat a little and simmer gently for a minute, while stirring. Remove from the heat and leave to cool for 5 minutes.

While the butter mixture is cooling, put the flour, bicarbonate of soda and spices in a large heatproof mixing bowl. Add the grated stem ginger and chopped chilli and toss everything together lightly. Make a well in the centre.

Beat the eggs with a metal whisk until smooth. Stir the milk gradually into the warm treacle mixture, then add the beaten eggs, stirring vigorously. Pour the treacle mixture slowly into the flour mixture, stirring constantly with a wooden spoon to make a thick batter. If there are a few floury lumps, give the batter a good stir with the metal whisk. Pour the batter into the prepared dish and bake in the centre of the oven for 35–40 minutes or until the sponge is well risen and a skewer inserted into the centre comes out clean.

While the sponge is cooking, make the toffee sauce. Put the ginger balls on a board and slice them thinly. Pile the slices from each ball up and cut through them to make thin matchstick strips, then scrape them into a medium non-stick saucepan.

Add the cream, sugar and butter to the stem ginger matchsticks and place the pan over a low heat. Cook together, stirring until the sugar dissolves, then bring the sauce to a very gentle simmer and cook for 30 seconds more, stirring constantly.

Take the pudding out of the oven and pour the hot sauce over the top, spreading the ginger pieces over the surface with a spoon. Vanilla ice cream, crème fraiche or single cream sets this off a treat.

Luscious lemon possets topped with tangy passion fruit jelly – just the kind of pud you need after a rich meaty curry. Dead simple to make too, and you can prepare these a day ahead and keep them in the fridge until you're ready to serve with a flourish. Best to use unwaxed lemons if you can find them, but if not, make sure you scrub the skins well before zesting. **Serves 6–8**

LEMON AND PASSION FRUIT POSSETS

- 2 or 3 large unwaxed or well-scrubbed lemons
- 600ml double cream
- 225g caster sugar
- 2 sheets of leaf gelatine (about 4g)
- 3 large, ripe, fairly wrinkly passion fruit
- 125–140ml cold water
- almond or pistachio tuile biscuits, for serving

Finely grate the lemon zest and squeeze the juice – you'll need 150ml. Put the cream and 200g of the sugar in a medium non-stick saucepan and warm together over a low heat for a couple of minutes, stirring with a wooden spoon until the sugar dissolves. Turn up the heat and bring the cream to a gentle simmer. Cook for 3 minutes, stirring, but watch the cream carefully so it doesn't get a chance to boil over.

Remove the cream from the heat and leave it to stand for 5 minutes. Stir in the lemon zest and juice. You should feel the lemon juice beginning to thicken the cream as you stir. Pour the mixture into a jug and divide it between 6 or 8 small ramekins or heatproof glasses. Leave to cool for 30 minutes, then cover and chill for about 3 hours or until just set.

While the lemon mixture is cooling, half fill a medium bowl with cold water and add the gelatine sheets 1 at a time. Leave them to soak for 5 minutes or until very floppy. Cut the passion fruits in half and scoop the pulp into a sieve set over a fairly wide measuring jug. Press the pulp with the back of a small ladle to extract as much of the juice and pulp as possible, leaving only the seeds. You should end up with about 75ml of liquid. Discard all but 2 teaspoons of the seeds. Add the cold water to the passion fruit juice until you have exactly 200ml of liquid. Put the reserved seeds in a small bowl.

Put the passion fruit juice and the remaining 25g of the sugar in a small pan and warm through very gently over a low heat until the sugar dissolves, stirring constantly. Remove from the heat. Take the softened gelatine sheets in your hand and squeeze them over the bowl to remove the excess liquid. Drop the gelatine into the warm passion fruit juice mixture and stir with a wooden spoon until it dissolves. Pour the mixture back into the jug and set aside but do not chill.

When the passion fruit jelly has cooled and the possets are just set, take the possets out of the fridge and uncover them. Divide the jelly between the ramekins or glasses to make a thin layer covering the lemon mixture. Dot a few of the reserved passion fruit seeds on top. Cover with cling film and return to the fridge for another 3–5 hours or until the jelly is completely set. Serve with little tuile biscuits.

Lassi is a yoghurt drink that's much loved in India and beyond – who says beer is the only thing to drink with curry? Traditional salted or spiced lassi can be beautifully cooling with a hot curry or you can enjoy sweet versions with added fruit. These are our favourites. **Both recipes serve 4**

MANGO AND LIME LASSI

- 1 ripe medium mango (about 300g)
- finely grated zest of 1 well-scrubbed lime
- 200ml plain natural yoghurt
- 400ml semi-skimmed milk, well chilled
- 8 ice cubes

Cut the mango in half either side of the large flat stone. Using a serving spoon, scoop the mango flesh away from the skin and put it in a food processor or blender. Remove the skin from the sides of the stone, carefully strip off the remaining mango flesh and add it to the rest.

Add the lime zest, yoghurt and milk, then blend until thoroughly combined. Divide the ice cubes between 4 tall glasses and pour the lassi over the top.

BANANA AND CARDAMOM LASSI

- 5 cardamom pods
- 2 ripe medium bananas
- 200ml plain natural yoghurt
- 400ml semi-skimmed milk, well chilled
- 1 tbsp runny honey
- ½ heaped tsp ground cinnamon
- 8 ice cubes

Put the cardamom pods in a pestle and mortar and bash them to release the seeds. Remove the papery husks and grind the seeds into a powder. Peel the bananas and put them in a food processor or blender.

Add the yoghurt, milk, honey, ground cardamom and cinnamon and blend until thoroughly combined. Divide the ice cubes between 4 tall glasses and pour the lassi over the top.

The Basics

HOW TO MAKE A GREAT CURRY

You don't need to be an expert to make a great curry. Follow our recipes and you'll soon be making a fantastic range of curries for any occasion. Even if you've never cooked a curry from scratch before, don't worry – it's much easier than you think. Making a curry really isn't any harder than putting together a Sunday roast or making a beef and ale stew. Just as in a stew, the flavour in a curry starts with the browning of the meat and the cooking of the onions. The element of a curry that sets it apart from a traditional stew is the spicing, and we're giving you plenty of help with that in this book.

We've had lots of the essential ingredients photographed so you'll know what they look like – check out our pages in this chapter on spices, chillies and other flavourings for tips on how to use them. Some of the ingredients lists for our recipes might look long and maybe a bit scary, but once you've bought the basic spices, you only need to add a few fresh ingredients for your curry to be complete. Here's some info that we hope will help you on your way to becoming a great curry cook.

What is a curry?

Some people make the mistake of thinking that a curry is a catch-all dish – that you can throw any old thing in the pan, add enough chilli to make it fiery hot, then dump it on a pile of rice. This couldn't be further from the truth. Curries are extraordinarily varied and very sophisticated, with an exquisite balance of spicy, aromatic flavours. Many are served with rice, but different types of bread are an equally traditional accompaniment.

In our book we've included lots of recipes from different parts of India, where each region has its characteristic dishes. There are chicken curries, curries with different meat and fish, pulse dishes and a wealth of wonderful vegetable recipes. We also feature curries from other parts of the world, including Jamaica and South Africa. Some of our favourites come from Southeast Asia where there is a particular emphasis on fresh aromatic ingredients, such as lemon grass and kaffir lime leaves. Rice is generally the staple in most parts of Southeast Asia, but noodles are also often served.

For most of the dishes in this book there are as many recipes as – well, we've had hot curries! We've tested and tasted and tested again to come up with versions that we love and we hope you will too. We advise that you follow our recipes carefully, measuring out the spices with a proper set of measuring spoons and weighing other ingredients to get the right balance of flavours. Then once you get accustomed to the methods of making great curries, try coming up with your own variations!

The basis of a good curry is a decent curry sauce. In the recipes in this book, we've made sauces in all sorts of ways, from quick sauces made with oil, onions and fresh tomatoes, to curries that start with blended onions, garlic, ginger and chilli, as well as rich curry paste and coconut sauces. It's well worth getting familiar with them all. You'll also find that lots of our sauces start off with slowly cooked and browned onions with an assortment of spices and perhaps some tomatoes. This is a great way to make a restaurant-style sauce.

Spices

It is the combination of spices that makes each curry unique and creates the wonderful balance of flavours. Once you have your selection of spices – and they will last for months in your cupboard – you are set to go. You don't need to get everything at once and can gradually build up your collection as you need. We suggest that you start with the following spices: cumin, coriander, cayenne,turmeric, fenugreek and cardamom. With these, and a supply of onions, ginger, garlic and chillies, you have the makings of a great curry.

We do use ready-ground spices, but for some recipes we like to grind our own in an electric spice grinder or a pestle and mortar – the mortar is a bowl made of a hard material such as wood, ceramic or stone and the pestle is a club-shaped tool used to crush and grind the spices. We find using a pestle and mortar satisfying – you can work out all your frustrations as you pound! – but an electric grinder does chop things very finely. Grinding your own spices means you can create your own garam masala, which is a warming, fragrant mix of spices that can be mixed and then dipped into whenever you need to (see our recipe on page 345). We don't tend to use premixed curry powders that often, except when making a very simple curry.

We usually get all the spices we need measured and ready before starting to cook a curry. They may all need to be put in together and you don't want to find you've run out of something crucial once your curry is bubbling away on the stove. We've tried and tested our recipes to give you as good a guide to spicing as we can, but always take your personal tastes into account. If you want your dish to have less (or more) heat, adjust the amount of chilli.

Cooking methods and equipment

You'll find that most curries are cooked on the hob – perhaps because the cooking methods were developed in countries where – and at a time when – an open fire was the best way of preparing a meal. As long as you've equipped yourself with a good non-stick frying pan (an extra-deep one is particularly useful), a couple of decent saucepans and a flameproof casserole dish, you shouldn't need lots of special cooking equipment. For recipes that involve deep-frying, a cooking thermometer is essential.

Assembling a meal

Different curries require different blends of spices and this means you can serve a number of curries at one meal and they will all taste deliciously varied. That's the way curry is traditionally eaten – with lots of small bowls of curries, pickles, chutneys, breads and yoghurts. Generally, in India and Southeast Asia, all of the dishes are served at the same time, rather than having a starter followed by a main course, but, in some parts of India meals are served in courses and you might like to do this too.

The rice and/or breads are the main part of an Indian meal and the meat and vegetable dishes are what are added. When you are putting together a meal, think about including at least one pulse-based dish or dhal too. Vegetable and lentil dishes will make the meal go further and if there's any left over they keep well to make part of another meal.

SPICES

What makes a curry special is the spicing and there is a wide range of amazing spices to choose from. On this and the following pages you'll find our favourites – the ones we use most for the recipes in this book. We hope you love them too.

Cumin

Cumin seeds come from a plant related to parsley that grows in the eastern Mediterranean region and in Asia. This spice has a lovely warm flavour, which is essential for many curries and is one of the ingredients in the Indian mixture known as garam masala. You can buy ground cumin, but grind the seeds yourself for the best results.

Cayenne

Cayenne is a hot spice made from the dried and ground seeds of the chilli pepper plant. Best used in small quantities, it adds a touch of fire to curries and other savoury dishes.

Cardamom

Cardamom pods are the fruit of a plant that grows wild in south India and Sri Lanka but is now cultivated in other parts of Asia. The pods can be added whole to add subtle flavour to dishes, lightly crushed, or split to extract the aromatic seeds. Green cardamom is often used in sweet dishes or more delicate curries, while brown cardamom has a stronger flavour – we always use green cardamom. You get the best flavour from using pods but you can also buy ground cardamom.

Asafoetida

This powerful spice is made from the taproots of a kind of fennel plant. It has a strong, not very attractive smell but this disappears once the spice is cooked. In fact, the second part of its name comes from the Latin word *foetida*, which means 'stinking'. Despite this, asafoetida is very popular in India and a small pinch makes all the difference to vegetable dishes such as masala potatoes. It is also said to help prevent flatulence!

Cloves

These are the dried flower buds of a tree that grows in Indonesia. They have long been popular in Britain for use in sweet dishes such as mincemeat and fruit cakes. Cloves have a strong flavour that can overwhelm if used too much, but they are very popular in Indian cooking. One of the ingredients in garam masala, cloves also enhance rich meaty dishes such as dhansaks and pasandas.

Turmeric

Turmeric comes from the root of a plant related to ginger. Most now comes from India, where it is loved for the yellow colour it adds to dishes as well as its spicy flavour. It is usually available in ground form but you can sometimes buy the dried root in specialist shops. Turmeric is one of the ingredients in ready-made curry powders and is also often used in fish dishes. It is believed to have some medicinal properties.

Coriander

Coriander seeds have a very fragrant, citrussy aroma. You can buy ground coriander or crush or grind the seeds yourself, which gives a fresher flavour. It's one of the spices in garam masala and used in Asian cookery for everything from chutneys to curries.

Cinammon

Cinnamon is made from dried tree bark and has a wonderfully warm sweet smell. You can buy it as little sticks of rolled-up bark or ground into a powder. In Britain, it is mostly used in sweet dishes, such as apple pie and Christmas pudding, but in the Middle East and Asia it's used to flavour savoury dishes. It is included in garam masala.

Cumin
Cardamom
Cayenne
Asafoetida
Cloves
Turmeric
Coriander
Cinnamon

Black mustard seeds
Yellow mustard seeds
Saffron
Fennel seeds
Kashmiri chilli powder
Nutmeg
Fenugreek
Ginger

SPICES

Black mustard seeds
Black, yellow and white mustard seeds come from different plants in the cabbage family. Black are the hottest and most pungent of the mustard seeds and they are the most popular in Indian cooking.

Yellow mustard seeds
These have a slightly gentler flavour than the black variety. Mustard seeds are often fried before use in Indian cookery to bring out their nutty flavour.

Fennel seeds
These little ridged seeds come from the fennel plant, which belongs to the parsley family. There are different varieties but the seeds most often used in cookery are sweet fennel seeds, which have mild anise flavour. You can buy the seeds whole or ground and their flavour works well in dishes such as spiced fish curry (see page 123).

Saffron
The most expensive of all spices, saffron is made from the dried stigmas of crocus flowers. It is said to take 70,000 flowers to make just 450g of saffron and the stigmas must be removed by hand. A little goes a long way, however, and a small pinch brings a lovely yellow colour to dishes as well as its characteristic flavour. Saffron is an essential flavour in our Rajhasthani kesar murg (see page 99), but is also used in some sweet dishes such as kulfi (see page 320).

Kashmiri chilli powder
This chilli powder brings a rich colour to dishes as well as a spicy flavour, and it's ideal for creating the red hue in dishes such as tandoori chicken (see page 75). Not as strong as some chilli powders but it has a great taste.

Nutmeg
Nutmeg comes from the fruit of the nutmeg tree, which grows in Indonesia, and now also in the West Indies. The nutmeg itself is found inside the fruit and is encased in a hard sheath, which can also be used as a spice called mace. Nutmeg can be bought whole or ground and its warm spicy flavour is popular in many sweet dishes, particularly custards.

Fenugreek
The seeds of the fenugreek plant are contained in most ready-made curry powders and have a strong, slightly bitter taste. These yellowish-brown seeds can be bought whole or ground and are often used in fish dishes, such as Keralan king prawn curry (see page 111).

Ginger
Ginger comes from the root of the ginger plant. The root can be used fresh (see page 352) or dried and ground – try our ginger pud (see page 324). The flavour of fresh and dried ginger is quite different and fresh is more commonly used in Asian cookery.

SPICES

Mango powder

This spice is made from unripe mangoes, which are sliced, dried and ground to form a powder. It can be used instead of lemon juice to add a tangy flavour to dishes.

Black pepper

Black peppercorns are the berry-like fruits of the climbing plant, which originally came from southern India but now grows in many tropical areas. It is one of the most important and most used of all spices and adds a warmth and tang to food. It also stimulates the appetite and helps to bring out the flavour of other ingredients. Black pepper can be bought ready ground, but the flavour is far better when it is freshly ground.

Star anise

True to its name, star anise is shaped like a star with eight points and has a aniseedy flavour. It is the dried fruit of an evergreen tree, which is grown in China and Southeast Asia. It is one of the ingredients in Chinese five-spice powder and we use it in our Malaysian chicken (see page 89).

Nigella seeds

These tiny black seeds are sometimes called black onion seeds but come from a completely different plant closely related to the popular country garden plant known as 'love in a mist'. It has a peppery, nutty flavour when warm and is often used in home-made breads such as naan (see our recipe on page 247).

Sea salt

Salt is the most popular of all flavourings and is used all over the world. Sea salt is the most prized variety. The best is gathered when pools of seawater left behind after the tide has gone out are evaporated by the sun, leaving salty crystals on the shore. Sea salt is more expensive than ordinary salt but has a fresher, stronger flavour that complements any style of cooking. It is available in flakes or finely ground.

Sichuan pepper

Sichuan pepper is not a true pepper but comes from the dried fruits of a tree that grows in the Sichuan province of China. It is one of the ingredients of Chinese five-spice powder and has a peppery taste with a numbing sensation.

Chinese five-spice

This mixture of powdered spices is popular in Vietnamese dishes as well as Chinese. Despite the name, it may include more than fives spices, usually star anise, cinnamon, fennel, cloves, Sichuan pepper and ginger or cardamom. Good for marinades for dishes such as Singapore noodles (see page 165).

Paprika

This rich red spice is made from the dried fruits of the capsicum pepper plant. It has a milder, sweeter flavour than cayenne so can be used more generously and it is very popular in Spanish and Hungarian cooking as well as Asian dishes.

Mango powder
Black pepper
Star anise
Nigella seeds
Sea Salt
Sichuan pepper
Paprika
Chinese five-spice

Fresh green curry leaves have a punchy flavour and are an essential ingredient in many curries.

Garam masala is a fragrant mixture of warming spices that is often used in Indian cookery to bring flavour to a curry without adding heat. Ready-made garam masala is a great store-cupboard standby, but the mixture is often bulked out with cheaper spices and is no where near as tasty as our simple home-made garam masala recipe – it will make all the difference to your curry. And it is definitely worth making a batch to have on hand. Double up the ingredients if you are likely to make more than a couple of curries a week.

Quite often, garam masala is added towards the end of the cooking time, but we like to sprinkle it over the curry early on in the recipe so the aromatic flavours have a real chance to permeate the other ingredients and become more mellow. With an electric spice grinder you can make the garam masala in a jiffy. An electric coffee grinder should also do the job. You can get great results with a pestle and mortar too, but it takes a bit longer. Pound the spices hard for several minutes until they reach a powdery consistency. **Makes 6 tablespoons**

OUR GARAM MASALA

- 12 cardamom pods
- 3cm piece of cinnamon stick
- 2 tbsp coriander seeds
- 1 tbsp cumin seeds
- 1 tsp whole cloves
- 3 dried bay leaves
- scant 2 tsp black peppercorns
- ½ whole nutmeg
- ½ tsp ground turmeric
- ½ tsp ground ginger

Put the cardamom pods in a pestle and mortar and crush them with the pestle until the pods crack. Tip them on to a board and open all the pods. Using the tip of a knife, scrape the seeds into a small frying pan and chuck out the husks.

Add the cinnamon, coriander and cumin seeds, cloves, bay leaves and peppercorns to the pan and toast over a medium heat for 1–2 minutes, stirring until you can smell the spices strongly. Watch them carefully so they don't burn.

Allow the spices to cool a little. Tip them into an electric spice grinder or a pestle and mortar, then grind or pound to a fine powder.

Finely grate the nutmeg and stir into the other spices. Add the turmeric and ginger and mix well. Use what you need and put the rest into a small screw-top jar. Keep in a dark place and try to use within a month.

TOP TIP

A scant teaspoon is just a little less than a full teaspoon, so the peppercorns shouldn't heap above the top of the teaspoon.

CHILLIES

Chillies vary in size, colour and shape. Every chilli has an individual flavour profile and can provide a very different level of heat to a curry so it's hard to predict the heat of each one. You may find that a curry cooked with chillies from the same shop one week could taste very different when you buy them next time, but this only adds to the excitement. One way to test the heat of the chilli is to take a tiny piece of the flesh from the middle (the stalk end will be hottest) and taste it – have a glass of cold milk or a some yoghurt handy to quench the heat if necessary! You can then adjust your recipe accordingly – and don't forget, the heat of a chilli can be reduced by removing both the core, membrane and the seeds from inside.

Long red and green chillies (Cayenne or Lombok)

In India, these tend to be from the cayenne variety but it is unlikely that your greengrocer or market will label them anything other than chillies and other varieties can look similar. Lombok chillies are usually slightly milder. The long red chillies are actually ripened long green chillies. Both types may provide a similar intensity of heat, but they do give a different flavour. We find the green ones have a bit more bite and the red more warmth.

Plump red and green chillies (Jalapeño or Serrano)

These short, plump chillies are the ones you see most often in the supermarket. As with the long chillies, there are varying species of plump chillies. On the whole, they seem to be a little milder than the long ones but there is no guarantee – Serrano should be hotter than Jalapeño. They are also green when first ripe and turn to a vibrant red colour as they continue to ripen.

Bird's-eye chillies

These small chillies have a high intensity of heat. They are green at first and ripen to become orange and then red. They are small and therefore are usually not deseeded, giving them added heat.

Scotch bonnet chillies

These are the hottest type of chilli that we've used in our recipes. They are sometimes used whole for flavour, but for a real kick they can be chopped before adding (as we have done). Scotch bonnets are commonly found in the Caribbean where they are popular in cooking. Like other chillies, they are green at first and ripen to yellow, orange and red. You can use habanero chillies in place of scotch bonnets if you come across them.

Chipotle

These are smoke-dried, red jalapeño chillies. They are great for mimicking the smoky flavour that might otherwise be achieved using a tandoor.

Dried red chillies

Dried whole red chillies are generally of the cayenne variety. Drying increases their shelf life to months rather than days, but they will lose flavour over time. They can be used whole, broken, chopped or ground and can also be soaked before use. Soaking is useful when you want to make a curry paste, as the chillies will then blend more easily with the other ingredients. If you want to remove the seeds from a dried chilli before using, snip along the side with a sharp pair of kitchen scissors and give it a good shake.

Dried extra-hot chillies

These are dried bird's-eye chillies and are great for storing for longer periods of time until they need to be used. They really are extra hot and should be used sparingly.

Dried chilli flakes

Chilli flakes are made from whole crushed, dried red chillies and include the skin, flesh, core and seeds. They have a high heat intensity and should be used with caution. Like other chillies the heat can vary from one batch to another.

Long chillies
Plump chillies
Bird's-eye chillies
Scotch bonnet
Chipotle
Dried extra-hot chillies
Dried red chillies
Dried chilli flakes

PREPARING CHILLIES

Chillies add fantastic flavour and they're an essential ingredient in curries. The usual rule of thumb is the smaller the chilli the hotter it will be. However, different chillies from the same batch can vary greatly in heat so watch out. If you are worried about making a curry too hot, start with a little and add more gradually, tasting as you go. Or you can always taste a small bit of the raw chilli before using. Chillies are great in your food but not your eyes! Be very careful not to touch your eyes or sensitive skin while you're dealing with chillies. Wash your hands thoroughly after handling or wear rubber or disposable gloves. Many people think much of the heat comes from the chilli seeds, but in fact a good deal comes from the white membrane surrounding the seeds. In many of the recipes in this book we have left the seeds and membrane in the chillies, as we like medium to hot curries. But if you prefer a milder curry, remove the seeds and membrane, or just use less chilli. Here are our methods of deseeding and preparing these little flavour bombs. Always wash chillies before using and dry them thoroughly.

Deseeding and chopping

- To deseed, trim off the stalk at the top of the chilli.
- Slit in half lengthways.
- Scrape out the seeds and membrane with the tip of a knife or a teaspoon and chuck them away.
- Slice each half lengthways into thin strips, without cutting through the tip (this holds it together for the next stage).
- Chop the strips across to get fine even dice.

Slicing

Trim off the top of the chilli. Using a sharp knife, slice it into thin rounds.

Slitting

For some recipes you only need to slit the chillies. Trim off the stalk and run a sharp knife down the length of the chilli just piercing the skin. Don't cut too deeply or you will slice the chilli in half.

Drying

If you have more chillies than you can eat, try drying them, but make sure they are really fresh and undamaged. And check that they are completely dry before storing them in an airtight container or they will rot. Traditionally, chillies were laid out in the sun to dry, but as we don't get much of that here you can try drying them indoors. Place whole chillies in a single layer on a tray and place them in a warm, well-ventilated area. Turn them regularly and within a week or so they will be dry and brittle.

To dry chillies in the oven, cut them in half lengthways and place them on a baking tray lined with greaseproof paper. Leave some space between each chilli. Put them in a low oven, about 100°C/ Gas ¼. The timing will vary depending on the size of the chillies so check them regularly, turning them from time to time so they dry evenly.

FRAGRANT LEAVES

These aromatic leaves all feature in the recipes in this book and add their particular aroma and flavour to curries. We think they're all best used fresh but some, such as curry leaves, fenugreek and bay leaves, keep their taste well when dried.

Curry leaves

These shiny green leaves come from a small tree that's related to citrus plants and they do have a warm, fragrant, slightly citrussy flavour. Curry leaves can be used fresh or dried. Fresh leaves are usually fried before being added to a dish, then removed before serving – frying helps to release their wonderful aroma. Curry leaves can be frozen and they also keep their flavour well when dried.

Fenugreek

The fenugreek plant belongs to the clover family and both the seeds and leaves are used in cooking. The leaves, sometimes known as methi, have a sweet earthy aroma and they can be cooked and served as a vegetable or dried and used as a flavouring in dishes such as lamb pasanda (see page 132).

Mint

There are lots of different varieties of mint, but the most popular in this country is spearmint. It grows very easily so it's well worth having some in your garden or in a pot on your window sill so you always have fresh leaves to use in your cooking. Its fresh zingy taste is perfect in dips such as raita and our fresh coriander chutney (see page 285), which make wonderfully cooling accompaniments to a hot spicy curry.

Bay leaves

Aromatic bay leaves come from the bay laurel tree and are a very popular herb, widely grown in Europe. They are one of the herbs used to make up a bouquet garni, and are an essential addition in many soups and stews. They can be used fresh or dried. Dried bay leaves should be crushed gently to release their oils. To dry bay leaves, pick a branch and hang it somewhere airy for a couple of weeks. You can then store the dried leaves in an airtight jar.

Kaffir lime leaves

Fresh or dried, kaffir lime leaves are used in many Thai recipes and have a fragrant citrussy flavour which makes all the difference to dishes such as our Penang fish curry (see page 125). Fresh leaves freeze very successfully and frozen packs of leaves are the easiest to find in the UK. Be careful not to eat the whole leaves.

Coriander

The coriander plant is related to parsley but has a quite different flavour. Both the seeds and the leaves of the plant have been used in cooking for thousands of years and fresh coriander is very popular in the Middle East and in most of Asia. The chopped leaves are best added at the last stage of cooking or sprinkled over a dish just before serving. Some people have an aversion to the smell but the flavour is excellent. Coriander is known as cilantro in the United States.

Fenugreek
Curry leaves
Bay leaves
Mint
Kaffir lime leaves
Coriander

OTHER ESSENTIALS

We reckon that no curry would be complete without at least one of these ingredients. Each of them adds flavour and aroma to your dish.

Onions

Onions add flavour and bulk to a curry and if you blend them to a purée, they can also bring a rich, creamy texture. You may be surprised at how many we use to make some of our curries, but don't scrimp on the quantities. We generally use the brown skinned medium onions and reckon they weigh about 150g each before peeling. If your onions are a different size, you can adjust the quantities accordingly. Red onions and extra-large onions can be milder but there is no guarantee.

Ginger

A fiery root, fresh ginger can be used finely chopped, grated, crushed or sliced and is often added to curry pastes. It has a peppery flavour with a sweetly pungent taste and is meant to be good for the digestion too.

Galangal

This is also a root, but harder and woodier in texture than ginger. It's prepared in the same way and has a fresh, slightly medicinal aroma with a faint hint of citrus. Best fresh, it can also be bought as a dried root or ground powder.

Garlic

Garlic comes from the same family as onions and leeks. There are many varieties but we use the common European ones that you should be able to find in every supermarket and greengrocer across the UK. They have a white, papery skin and streaky pink cloves. Break open the bulb and it should be easy to separate the cloves ready to peel. Avoid any with little green stems and give your garlic a good sniff. Sometimes it can be a bit musty which will taint the flavour of your food. The more finely chopped or crushed the garlic, the stronger it will taste. At all costs, avoid burning your garlic as you cook it; the bitterness will wreck your dish.

Shallots

Shallots are usually milder than onions and have a slight sweetness that really comes out as they are cooked. They are small with a pale brown skin and sometimes contain more than one bulb. Banana shallots are long with a brown skin and have a similar flavour. They are less of a fiddle to prepare but can be more tricky to get hold of. We've given shallot weights in our recipes, so you can use either. Thai shallots are smaller, pinker and slightly more pungent. Always peel shallots before using. If the skins are a bit stubborn, try soaking the shallots in a bowl of just-boiled water for a couple of minutes.

Lemons and limes

These little beauties are essential for bringing out the flavour of the spices and for adding a sour note to some curries. The juice is also great for marinades as the acid helps tenderise meat. If you roll a lemon or lime firmly with the palm of your hand over your work surface a few times before you squeeze it, you will be able to extract more juice. If your fruit isn't unwaxed, give it a scrub under warm water before grating to help remove the protective coating. You'll find that knobbly-skinned lemons will give more zest than smooth skinned ones. Make sure you only grate the coloured part as the white pith will taste bitter. We use a fairly fine side of the grater but not the finest as you could end up with lemon mush.

Lemon grass

A native of India and southern Asia, this is a variety of grass and has a strong citrussy flavour. It's an essential ingredient in Thai and Southeast Asian cooking and can be used whole, crushed or chopped. If not using whole, remove 3 or 4 of the outer layers to reveal the more tender inner parts which are less fibrous and easier to chop. Most of the flavour is in the thicker end of the bulb.

Galangal
Ginger
Garlic
Onions
Shallots
Lemons
Lemon grass
Limes

PREPARING PRAWNS

Prawns are great in a curry and go brilliantly with chilli, lemon grass and all those fab flavours. What's more, they are easy to prepare and very quick to cook. You can buy raw or cooked prawns and they can be fresh or frozen, peeled or unpeeled. When buying raw prawns, check that they smell really fresh. They should be moist, shells intact and be blue-grey in colour – they turn pink when cooked.

Peeling

Peeling is what you do when you remove the shell from the outside of the prawns. To peel a prawn, start by removing the head – just twist it off the body. Turn the prawn over and pull the shell open along the belly, working from head to tail, and then carefully peel it away from the flesh. It should come away easily, taking the legs with it.

Deveining

Before cooking larger raw prawns it's best to remove the intestinal tract – the black line along the back of the prawn. It shouldn't do you any harm if you eat it, but it can be a bit gritty and may taint your food. It's also worth checking for the intestinal tract on cooked and peeled prawns, as they aren't always properly cleaned.

- Using a small sharp knife, make a shallow cut along the curved back of the prawn.
- Lift out the 'black line' with the tip of your knife. Wipe any gunk away with some kitchen paper.

Butterflying

To butterfly a prawn, peel as above but leave the end part of the tail attached. Devein in the same way but make a deeper cut – about half way down. The prawns will open as they cook, revealing the milky white centre. This is a great way of getting extra flavour into really large prawns.

Cooking

We often use big king or tiger prawns for our curries and usually cook them from raw for a more prawny taste. The small north Atlantic ones aren't as meaty but they have a really great flavour. Whichever you use, be careful not to overcook them, as they will become tough. Just 2–3 minutes is usually enough, depending on the size of the prawns.

Storing and defrosting

It is best to use fresh prawns the day you buy them, but you can keep them in the fridge for one or, at the most, two days. Most will have been previously frozen and then thawed for sale. We like to keep some frozen ones as a standby in the freezer. If they have already been cleaned, you can even cook them from frozen if necessary.

If you buy frozen prawns, keep them in the freezer until they need to be defrosted, then once defrosted, use them straight away. It's best to defrost prawns in the fridge for a few hours, but if you're in a rush you can defrost them at room temperature – don't leave them for too long, though.

Our basic curry sauce is full of big, fresh flavours. Even if you're a fan of ready-made sauces, give this a go and you'll really notice the difference. You can make it in large quantities – enough to serve 16 – and then freeze it in portions, ready to transform into an amazing meal in next to no time. You can also halve all the ingredients to make a smaller quantity if you prefer.

We've suggested a few ways to use your basic sauce, but you can mix and match other ingredients to suit your taste. If you like a very hot curry, add some extra chillies. For something milder, deseed the chillies and stir some double cream or yoghurt into the sauce. Add extra spices, some curry leaves or herbs to vary the flavour. If you have some chicken handy or some prawns in the freezer and perhaps some vegetables leftover from a busy weekend, try using them in a curry. This sauce is versatile enough to suit almost any ingredients. **Makes enough sauce for about 4 curries to serve up to 4 people**

GOOD BASIC CURRY SAUCE

- 6 tbsp sunflower oil
- 8 medium onions, halved and sliced
- 12 garlic cloves, finely chopped
- 80g chunk of fresh root ginger, peeled and finely chopped
- 2 plump green chillies, finely chopped (deseed first if you like)
- 4 tsp cumin seeds
- 4 tsp ground coriander
- 2 tsp ground turmeric
- 1 tsp garam masala
- ¼ tsp asafoetida (optional)
- 2 x 400g cans of chopped tomatoes
- 500ml cold water
- 2 tsp flaked sea salt

Heat the oil in a large non-stick saucepan and add the onions, garlic, ginger and chillies. Cover the pan and cook over a low heat for 20-25 minutes or until the onions are very soft. Remove the lid and stir occasionally. Uncover the pan, increase the heat and cook for 10–15 minutes more, stirring frequently until the onions are a nice, rich brown. This will add lots of flavour to your sauce, but watch the onions carefully to make sure they don't burn.

Sprinkle the cumin seeds, coriander, turmeric, garam masala and asafoetida over the onions, then cook for 2 minutes, stirring constantly. Add the tomatoes, water and salt to the pan, then bring to a gentle simmer and cook for 20 minutes, stirring regularly.

Remove the pan from the heat. If you want a smooth sauce for your curry, blitz the onion mixture with a stick blender until it's smooth. You can also do this in a food processor but leave the sauce to cool for a while first. You might like to try dividing the sauce in half, then blitzing one half until smooth to give you variety. Use as much as you need, then freeze the rest. The freshly made and covered curry sauce will keep in the fridge for up to 3 days.

To freeze, divide the curry sauce into 4 equal portions and spoon or pour them into large freezer bags. Press out as much air as possible and seal the top, then freeze for up to 2 months. Defrost in the fridge overnight or at room temperature for a couple of hours before using.

TOP TIP

If you can't get any green chillies for this recipe, use ¼ tsp cayenne pepper or hot chilli powder if you like. If you prefer a mild curry, just add a pinch.

This is a brilliant standby and a great way of using up cold roast lamb too. You can serve it with rice to make it go a bit further or leave just as it is – a great one-pot supper. **Serves 3–4**

LAMB, POTATO AND PEA CURRY

- 500g lamb neck fillet, well trimmed
- 1 tbsp sunflower oil
- 1 portion of good basic curry sauce, unblended
- 350ml just-boiled water
- 1 bay leaf
- 400g potatoes, preferably Maris Pipers
- 150g frozen peas
- flaked sea salt
- freshly ground black pepper

Trim the lamb and cut it into chunks of about 3cm, then season them with salt and plenty of freshly ground black pepper. Heat the oil in large non-stick saucepan and add the chunks of lamb. Fry them over a high heat, stirring regularly for 5 minutes or until well browned.

Pour the curry sauce over the lamb, stir in the water and add the bay leaf. Bring everything to a simmer, reduce the heat slightly and cover with a lid. Simmer gently for 20 minutes, removing the lid and stirring the curry every now and then.

Peel the potatoes and cut them into 2.5cm chunks. Add the potatoes to the pan with the lamb, stirring to make sure that they are well submerged in the liquid. Cover the pan and continue to simmer for 25 minutes or until both the lamb and the potatoes are tender, stirring occasionally. Stir in the peas and simmer uncovered for 2–3 minutes until the peas are hot. Season to taste with more salt and black pepper.

A luscious Thai-style curry, this can be made with our basic curry sauce too. Add extra peppers, peas, sugar snaps or beans if you like. Or bump up the quantity of prawns to make it go a bit further. This also works well with chicken, fish or duck. **Serves 3–4**

COCONUT PRAWN CURRY

- 1 portion of good basic curry sauce, unblended
- 400ml can of coconut milk
- 2 tbsp Thai red curry paste
- 1 tbsp Thai fish sauce (nam pla)
- 1 yellow pepper, deseeded and cut into 3cm chunks
- 100g mangetout, trimmed and sliced in half diagonally
- 400g cooked king prawns, thawed if frozen, and peeled

Place a large, non-stick frying pan over a medium high heat and add the sauce. Cook the sauce for a few seconds, stirring constantly, then add the coconut milk, Thai red curry paste, fish sauce and the yellow pepper. Bring everything to a gentle simmer and cook for 5 minutes, stirring occasionally.

Stir in the mangetout and simmer for a minute more. Add the prawns, along with any juices left from thawing, and cook for a further minute, stirring until the prawns are hot.

A lovely, quick version of the classic, this can be made in no time. The smoked paprika helps add a smoky tandoor flavour to the chicken but you can leave it out if you prefer. **Serves 4**

CHEAT'S CHICKEN TIKKA MASALA

Cut each chicken breast into 8 bite-sized pieces and season them with the paprika, salt and some freshly ground black pepper. Heat the oil in a large, non-stick frying pan and add the chicken, then stir-fry over a medium-high heat for 2 minutes until lightly coloured.

Pour the curry sauce over the chicken and stir in the cream, sugar and water. Bring to a simmer, reduce the heat slightly and cook for 6–8 minutes, stirring regularly, or until the chicken is cooked through and tender. You can check it by cutting one of the larger pieces in half – there should be no pinkness in the middle.

- 4 boneless, skinless chicken breasts
- ½ tsp smoked paprika (optional)
- 1 tbsp sunflower oil
- 1 portion of good basic curry sauce, blended
- 5 tbsp double cream
- 1 tsp caster sugar
- 200ml cold water
- flaked sea salt
- freshly ground black pepper

You'll find our light chicken korma and creamy chicken korma in this book, but it's such a popular dish that we think you'll like to have our extra-quick version too. This one is very popular with kids and can be knocked together in less than 10 minutes once you have made (or thawed) the sauce. **Serves 4**

QUICK CHICKEN KORMA

Cut each chicken breast into 8 bite-sized pieces and season them with salt and some freshly ground black pepper. Heat the oil in a large non-stick frying pan and add the chicken, then stir-fry over a medium-high heat for 2 minutes until lightly coloured.

Pour the curry sauce over the chicken and stir in the cream, ground almonds, sugar and water. Bring to a simmer, reduce the heat slightly and cook for 6–8 minutes, stirring regularly, or until the chicken is cooked through and is tender. You can check it by cutting one of the larger pieces in half – there should be no pinkness in the middle.

- 4 boneless skinless chicken breasts
- 1 tbsp sunflower oil
- 1 portion of good basic curry sauce, blended
- 150ml double cream
- 4 tbsp ground almonds
- 1 tbsp caster sugar
- 100ml cold water
- ½ tsp ground turmeric
- flaked sea salt
- freshly ground black pepper

YOUR STORE CUPBOARD

Don't feel you have to rush out and buy all the ingredients described on these pages, but it is worth getting familiar with them and gradually building up a selection. With these in your store cupboard you need never be short of a good meal.

Pastes

Green, red and yellow Thai curry pastes

Authentic Thai curry pastes are widely available in supermarkets and are a very useful addition to your store cupboard. Keep them in the fridge once opened. Basic ingredients in these pastes include chilli, garlic, onion, lemon grass, salt, galangal, kaffir lime leaves or peel and spices. Red chilli paste tends to be hotter than green, as it contains more red chillies. Yellow curry paste is the mildest and much of the colour comes from ground turmeric.

Massaman curry paste

Massaman curry comes from the south of Thailand and the Muslim influence here makes these curries quite different to other Thai food. The paste is usually made from red chilli, lemon grass, sweet basil leaves, garlic, salt, ginger, shallot, shrimp paste and spices.

Tamarind

You can buy tamarind in many forms – as a block, paste or juice and occasionally you can find whole pods. But it all comes from the same source – the fruit of the tamarind tree. Tamarinds look like long beans and the tart flesh is used as a spice and as a souring agent. If you can't get any, you can use lime or lemon juice instead.

Shrimp paste

This Thai ingredient is made from fermented, salted shrimps, which are pounded into a concentrated paste. It might sound strange, but it gives a great authentic flavour to Southeast Asian food, adding a savoury saltiness to dishes. Unlike fish sauce, it needs to be cooked first. Typically, a small amount of shrimp paste is fried as part of a spice paste, then other ingredients are added to it. You can find shrimp paste in Asian supermarkets where it is sold in brown blocks, tins or jars. It may also be called balachan, blachan or terasi.

Flours

Atta flour

Atta is the flour most often used to make Indian breads and often has a fine texture and slightly nutty taste. Atta flour is milled from durum wheat and so has a higher gluten content than traditional plain or wholemeal flour. This means the resulting dough will be strong enough to roll out thinly. Atta flour is perfect for making chapatis and puris.

If you can't get atta flour, make the dough with a mixture of strong white flour and fine wholemeal flour instead. We have listed the quantities in the recipes. We've found that traditional stoneground wholemeal flour is too coarse, so make sure you choose a finely ground variety.

Rice flour (gluten free)

Rice flour is made from ground uncooked rice. In Asia it is used to make rice noodles and for some pancakes, such as our dosas. It's great for thickening sauces too.

Cornflour (gluten free)

Cornflour is finely powdered white starch, which comes from maize. Unlike other flours, it is virtually tasteless and its main use is as a thickening agent when it is blended with liquid to form a smooth paste. Cornflour is also good in light batters, as in our salt and pepper squid recipe, as it makes a thin and crispy coating. Delicious!

Gram flour (gluten free)

Widely used in Indian cooking, gram flour (also known as besan) is made from ground chickpeas. Despite being gluten free, it has a high protein content compared to other flours and is yellow and crumbly in appearance.

Pulses

Lentils have been part of the human diet for centuries and it is believed they were one of the first crops ever cultivated. Nowadays they come in all sizes and colours, from yellow to red, green and black, and with or without skins, whole or split. What's great about them is they readily absorb a variety of wonderful flavours – perfect for curries!

Red lentils

These are orange in their dried form, but they turn golden and mushy when cooked. They cook faster than other lentils and are excellent in dhals.

Toor dhal

Toor dhal is also known as tuvar dhal, arhar dhal, yellow lentils or tur dhal. Whole toor lentils are yellow with tan jackets, but they're usually sold skinned and split. They have a mild, nutty flavour, and they're often cooked as a side dish or ground into flour. They're sometimes sold with an oily coating, which you should rinse off. Look for them in Asian supermarkets.

Chana dhal

Chana dhal are a small relative of the chickpea. These dull yellow lentils are split in half before use and are sweet and nutty in flavour, making them one of the most popular of all pulses in India.

Oils and seasonings

Sunflower oil

We like to use sunflower oil in most of our recipes as it has a neutral flavour, but you can also use groundnut oil or vegetable oil. Avoid olive oil as it can alter the taste of your curry.

Fish sauce

Fish sauce, or nam pla in Thai, is one of the basic ingredients in East Asian cooking. It has a pungent smell, tastes very salty and is used for seasoning, like we would use salt and pepper. It adds a layer of flavour which is difficult to describe but is essential to many dishes.

Fish sauce is made from a fermenting small whole fish, such as anchovies, in brine. The liquid is then drawn off and bottled. It is now widely available in supermarkets, but you will find more authentic versions in Asian food shops. Fish sauce is also known as nuoc nam in Vietnam, patis in the Philippines, and shottsuru in Japan.

Soy sauce

Soy (or soya) sauce is made from fermented soya beans, salt, barley and wheat flour and is a staple in Asian cooking. There are many varieties of soy sauce and they vary in consistency and flavour. Dark soy is thicker and richer than light soy sauce and also makes a good dipping sauce. Try ketjap manis too, an Indonesian sweet soy sauce. We've found it good for marinades.

Other ingredients

Canned tomatoes

Fresh, ripe, good quality tomatoes often have a better flavour, but canned tomatoes add a more vibrant colour to curries. In some recipes you'll see that we use only a small can of tomatoes. Don't be tempted to add more and use a whole large can, as we've found that the distinct flavour can sometimes overpower the flavour of the spices.

Coconut

Coconut milk is used in curries from a number of different countries. It's made by straining the grated coconut flesh with water. Many cans of coconut milk sold in the UK contain stabilisers in order to prevent the liquid from separating. However, some manufacturers don't use them, so just check the label if you would prefer it without stabilisers or if the recipe lists this type of coconut milk. If the coconut milk doesn't contain stabilisers, just give the can a good shake before using.

Coconut milk can also be made using coconut milk powder, which is mixed with water. This is not to be confused with coconut powder, which is dried coconut flesh that has been ground to a powder and does not dissolve when mixed with water.

Desiccated coconut is dried coconut flesh that is finely shredded. It can be used to add a coconut flavour to a dish, without adding extra liquid. You can also soak the desiccated coconut in a small amount of water to soften it so the flavour disperses more effectively.

Ghee

Ghee is a clarified butter used in cooking in South Asia. The butter is heated and separated to leave the clear liquid, which is left to set. Ghee can be made from both cow's milk and from buffalo milk. It adds a rich, buttery taste to curries but can be heated to a higher temperature than butter without burning.

Pickles and chutneys

Supermarkets now sell a wide range of pickles and chutneys, which can be a great accompaniment to any curry. Chutneys can be made with a variety of different fruits, vegetables and spices. They add another great element of flavour to a meal and go well with a rich curry. We have come up with recipes for lime pickle and mango chutney as well as a few other traditional accompaniments.

Unlike British chutneys that are usually stewed with lots of vinegar and sugar, Indian chutneys are often very light and fresh, requiring little or no cooking.

Rice

Basmati rice is a long-grain rice that, when cooked, should not be sticky but should remain as long, separated slender grains of rice. White basmati rice is the most widely available type, but brown basmati rice can also be used – remember that brown rice takes longer to cook. Basmati is known for its distinctive fragrance, which is more pungent than that of other rice with the exception of jasmine rice.

Thai sticky rice (also referred to as glutinous rice) is most commonly used in sweet dishes but may also be used to accompany some savoury curries.

Stock cubes

Stock cubes are not often used in traditional curries. However, they can be a good way to add extra flavour and depth to a curry, especially in a quick, simple recipe. In most instances, you can use chicken or vegetable stock cubes, unless the dish is specifically vegetarian.

Yoghurt

Yoghurt plays an important role in Asian cooking, especially Indian cuisine. Most yoghurt sold in the UK is made from cow's milk, but other types of yoghurt, such as sheep and goat, are popular in some parts of the world. Yoghurt is often used in marinades, which are a great way to keep your meat moist and make it really tender. We have used this technique in several of our recipes, for example in our chicken tikka (see page 20) and lamb biryani (see page 134). Yoghurt is also great for cooling the mouth when eating a spicy curry and is used as a base for traditional condiments such as raita.

A CURRY & A BEER

We've all been there haven't we? You're in the pub with friends, having a bit of a catch-up, time passes and the inevitable hunger sets in. It's not long until someone says 'Anyone fancy a curry?' Off you troop to the local curry house. Naturally you order some beers. Or maybe it's a takeaway feast. You've phoned in your order and in the 45 minutes you have to wait you crack open a beer from the slab pack that was on offer at the supermarket. Or maybe you're going to have a go at cooking one of our curry recipes from scratch. You've got your shopping list for your ingredients and I bet you're going to buy something to drink. We love a beer with our curry but we wanted to find out more about what goes with what so who better to help than our friend and beer expert, Jeff Pickthall. This is what he has to say.

In my view there's nothing better than a beer with a curry, but I'd like to encourage you to be more adventurous with your choices. The UK now has almost a thousand breweries and hundreds of foreign beers are imported. The pub trade is in decline but don't let that fool you – beer is booming. Being a beer enthusiast is trendy! New-wave beer geeks are young, fashionable, sociable and discerning. Beer drinkers are no longer divided into the two clichéd categories – real-ale bore or lager lout. In towns and cities across the UK, specialist beer pubs and bars are thriving. The term now favoured is 'craft beer'. Put that in a search engine and you'll find the internet is buzzing with well-informed beer talk.

Wine people know that their favourite beverage can enhance a dish. They go to great lengths to find wines to drink with food. When a great match is found the effect is spectacular. The wine and the food seamlessly integrate, the flavours sing harmoniously. But ask a connoisseur for wine recommendations for curry and he'll look at his feet and mumble something about having an appointment he must keep.

International food – and drink

'Curry' is the vague term applied to spicy foods with strong historical roots in India. In the days of the British Empire, Indian workers travelled the globe in the service (not always entirely voluntarily) of the Empire and they took their food culture with them. Often finding themselves in far-flung places where familiar ingredients were unavailable, they improvised with local foods and in doing so created entirely new dishes to add to the broad category 'curry'. Curry is now international food. From the Caribbean in the west to Japan in the east the curry diaspora feeds the world. And beer is the international alcoholic drink. Mirroring the way curry culture conquered the world via the British Empire, European beer styles colonised the world. In the era of expansionist empires, we conquering Europeans took our beer with us and we brought exotic food back.

Fortunately, beer and curry are made for each other! But curry means big tastes, spice and heat. Your ice-cold thirst quencher isn't going to get a look in where flavour is concerned. If you've gone for hot, a beer may give you a few seconds of relief from the chilli burn, but big curry flavours eclipse the more timid types. Supermarkets now carry large beer ranges but the choice can be daunting; little information is provided on what any beer actually tastes like, never mind what food it would suit. Some brewers make food-matching recommendations on their beer labels, but there's no substitute for a consultation with a specialist and again, the internet is your friend. Search for 'specialist beer shop' and you'll find beer sellers who love nothing more than a bit of beer and food chat. Alternatively you can get involved in beer chat on Twitter – you can make a start by following me, @jeffpickthall.

Si and Dave's recipes represent an excellent overview of the curry world and all the classics are there. The chicken korma, for instance, with its key ingredients of almonds and cream is delicate, and so partners well with subtle beers. The style I would recommend is golden ale and most UK brewers now brew one or more. They're pale, light and usually possess some exotic fruity flavours. My favourites are 'Kipling' (5.2% a.b.v.) by Thornbridge Brewery, and one Dave and I enjoy in our home county of Cumbria, 'Loweswater Gold' (4.3% a.b.v.) by Cumbrian Legendary Ales.

The term 'lager' is as broad as the term 'curry' and it covers a range of beer styles with historical roots in Germany and the Czech Republic. I'm particularly partial to a German 'Dunkel'. They're dark but easy-drinking and they work well with meaty curries with tomatoes such as Rogan Josh or Madras. Erdinger Dunkel (5.6% a.b.v.), widely available in the UK, possesses a touch of soy-like meatiness and a hint of sourness that cuts through oiliness. If you're lucky you'll find my favourite Dunkel, which is by Klosterbrauerei Andechs. Thai curries are typically delicate and fragrant, requiring a different type of beer. The Thai lager 'Singha' (5% a.b.v.) is rather good but often overlooked by beer lovers. Singha is ubiquitous in Thai restaurants but at home you can be more adventurous and perhaps try a Belgian wheat beer with a Thai curry. In Flemish they are 'witbiers', in French they are 'bière blanche'; either way they are brewed with both wheat and barley malts giving them a cloudy pale yellow look. Typically, they are flavoured with coriander seeds and Curaçao orange peel for a fresh zesty flavour. The most well known is Hoegaarden but there are plenty of others, such as St Bernadus Blanche by the St Bernadus Brouwerij, which is more complex. Hop Back Brewery of Salisbury, Wiltshire brew 'Taiphoon' (4.2% a.b.v.) with lemon grass, which fits right in with Thai foods.

Flemish red ale

The vindaloo is a serious curry and the perfect beer style to match can be something of an acquired taste: the Flemish red ale. This beer style is sour – I kid you not! The surreal Belgian brewers delight in using the naughty yeast strains that other brewers dread – the ones that create sourness. The beer is matured for more than 12 months in oak casks before being blended with fresh beer to give the correct flavour profile. The entry-level Flemish red ale is 'Duchess De Bourgogne' (6.2% a.b.v.) by Brouwerij Verhaeghe. It's a sweet and sour beer with fruity flavours redolent of plums and dried fruits. If you're feeling brave and wish to qualify as a premier league beer geek you should go for the 'Grand Cru' (6% a.b.v.) by Brouwerij Rodenbach. Drink it with the richest vindaloo and you'll have a meal to remember.

India Pale Ale (IPA)

The British Empire gave curry to the world and Britain gave one very special beer style to the Empire – the India Pale Ale or IPA. The journey to India and other far-flung outposts of empire was arduous, not only for the passengers but also for the precious cargos of beer, and the beers that survived the journey best were those with the most hops. Hops have antibacterial qualities as well as contributing bitterness and attractive fruit and herbal flavours and aromas to beer. IPAs disappeared just as the empire did, but the craft-brewing revival of the past 30 years has seen brewers recreate old styles. In fact, IPAs now dominate the craft-brewing sector in the USA and the revival has fired up British brewers to once again brew the style. The great thing about IPAs is that they work brilliantly with the big spicy flavours of curry. I would happily recommend IPAs for every recipe in this book! IPAs are typically 5–7.5% a.b.v., pale to mid-brown in colour, highly bitter, highly aromatic and often possessing exotic fruity flavours. There are loads to choose from now. 'Worthington's White Shield' from Burton on Trent is one of the originals and from Si's patch in the northeast there's the IPA by Mordue Brewery – a medley of exotic hoppy fruit loveliness. Lovibonds of Henley-upon-Thames brew '69' IPA. Thornbridge brew 'Jaipur' and Goose Island IPA from Chicago is on British supermarket shelves. There are plenty to try. You have no excuse. Go curry; go India Pale Ale. You can't go wrong.

GREAT CURRY MEALS

Now you've had a look through our book and hopefully tried some of the recipes you might like to think about preparing some great curry meals. Instead of just making and serving one curry at a time, have a go at cooking up a combination. Many of the curries can be prepared ahead and warmed up the next day – some are even better that way – and others are very quick to prepare from the start.

Always serve a good selection of pickles and chutneys to accompany your curries and make a few chapatis or even some puris if you are feeling bold. There is no better way of impressing family and friends than a colourful collection of home-made curries – and only you will know how easy they are.

It's nice to start meals with a few poppadums served with our minted yoghurt sauce, mango chutney, lime pickle, coconut pickle and fresh tomato and onion relish. You don't have to make everything from scratch, but look out for good-quality pickles and chutneys and snap them up when you see them. They will last for ages in the fridge once opened. A packet of uncooked poppadums can be stored in the cupboard and half a dozen will take less than 5 minutes to fry. And try some of the flavoured ones too – they're delicious. Or you can pick up ready-fried poppadums in most large supermarkets.

We've checked out how many servings each of the recipes makes, so increase the recipes where we've suggested. You don't need to increase everything though as a selection of different curries can be very filling. If there is anything left over, you can always heat it through and serve it the next day or even freeze it for another occasion. Here are our suggestions for some meals you could make and we are sure that once you get started there will be no stopping you!

Casual meal with mates

Nothing beats an informal meal with a few friends. All the main course recipes can be made the day before, although we recommend that you add the grilled chicken to the tikka masala sauce on the night so it stays tender and succulent. It can be grilled earlier in the day if you like, then cooled and chilled. **Serves 8–10**

Onion bhajis

–

Lamb dopiaza
Chicken tikka masala
Dry Keralan beef curry
Vegetable coconut curry
Pilau rice x 2
Naan bread

–

Chilli chocolate pots x 2

Sunday lunch

Instead of a trad roast, try serving a curry Sunday lunch for a gathering of friends or family. The puddings can be made before and the chicken marinated overnight. You can fry your pakoras in advance then reheat them on a baking tray in a very hot oven just before serving if you like. **Serves 6–8**

King prawn pakoras
Lamb chop pakoras
-
Masala roasted chicken x 2
Seekh kebabs
Aloo gobi x 2
Coconut rice
Red onion, orange and pomegranate salad
-
Lemon and passion fruit possets

Quick Friday night fix

Quick to prepare, this simple supper could be ready to eat in under an hour. Serve with mango sorbet or coconut ice cream from the freezer, or knock up the sticky rice with mango recipe if you have a bit more time. **Serves 4**

Salt and pepper squid
-
Filipino spicy curry
-
Mango sorbet

Summer picnic

Easy to pack, this spicy selection will make a great change from the traditional al fresco fare. Don't forget to take along some minted yoghurt sauce, mixed salad and an assortment of pickles and chutneys too. **Serves 8**

Samosas
Goll bhajis
Tandoori chicken
Nargis kebabs
Mooli salad
-
Tropical fruit salad

Party for 25

Curries make the perfect party food and this flavoursome spread will keep everyone happy. You can do lots of the preparation in advance too. Make sure you have plenty of poppadums, pickles and chutneys on offer for people to pick at. Mini poppadums are a useful addition as you can pile them into a bowl and serve with a selection of dips. You'll find them in the crisps and snacks aisle of the supermarket. **Serves 24–26**

Chicken tikka x 2
Prawn tikka x 2
Shami kebabs x 2

-

Lamb rogan josh
Creamy Kashmiri chicken curry
Vegetable biryani x 2
Mushroom rice x 2

-

Pistachio meringues with raspberries x 4

Perfect dinner for eight

Lots of elements of this menu can be made well in advance and we've given you a really easy starter to take the pressure off. If you want to make something a bit more unusual, try the prawns on puri instead of poppadums and swap the Keralan prawn curry for one of our fish curries instead. **Serves 8**

Masala poppadums

-

Chicken jalfrezi
Lamb pasanda
Keralan king prawn curry

-

Aubergine and tomato curry
Green beans with coconut
Saag aloo
All-in-one split pea dhal

-

Mango ripple fools

Special dinner for two

This is an Asian-inspired dinner for two. You'll have some chicken satay and a couple of pears left over but they will keep for a day or two in the fridge. **Serves 2**

Chicken satay

–

Penang fish curry
Asian greens with ginger
Jasmine rice

–

Spiced poached pears

Family supper

This is no more difficult to put together than shepherd's pie and apple crumble and the kids will love it. **Serves 4–6**

Lamb kofta curry
Perfect basmati rice
Fresh onion and tomato relish

–

Pineapple fritters and coconut ice cream

Vegetarian dinner

There's no better way of putting together a veggie meal than with various curries. With all this flavour, who needs meat? **Serves 6–8**

Stuffed parathas
Chilli pickle

–

Lentil and vegetable curry
Crunchy palak paneer
Chana masala
Si's bhindi bhaji

–

Pistachio and rose kulfi

INDEX